Veering Off

MY SEARCH FOR FREEDOM

Veering Off

MY SEARCH FOR FREEDOM

by

KEVIN CROMLEY

ADAMS AVENUE PUBLISHING

Veering Off

MY SEARCH FOR FREEDOM

Published by ADAMS AVE. PUBLISHING – USA
info@aperfectfind.com
ISBNs 978-1-7321989-0-6 (soft back),
978-1-7321989-1-3 (e book)

10 9 8 7 6 5 4 3 2 1

To the Reader,

This book is a memoir, reflecting the author's present recollections of experiences over time. Some names and characteristics have been changed, some events compressed, and some dialogue created.

Enjoy!

To Kevincito and Kristi,

May your lives be filled with adventure!

TABLE OF CONTENTS

CHAPTER ONE

SEARCHING

What if everything you knew, or thought you knew, fell away in an instant. Like an anchor hurtling through the sea...

Imagine your life, your essence, all that makes you... you, compressed into a single element, an atom... a speck of dust floating through the infiniteness of space...

What would be at your core? What makes you... you?

I was just 26 years old, and already cynical with life, the night the cosmos reached out and gave me a nudge.

* * *

I'm running around my bonfire, naked, and chanting like a madman. I spit a mouthful of Tequila into the flames and scream at the wind.

My quest for... something—anything—has been leading me deeper and deeper into Mexico. What am I searching for, direction? Some deeper purpose to my existence? Perhaps, but as the fire roars and the flames lick the night sky, I'm blind to such things. What I do know, is that something is missing inside me, some gaping hole that can no longer be filled with booze and solitude.

Then I hear it. A voice? I look towards the boombox sitting on the roof of my VW van. Led Zeppelin jams out through scratchy speakers. I stop running. Kev, you're on an empty stretch of coastline in El Socorro, Mexico—halfway down the Baja peninsula—miles from civilization. Nobody is here... nobody is ever here.

I listen to the wind, the ocean and the crackle of fire, craving more. The sand caves beneath my toes. I stagger and drop to my knees. Then I hear it again. It's not a voice, it's more like a feeling, something inside. I want fucking answers.

I look to the sky, waiting, listening. But there is nothing—only the indifference of the stars flickering in silence, billions of miles away.

I thrust my fists into the air and scream. But still, there is nothing.

Rocking back on my ankles, I close my eyes and drop my head to my chest, defeated. I'm a leaf on a vine, waiting for a gust of wind to tumble me on down the path.

But just as my world seems small and inconsequential—a life teetering on a plane of uncertainty—silence descends upon the beach.

She wraps her arms around my body, permeating my skin and reaching into my core. I shiver at her touch and open my eyes.

Flames dance before me, flickering from side to side like a snake, creeping higher, casting shadows. The heat pierces my sunburnt skin, one patch at a time, spreading along the contours of my body. My shivers cease as the flames burrow deeper, penetrating my organs, my blood, my soul. I have fused with the fire before me.

I stand tall and straight and flex the muscles in my shoulders. Looking out to the sea—fire blazing, power radiating—the message is clear. It's time to grab the reins of my life, open the cage, and ride the beast. To where? I have no fucking clue.

* * *

When I returned to my home in San Diego, I was focused—driven. Something I'd lost over the years. I knew I was going somewhere, but where? Breaking free from my life became my guiding force, my beacon, pushing me forward, steering me away from the shoals of conformity; Inevitability.

The Peace Corps flashed through my brain. I'd heard about it before, once while talking to a counselor in the Career Placement Office in college. It sounded like such a wild idea at the time as I prepared to tackle the business world, but now the idea of joining burned inside me like the fire from Mexico. I sharpened my pencils and did my homework, driving to the local library and getting my hands on every book, pamphlet, form, and document available. I quickly discovered the Peace Corps would be a two-year and three-month commitment.

My analytical side appeared, reminding me of my long-term goals of scaling the corporate ladder, and how the Peace Corps didn't fit into any of my business plans.

I decided to pay creepy, left-brain voice some credence and called my mom. She'd traveled a rocky road and somehow managed to find her center of gravity. She'd steer me back on course, back to the practical, business path I'd always envisioned.

"Mom," I said, trying to mask my excitement, "what's going on?"

"Hi Kevin... What's up?" I sensed worry in her tone. "Surely there must be some reason my son is calling me out of the blue. You need money?"

"No," I assured her. "I'm thinking about doing something a little wild."

"Oh shit, what now?"

"Uh... joining the Peace Corps."

There was a long pause. I dipped my head, waiting for the blow, waiting for her to tell me all the reasons I shouldn't do it. The Man of Fire from the beach had disappeared.

"You know Kevin," she finally said, "I think that's the best thing for you right now."

"Wait, what?" I said indignantly. "This is supposed to be when you tell me what a crazy idea this is."

I heard her take a long drag from her cigarette and exhale. "Just go," she said.

"Well, now I'm just getting offended. Are you trying to get rid of me?"

"No, I just think that you need to do this."

"Really?"

"Yes, besides, I can tell by your voice you've already made your decision."

She was right, I had made my decision. She'd always been able to see straight through me. It was time for me to make my move before life kicked up a storm and pushed me further down the path of inevitability. I wanted her approval, her affirmation. I suppose I always have.

* * *

I'm 7, the school bell rings, and I fly out of my classroom into the bright San Diego sunshine. I run past the office and a sea of kids rushing down the busy hallways. I jump off the stairs to the awaiting sidewalk and hear a voice that stops me dead in my tracks.

"Kevin!"

I look up. Mom is leaning against her red, convertible Fiat. I look past her. My baby sister, Kerry, and two older sisters, Stephanie and Michelle, are sitting in the car with worried looks scrawled on their faces.

"Get in, we're going for a ride," she says with a grin.

"Where to?" I ask, eyes wide.

"We're going on an adventure. Oh, and say goodbye to San Diego!"

"Huh? We're going where?"

"Get in!"

I step slowly into the Fiat. She slams the door behind me and walks to the driver's side. Her energy is like a vortex, pulling me into her world. My head slams back as she throws the car into gear and peels away from Alice Birney Elementary.

We hop on Interstate 8 and head east, convertible top down, sun beating on our heads. We travel across Arizona, New Mexico and Texas, occasionally stopping to nap on the sides of dusty roads. Grit and sand stick to my teeth when I wake. Mom's pushing hard on the gas pedal, wind gusting through her hair. Glenn Campbell sings Rhinestone Cowboy as the Fiat chews up the miles.

Crammed tight amongst each other, my sisters and I attempt small talk over the howling wind, pretending to be happy travelers on an impromptu adventure. But we're really just scared kids. Mom is on another crazy streak, and we all know it—no matter how brave we act.

We continue racing down the highway for several days, sleeping off and on, skin sticking to the vinyl seats.

Mom finally rents a room in a beat-up, Norman Bates motel right off the freeway—blinking "Vacancy" sign and all. We drive right up to the door. We're all in desperate need of a bed and shower, our dirty, sweaty faces, and stinky clothes, making us look more and more like a homeless family.

"Mom, where are we going?" I ask for the 100th time as she fidgets with the key in the lock.

"Yeah Mom, where are we going?" Michelle chimes in, pushing strands of long blonde hair from her eyes.

My oldest sister, Stephanie, looks on pensive, absorbing information, always the studious type.

"Well aren't we all having fun?" she asks as we enter the room.

"But Mom…"

"Well?" she asks again. We all take turns falling backward onto the beds, exhausted. "Isn't this a great adventure? Or would you rather be back home doing chores?"

"No, no, no!" Michelle and I cry out. My baby sister, Kerry, is already fast asleep on one of the two beds, her chubby legs curled up to her chest.

"Look," Mom says, "I needed to get away from my life. You know

I love you kids with all my heart. We're going to be just fine. I'm your mother, let me do the worrying."

I jump up, wrap my arms tight around her neck and whisper in her ear, "Don't worry Mom, I'll protect us."

Michelle begins to bounce on the bed, annoying Stephanie, who has opened her Zane Grey book and become lost somewhere in the Old West.

Mom says she's going out for a while, but we all knew what that really means; that she's going to some stinky bar for hours and hours.

"I'll be back soon," she says, walking out the door.

"Leave the light on," I whisper.

* * *

Executive Order 10924, issued by John F. Kennedy, March 1, 1961, established the Peace Corps with a mission "to promote world peace and friendship... to help the peoples of such countries... in meeting their needs for trained manpower."

Translation: Peace Warriors. Grunts!

Two hundred and twenty thousand Americans would go on to serve in the Peace Corps over the next 55 years, serving in 141 countries. I worked out the math, determining the percentage of people in the U.S. that join the Peace Corps is approximately .00001%. That's a bad-ass club, and I wanted to be a member. My quest was on!

Joining the Peace Corps is a competitive process. Simply having a desire to be transported from your life for two years, is not—strangely—a sufficient prerequisite. They require quite a bit more.

As with all jobs involving the Federal Government, step one included filling out reams of forms. For once, I had a leg up, as my current two-year stint with the Department of Social Services had educated me in the fine art of pushing paper.

After plowing through the mounds of paperwork and reaching the final page, I looked closely at the fine print where I was to affix my signature. It read as follows: *Cut a 1/4" slice in the uppermost portion of your thumb with a blade no longer than 3", let blood pool sufficiently and then press the aforementioned thumb on the document here, here, and here.*

I signed on the dotted line instead, stuffed all the papers inside the large envelope provided, and mailed the packet into the void of bureaucratic space.

I refrained from telling any of my coworkers or friends my plans.

I figured I'd jinx myself if I suddenly became that asshole dude who can't stop talking during his last two weeks on the job. You know the guy.

Whether I was eating in a restaurant, driving to work or paddling out to the waves, the Peace Corps was always hovering above me—just outside my grasp—waiting, contemplating. Would it burst and crush all my dreams? Or sweep me into the clouds and carry me away to distant lands?

My anxiety grew with each passing day, palpable, close to the surface. I began walking quicker, working faster. Days turned to weeks. Was this not my fate? Self-doubt can be a motherfucker.

I had a good old-fashioned stare down with our mailbox every day. Always sitting there on its weathered, wooden post, so smug—my nemesis! Taking a deep breath, I'd grab the latch and pull down the door. Was my future lying amid the envelopes and magazines? I'd quickly flip through the pile. Nothing!

Then one day—when I'd all but given up hope—I spotted the red, white and blue Peace Corps logo. The moment of truth. My heart sank when I felt the thin envelope, remembering all my college rejection letters arriving in thin envelopes my senior year of high school.

I tore it open, yanked out the papers and quickly scanned for the word "Congratulations." It wasn't there. Fuck! I began trembling. Slow down, Kevin. I re-read the letter. I'd passed the initial application process, but still needed to complete a full physical and an in-person interview.

Anxiety traveled as my copilot over the next two weeks, pinching and prodding me, relentlessly tapping its fingers on my temple, always questioning. What will they ask in the interview? How should I answer? What should I wear? Am I worthy?

A week later I found myself fidgeting nervously in the doctor's office. "Lift up your gown and lie on your side," the doctor said as she pulled a latex glove from a cardboard box.

Snap!

The sound of doom echoed off the walls as the glove smacked her wrist and she walked behind me. Then came the dreaded words, "This is going to hurt!"

It did. A LOT! I passed my physical and prostate exam. I didn't bother sending a thank you card.

Interview day arrived. I opted for my best navy-blue suit, hopped in my VW camper van and began the two-hour drive north to Los Angeles. My copilot, anxiety, informed me that this was the most important trip of my life. Don't Fuck It Up!

One o'clock arrived and I found myself stuck amid thousands of cars all inching along the 110 freeway towards downtown. My 1:30 appointment appeared to be in serious jeopardy. Unbelievable! I'd allowed plenty of time for delays.

The gears on my watch found a fast-forward function. The minute hand screamed, "Tick, tick, tick, tick…" The sound of all my dreams slipping through my fingers. My copilot poked me in the temple and scoffed, "Well look at you, stuck here on some ungodly Los Angeles freeway, sweating your ass off, in your cheap little suit and tie, in your rickety old camper van. HA! Either turn around and go back to your monotonous, preordained life or do something about it—NOW! Tick tock."

I pounded my fist on the ceiling, straightened up in my chair and yanked the wheel to the right, clawing my way through the mountain of cars to reach the next exit. Pay phone, pay phone… found you, in the corner of a beat-up gas station. I grabbed my Peace Corps paperwork, fumbled through my pockets for a quarter and dialed the number below the logo.

"Hi, this is Kevin Cromley. I have an appointment today. I'm so sorry, but I'm running a little late. I should be there in twenty or thirty minutes." I noticed a scruffy guy wearing a ripped-up jacket eyeing me curiously from the alley behind the gas station.

"Ok, no problem," the secretary said. "We'll see you when you get here."

I flung open the phone booth doors and sprinted back to my van—jacket and tie blowing behind me—a modern-day Superman in the middle of Watts. The guy in the alley gave me a parting nod. He was rooting for me now.

Thirty minutes later, I arrived in gritty downtown Los Angeles, parked my van in a lot with crumbling asphalt and raced the two blocks to a high rise where the Peace Corps office was located. I ran my fingers through my short brown hair and straightened my tie in the elevator. I entered the office, sweating, late and disheveled; undoubtedly blowing my only chance of fleeing from this world I found rapidly closing in around me, of escaping from the "inevitability" of it all.

"Hi, I'm Kevin. I'm here for my Peace Corps interview," I said breathlessly. "I'm really sorry I'm late."

"No problem, just have a seat and somebody will be with you shortly." I sat down on a small blue couch and scanned the room. Several people were working at their desks. I realized I was the best-dressed person in the office. *Hope?*

A young lady came over and smiled, "Kevin? Come with me back to our conference room."

"Sure," I said, repeating for the millionth time, "I'm so sorry I'm late."

"Don't worry about it," she said. "Most people forget to factor in Los Angeles traffic." *Still hope!*

We walked into a small room with a rectangular desk and sat down. She told me a little about her time in the Peace Corps. She was a Returned Peace Corps Volunteer (RPCV) along with the rest of the staff. I didn't understand what that meant at the time, but what I did understand was that our interview felt more like a conversation between two good friends than an inquisition into my sanity—which I most definitely would have failed. She was cool and friendly and a sense of calm—missing for so long— flooded over me as I leaned back in my chair.

We talked about my job, my education and my background. She asked about my family and about any relationships that might affect me leaving the country.

"I don't have a girlfriend," I told her. "Nothing is holding me back."

"Do you understand the commitment you'll be making? Two years and three months is a long time."

"I do," I told her. And at that time, I thought I did.

As the interview was wrapping up, she leaned in, "Kevin, I just have one final question for you. What are you running from?"

I didn't hesitate, looked directly into her eyes and said, "I'm not running from anything, I'm running to something. The Peace Corps is calling me and has been for a while."

She looked at me curiously for a few moments then smiled, "Wow, I've never heard that before!"

I knew I was in. Everything I said was true. I'd opened my heart to the Peace Corps, and there was no other destiny for me.

* * *

"Rise and shine Sunshine!" Strands of Mom's hair fall on my forehead as she shakes me awake.

My sisters and I crawl out of bed and back into the cramped Fiat. Mom reeks of booze and cigarettes, a familiar smell. She stops at a gas station to fill the tank and goes inside the mart. When she returns, her arms are full of Coke bottles, Lay's potato chips, and Hershey bars.

"We're going to have to make this last kiddo's," she says, handing us the snacks and starting up the car. "I'm down to my last $12."

"What!" Stephanie yells. Oh shit, I know if Stephanie is worried, we're in trouble. "How are we supposed to live on $12?"

"We'll be just fine," Mom says.

"Why are we even leaving San Diego?" Steph's piercing blue eyes shoot daggers at Mom.

"I need a change of scenery."

"But where are we going to live?" I ask, my voice breaking.

"Yeah, where are we going to live Mom?" Michelle asks.

"Everybody just relax!" Mom shouts, her hand dangling over the steering wheel, cigarette burning between her fingers. "We'll figure it out when we get there."

I bite down on my lip, fighting back the tears, "Get where?"

Mom takes a drag on her cigarette and stares deep into my eyes, "Wherever the road takes us."

CHAPTER TWO

BREAKING AWAY

A month later, the letter appeared in the mailbox. I held the envelope tight in my hands, knowing my fate lay just inside. When I couldn't take the suspense any longer, I ripped it open and read the magic words: "Congratulations! You have been selected to serve as a Peace Corps Volunteer in Nicaragua."

"Yes, Yes, Yes!" I danced in circles right there in the middle of the street not giving a shit who saw me. It was official, I was leaving my life behind.

Wait! Where in the hell is Nicaragua? I had wanted to live on some exotic island in the Caribbean or South Pacific near the coast and waves. I envisioned living in a hut, Robinson Crusoe style, with my surfboard "Friday" as my only companion.

I was tearing through the living room in search of a map when I spied my roommate's globe. Spinning the sphere, I found Central America, the tiny isthmus connecting North and South America. I focused in on a triangular country, noting how the Pacific Ocean wrapped around its' west coast and the Caribbean Sea ran the length of its' east coast. A goofy grin spread across my face, the best of both worlds; Nicaragua it shall be! I even liked how the name rolled off my tongue.

Wait! Is Nicaragua safe? Fuzzy stories of Ollie North, Iran Contra, and Sandinistas raced through my mind. Images of guerrillas carrying AK47's and patrolling the jungles just outside my hut. I was a little scared, I'm not gonna lie. But the Peace Corps wouldn't steer me wrong. They'll protect me. *Right?*

I finished reading the letter. If I accepted the assignment, I'd be departing for Miami in four weeks for a two-day orientation. And from there, I'd fly to Nicaragua, for the next two years and three months of my life. Gulp! Well, I accept. Nicaragua here I come!

I gave notice to my roommates and the Department of Social Services, then began purging all the meaningless shit I'd acquired since graduating college.

I was walking on air and wanted to scream to every person I met, "Hey, I'm leaving for the Peace Corps!" Even devising ways to slip it into conversations.

"Yeah, I won't need that baseball glove in the Peace Corps," I'd tell strangers as they picked through my things during weekend yard sales.

"I'll take fifty bucks for the bike. I can't ride it down to Nicaragua, where I'll soon be living in the Peace..."

I was only allowed to bring two pieces of luggage, so I headed to REI. The salesman was more than happy to listen to me babble on about the Peace Corps while he sold me a sleek internal frame backpack, sleeping bag, stove, tent and lots of other camping gear I'd concluded I couldn't live without. From the literature they sent, I knew I'd be living in a house, but for some reason I couldn't shake the image of me traipsing through the jungle, whacking down rope-sized vines with a machete.

For my second piece of luggage, I decided an oversized duffel bag was a must, remembering how we'd stuffed our ninety-eight-pound wrestler in one during practice one day in high school. My roommate had the perfect bag, but the zipper was broken and a seam needed stitching. He worked in the Athletic Department at San Diego State University and assured me he'd have it repaired. Two weeks passed, and I grew frustrated.

"Did you bring it?" I asked Jon the second he stepped inside the house.

"No, just relax. I've already told you three times that it'll be ready soon."

Everything needed to be in order; organized and in its place. It's always been that way with me, my eternal battle; rifles drawn and at the ready, beating back the enemy—the disorder which marked my youth.

Jon arrived with the duffel bag folded up under his arm. "Here's your bag, you whiny bitch."

"Thanks," I said, snatching it from his arms. I ran into my room, tossed it on the bed and spent the next three hours stuffing clothes, books, headlamp, water bottle, essential papers, journals, pens, camera, toiletries and the entirety of my life into a backpack and duffel bag. Each time I thought everything was perfectly packed and secured away, I'd remember a particular cassette or pair of camping socks I had to bring and was forced to pull everything out and start over.

I purchased last minute items I couldn't live without such as beef jerky, sunflower seeds, a Zippo lighter and harmonica, and crammed them into the bags. Finally, I made the determination that my bags were sufficiently organized, and I was ready to go. Party Time!

* * *

My farewell party was epic, a tale of two parties really. The PG version played out during the day as my mom, sisters, co-workers, and friends came to see me off. Two truckloads of wood-chips had been spread around picnic tables in the backyard, and a bar, made from scraps of wood and palm fronds, greeted the guests with a sign that read, "Nicaragua or Bust!" The letters, painted in jungle green, sat above a row of rum bottles.

Mom pre-cooked over fifty pounds of both, baby back and spareribs. I lathered them in homemade barbeque sauce, tossed them on the grill and finished them with a nice char. Kerry, my younger sister, brought two big batches of baked beans topped with caramelized onions and strips of bacon. Jon tossed a giant salad filled with tomatoes and diced up cucumbers, while I chopped up pineapples and mangoes. Kegs of beer, sitting in tubs of ice, caught shade from the bar's palm fronds.

Under the bright sun, friends and family talked and laughed, barbeque sauce dripping down their chins with each bite of the tender meat. They washed it all down with cold beer in red plastic cups, as reggae music and classic rock rang out. When the sun turned orange and began to dip, they gave me giant hugs and wished me well, then they walked away and disappeared from my life.

Mom pulled me to the side and gave me a big hug. "Be safe down there," she whispered as strands of her gray hair slid across my shoulders. "But have the time of your life."

"I will." As I pulled away, I caught a glimmer of pride in her dark green eyes.

Night made her arrival and the music, sensing her presence, rose to greet her. The PG party quickly faded away as I poured vodka, rum, tequila, 7-Up, champagne and white wine into a large vat. I added a gallon of fruit punch to the brew and tossed in chunks of pineapple, oranges, lemons, limes and mangoes. The result: a sweet, sticky red concoction that went down way too easy—Jungle Juice!

Cars filled the streets, and young people stumbled in—one after another—a seemingly endless parade of revelers. The party was in full effect. Stevie, my best friend from high school, fetched beers and helped keep the booze flowing and music pounding. He had traveled down from San Jose in Northern California with his two cousins, Kira and Amy.

"Um... Can I help you with something?" Kira chided as she caught me checking her out. We had met once before when I visited Stevie in San Jose. She was cute and down to earth with sandy blonde hair.

"Sure, fetch me a beer," I joked. Kira rolled her sexy green eyes and walked away. I figured I'd steer clear. She was Stevie's cousin after all, and besides, I was leaving for the next two years of my life.

"Dude, there's no alcohol in this Jungle Juice," Stevie complained.

"It sneaks up on you!" I warned.

Others began chiming in, "This is Kool-Aid!" and "Hey Kev, are you going to Nicaragua or Hawaii? Because this shit's Hawaiian Punch!"

Nobody wanted to heed my advice, so I shook my head and dumped another bottle of dark rum into the red soup. That seemed to do the trick. People were soon singing and dancing and running wild—not a care in the world. Some snuck off to dark corners of the house to engage in "non-PG" activities.

I walked outside. The jacuzzi was packed. I counted heads as they passed cake back and forth. I had just reached twenty-two when an explosion rocked the side of the house.

I ran towards the noise and found Jon lying on his back with a group of people around him. "Call an ambulance!" somebody yelled out. They picked him up, carried him to the front yard and laid him in the grass. Within minutes, an ambulance was flying down our road, sirens blaring. They loaded Jon on a stretcher and hauled him away.

"Dude, what happened?" Stevie yelled. "It sounded like a bomb went off."

"I don't know," I said walking back to the side of the house.

I discovered the gas line attached to the propane tank had ripped, allowing propane to leak out. When Jon lit the barbeque, the built-up propane exploded, knocking him back five feet. He received third-degree burns on his elbows and knees. The hospital bandaged him up, gave him some pain meds and sent him on his way.

Apparently, it's not a party until there's an explosion because the party went right on without him.

The next morning, I woke to the sun burning holes in my eyelids through my bedroom window. I pried open my eyes and made my initial assessment. Hangover? Check. Limbs intact? Check. House still standing? Partial check.

Kira was lying next to me. Hmmm. I pulled a sheet over her naked body and crawled out of bed. As I made my way into the living room, I found several people sprawled about and red blotches splattered all over the carpet—Jungle Juice puke!

I hopscotched over the bright red chunks and made my way outside. The sun was baking down hard on San Diego. The jacuzzi, filled with cake and empty beer cups, had become a science project overnight. Frothy green algae blooms floated on top of the red soupy mess, and a shadow lurked at the bottom. Moving closer, I made out the hazy outline of a lawn mower sitting on the bottom.

I glanced around the corner. Broken bricks and black soot sat where the barbeque used to be. Cleanup was going to be a bitch, but not for me!

I boarded a plane at noon for Miami.

CHAPTER THREE

PEACE CORPS

A thin white kid was sitting on one of the beds, hotel phone pressed to his ear and babbling in Spanish when I entered my hotel room in Miami. I assumed he was another volunteer.

I couldn't understand a word he was saying, and a flash of panic came over me. I'd told the Peace Corps I spoke a little Spanish, but frankly, my Spanish sucked. Five years of studying had only taught me a few basic phrases, albeit important ones, like "*Yo quiero cerveza*" and "*Donde esta el baño?*" Would I be the only volunteer in my group not fluent in Spanish?

I placed my duffel bag—so heavy it felt like I'd stuffed my VW engine inside—in a corner and sat on the bed.

"Hey, what's up?" I said after he hung up the phone minutes later. "I'm Kevin."

"Hi, I'm Craig," he replied, a mischievous grin spreading across his unshaven face.

I moved towards the edge of the bed, "So, are you going to Nicaragua too?"

"Um... yeah," he said dully.

"Aren't you excited?" I asked, taken aback by his muted tone.

"I guess... Why, should I be?"

"Should you be... Are you kidding me?" I stood, held my arms out wide and found my deep sermon voice, "Dude, we're leaving for Nicaragua in two days, for the next two years of our lives. Yes, you should be excited, you should be jumping up and down on your bed right now!"

Craig just stared with his droopy eyes and big smile—as if I was the crazy one amongst us. Perhaps I was.

"Are you on Valium or something?" I asked.

"Not that I can remember. Why?"

"Peace Corps. Nicaragua. Hello? You act like we're here in Miami to play golf."

"Oh yeah... that." Craig patted his short black hair, apparently bored by the conversation. Was he messing with me?

I headed for the door, "Come on man, let's go get a beer somewhere."

Craig grabbed the hotel key off the nightstand and walked to the door. "You mean we're not going golfing?"

We made our way to the Metro, an aboveground monorail, and ten minutes later found ourselves wandering the streets of Miami, Salsa music blasting from open doors. We ducked inside a local Latino bar and sat on black leather stools while Spanish conversations and music whirled around my head. Would I ever learn this elusive language?

"Dos cervezas por favor!" I hollered, content I'd always be able to order a drink. I hoisted my beer to Craig, "Here's to the next two years of our lives!" Craig gave my mug a lazy clank, seemingly unfazed.

We were chucking all we'd ever known to serve in a land we'd never seen. The gravity of my decision was not lost on me. Craig, on the other hand, seemed like he was heading off to summer camp.

"Where are you from?" I asked.

"Longmont," he said. "It's a small town outside of Boulder, Colorado. We're famous for our boulders."

"What?"

"Never mind. What about you?"

"San Diego."

"Oh," he said and took a drink from his beer. "I hear you're famous for your sand."

I scrunched my eyes and shook my head, trying to decide if he was serious or just pulling my leg—something I'd be doing for a long time to come.

Craig was fresh out of college, and perhaps, hadn't absorbed the same punches life had thrown my way, but something about him made me laugh and I started to feel like I could talk to him about anything—a rare commodity in my life.

"Otra!" I shouted to the bartender, gulping down the last of my beer and heading to the bathroom.

When I returned, Craig was slumped over, his face planted on the bar. I shook his shoulder, "Hey are you ok?"

Heart attack, stroke, mad cow disease—my mind flipped through its card catalog of medical knowledge. "Craig, Craig!" I was on the cusp of asking the bartender to call an ambulance when I heard him speak.

I lowered my head and listened, but he was mumbling incoherently. I moved closer, putting my ear next to his mouth. Wait! Is he... babbling in Spanish again? Yes! Craig didn't have Mad Cow Disease. Craig was drunk. Who gets drunk off one beer? Apparently, Craig.

"We need to get out of here." I shook his shoulder. "Can you hear me?" More Spanish. I put him in a bear hug and lifted him off his stool. He wobbled and nearly fell. I draped his arm around my neck and guided him towards the door as people looked on. Laughter trailed us into the balmy night.

We stumbled onto the Metro and found our way back to the hotel. I shoved him into the elevator and propped him against the wall. The elevator dinged, and I dragged him down the hallway past wide-eyed guests. Don't mind me and my roofied date, Craig! I gave him a nudge, and he fell into bed, face first. I turned and headed straight down to the lobby bar.

"Shot of Jack!" I hollered to the English-speaking bartender. He had an emerald glow from a set of neon lights strung along the counter. I thought about Craig—snug in bed—sleeping off his one beer and tossed back my whiskey. Records were hung on powder blue walls, giving the bar an art deco vibe. I leaned over and read the artist's names: Elvis Presley, Beach Boys, the Beatles...

"Hey!" somebody hollered. I spotted a guy across the bar with short brown hair and stubble on his chin looking my way.

"Hey, did you..."

"What's that?" I yelled over Buddy Holly.

"Did you go to San Diego State?"

I looked from side to side, wondering if he was talking to me.

"No, I went to Chico State." I said, trying not to give him my 'who the fuck are you?' looks.

"Whatever," he said. Apparently, I failed.

It struck me, I should ask him why he thought I went to San Diego State. He seemed like a cool guy, and it would give me a reason to tell him all about me joining the Peace Corps. But, when I looked up, he was walking out the bar.

I drank a large swig of beer which dribbled out the corners of my mouth and down my shirt. As I sopped it up with a napkin, I noticed the block letters on my chest spelling out, *San Diego State*. It's official—I'm an idiot.

Craig was beginning to stir when I went back to the room. "Dude, you're alive. What happened to you?"

He mumbled something I couldn't make out.

"You better not be talking in Spanish!"

He sat up and wiped away the drool from the side of his mouth.

"Hey man," I told him. "I'm going back out. Sleep it off, and I'll see you in the morning."

"No, wait, I'll go with you."

"Ha, Ha."

"No, really," he said, standing up. "I'm ok."

"No way. I'm not carrying your ass home again! You're a lightweight bro. No offense."

"I was just tired from my flight. I'm fine, really. I want to go."

I looked him over. He appeared sober. "Ok fine," I said. "Let's go. Just take it easy." It wasn't like I had anybody else to hang out with.

For the second time that evening, Craig and I headed out the lobby doors and into the Miami night. We didn't have to walk far this time. The bellhop pointed us to a bar across the street on the 12th floor of a high-rise.

The elevator doors opened to pink and blue lights dancing across the tile floors and flashing off panoramic windows. Bottles of booze glistened in the mirrors running from floor to ceiling, while fast-paced merengue music pulsed through the room and the Miami lights lit up the city below.

"Beers!" I screamed to both Craig and the bartender. Two cute girls were chatting in Spanish a few seats down. Good lord, am I already in Nicaragua? My whiteness was becoming more and more apparent. Funny how race doesn't play much of a role in your life until you slip from the majority to the minority.

Two beers and two shots later, I was feeling good. Even kicking some rust off my Spanish as I talked to a pretty Cuban girl.

"Quieres una cerveza?" I asked, but before she could answer, I remembered Craig two seats down. "Hey Craig, you want another..."

Craig didn't want another. In fact, Craig was... well, I'm sure you can guess. Craig was face down on the bar. Again! Déjà-fucking-vu! Is that even humanly possible? Apparently, all things were possible with Craig.

* * *

The next morning, we had our orientation. Craig woke up spry and sober, while I was moving much slower. We headed down to the lobby and into a conference room. I poured myself a large cup of coffee and dumped in nine spoons of sugar, hoping to clear away the cobwebs. Twelve other young people were milling about, and I wondered if they, too, were going to Nicaragua.

I thought I recognized somebody. Looking closer, I realized it was the guy from the bar who'd asked if I went to San Diego State. I ducked my head, but he saw me and gave me a knowing nod. Yes, it's me... the asshole.

They taught us some basic Spanish phrases and health tips over the next two days. I discovered, to my relief, I wasn't the worst Spanish speaker in the group.

"Look around," the speaker told us in our final workshop. "Out of the thirteen people in your group, three of you won't make it the full two years, and another three will end up marrying local people. Those are the odds."

I looked around the room and smiled. I'd been busting my ass my whole life to get to this point. There was no way in hell I was going home early, and as far as marriage was concerned, well, let's just say I had decided long before that marriage and me would be a toxic mix. But I bet that goofy guy in the corner marries a local!

I noticed a woman in the corner pulling out handfuls of syringes from a black bag. She loaded them with a clear liquid and flicked the sides. Before leaving for Miami, I'd already received a dozen shots. Turns out, I needed more. She told us to form a line and pull down our pants—men and women alike. Welcome to the Peace Corps!

"You're going to need each other," we were told repeatedly, so much so that I began to wonder if I'd joined the Peace Corps or the Marine Corps.

There were several cute girls in our group, but one caught my eye. She was 5'6" give or take, with sandy blonde hair and piercing blue eyes. A bucket of freckles spilled out over her nose and cheeks. If they really were sending us to war, I wouldn't mind being stuck in a foxhole with her.

Like Craig, Stephanie had recently graduated from college, along with half of the group. The rest having bounced around in the struggling economy for the last few years.

We all had two things in common: business degrees and a burning desire to get to Nicaragua. With the possible exception of Craig, but then again, Craig was in a class of his own.

I'd made my first baby steps down this new, unknown path. As I looked ahead, the view was blocked by rugged terrain still to be traversed, but I forged ahead, solid and strong—eager and hopeful. Never looking back.

We *were* going to need each other down there; often being each other's sole link to sanity. We would be the sixth group in Nicaragua since the Sandinista regime. *Peace Corps Nicaragua, Group 6* was our official title, but we quickly whittled that down.

On April 4, 1995, *Nica 6* boarded a 747 bound for Nicaragua and unknown adventures.

CHAPTER FOUR

NICARAGUA

As we banked right and began our descent, I caught my first glimpse of Nicaragua and all her beauty spread out below. She was lush and green, spotted by lakes and rivers and flecked with volcanoes punching up through her clouds. What adventures awaited down in that rugged terrain? Would her secrets be mine?

Dark-skinned men wheeled a giant set of stairs across the runway and up to the side of our plane. The big door swung open, and passengers began filing out. My turn couldn't come fast enough.

I grabbed my backpack and stood behind Craig and the rest of the group. My sense of purpose—once nearly extinct—began to grow with each step I took and every row I passed. And before I knew it, I'd reached the door, the exit, the portal to my future. With my heart racing, and Nicaragua within grasp, I paused and took it all in. Here we go Kev; Hang on!

A blast of hot air smacked me across the face as I poked my head out of the plane. Heat so intense it jerked me back. Sweat poured from my scalp as I descended the stairs and made my way across the tarmac. God had pointed a giant hair dryer towards my head and turned it on high.

"Agustino Sandino" was painted in dark blue letters on a cement block wall leading to Immigration. The inside looked like a neglected, old elementary school—dingy walls painted in two shades of blue, peeling from every corner.

Nica 6 formed a line and inched forward. My muscles tightened as if a Boa was constricting around my limbs. I glanced at my fellow volunteers, horror in their eyes—sheep to the slaughter. It was real now. We bunched closer as the Immigration booth neared. Stephanie looked my way, her eyes mirroring my fear. We furrowed our eyebrows and laughed at the tension, breaking its hold, if for only a moment.

A short, thin man wearing a Panama hat and sporting a trimmed mustache appeared out of nowhere, as if by magic. "Hi, I'm Diego, your Training Director. Welcome to Nicaragua." A collective sigh of relief rang out through the group. We all took turns shaking his hand. "Take out five dollars and have it ready to pass through Immigration," he told us as we huddled around him, like moons orbiting a planet.

The terminal was chaotic, people pushing and shoving and cutting in line, everybody screaming and shouting, waving hands in the air. Just past Immigration, swarms of children were running wild, pointing and yelling, motioning for us to follow them. The order I so craved, so desired, the order that had protected me and been my fortress and my shield—was dissolving before my very eyes.

Diego pushed his glasses higher on his nose and reminded us to have our five dollars ready. Were we bribing our way into Nicaragua? The short, stocky man behind the counter didn't seem at all happy to see us. Had he missed the memo that said Nica 6 was arriving today to save his country? He looked at me and barked something in Spanish, which I assumed meant he wanted me to come forward.

I approached his booth and handed him my crisp, new Peace Corps-issued passport. He took a long, slow look at me and then at my passport. He growled in Spanish and stared into my eyes. Had he caught a whiff of the Jungle Juice and fear oozing from my every pore? Had he determined I posed a threat to Nicaraguan society? I remembered the crumpled up five-dollar bill in my sweaty hand and handed it over. He grabbed the money, grunted and stamped my passport with a thump. With a wave of his hand, he motioned me to pass. Bienvenidos a Nicaragua!

My giant blue and gold duffel bag stuck out amongst the sea of luggage being tossed around baggage claim. As the others dug through the pile, I sat in a corner and wrote down my first impressions of Nicaragua. "Well, I'm either in Nicaragua or on the surface of hell, it's so fucking hot here!"

The bags all found their owners and we made our way out of the airport. Hundreds of shoeless kids with outstretched hands circled around us as if we were rock stars, shouting, "Regalame un peso." Give me a peso. They had dirty, sad little faces. I reached into my pocket and pulled out a pile of change. The children pushed and pulled me in different directions, reaching their hands into my face and tugging on my arms as I passed out the coins. I realized I was being separated from the group. Alarmed, I locked my eyes on Diego's hat in the distance.

I swam through the children, moving them gently aside, and pushing forward, until I made it back to the safety of Diego's Panama. We plowed further away from the terminal, reaching a curb where two passenger vans awaited. The crowd thinned, allowing us to throw our luggage in one van and climb in the other. The air conditioning was blasting as we made our getaway. I settled into my seat and exhaled.

"Hola!" Diego said, popping his head around the front passenger seat. "How was your flight?"

Everybody began peppering him with questions.

"Hold on, hold on," he said. "One at a time."

I looked out the window as we passed what I could have sworn was a Woolly Mammoth pulling a wooden cart stacked ten feet high with firewood—extinct my ass.

"Those are oxen," Diego clarified, destroying my theory we had landed during the Pliocene Epoch. We sped down a two-lane highway, past horses, pigs and mules. Women sat sideways on motorcycles, holding babies wrapped in bright red and purple blankets. The cars zipping in and out of traffic seemed different, older and boxy.

"Diego, what type of cars are those?" I asked.

"They're called Lada's." He went on to explain how the Lada and other Russian vehicles were brought over during the 1980's, after the Sandinistas won their civil war against the dictator, Samoza. At the time, Russia and Cuba provided support for the fledgling communist government. "They left the vehicles behind when they pulled out of Nicaragua." Diego had given me my first lesson into the complexities of Nicaragua.

I looked out the window once again to this strange new land, a mixture of excitement and fear rumbling inside my belly. An old man, wearing a wide-brimmed hat, rode his horse down a dusty road, disappearing into a wall of green foliage and tropical trees. Perhaps our 747 had been a time machine... Perhaps I just needed a beer.

* * *

We arrived at a small hotel in the city of Granada. As I stepped from the van, the sweat returned with a vengeance. We had come in April, the dry season, and hottest month of the year. High 90's was the norm, with the same degree of humidity. Tropical hell! My clothing became less a means of covering my body, and more a mode of absorbing the buckets of water and toxins oozing from my every pore.

"Drop your bags in your rooms and meet me in the dining room," Diego said, as he passed out room keys. I snatched mine out of his hand and flew to my room. Once inside, I raced into the bathroom and jumped in the cement shower. I cranked on the scratched-up metal handles and waited for relief from the ungodly heat. Water barely trickled from a flimsy showerhead hanging from the wall. Calculating it might take over an hour to wash away my sweat, I wrapped a towel around my waist and rushed out of the bathroom.

"Hi, Kevin."

Well, what do you know! It was my old drinking buddy, Craig. Partners in crime yet again. "What's up man?" I asked, attempting to give him a high five. After several failed tries, I decided Craig and I would stick to handshakes going forward. I changed into a fresh pair of clothes and felt semi-human again, but as we headed out the door, and before my foot had even touched the ground, the sweat gushed from my forehead. There was no escape.

The Peace Corps nurse, Samantha, stopped by and gave us a rundown on all the maladies we might contract while in-country: Malaria, Dengue Fever, Cholera, snake bites, bugs, scorpions, amoebas, worms... she tossed scary words around like they were candy—Blow Pops or M&M's to enjoy.

"Oh, and you must take Chloroquine every day," she said, handing out packets of pills to ward off the dreaded Malaria. "The side effects include headaches, nightmares and dizziness."

Oh boy, can't wait. The kicker; if we didn't take the pills, and got Malaria, we could be kicked out of the Peace Corps. Nurse Ratched, er... Nurse Samantha was a real barrel of laughs, especially when she grabbed her bag o' needles and told us to drop our pants.

Diego took us into town the next day. We walked past adobe houses splashed in vibrant blues and oranges. The locals took pride in their sleepy, colonial village on the shores of Lake Nicaragua. The mega volcano, Mombacho, stood nearby, looming high over the city as if it were her bodyguard. "I am Granada's protector!" it screamed in silence.

Tiny islands, some with small houses, dotted the lake. Pangas and other small boats moved from island to island ferrying people and supplies. Near the center of Lake Nicaragua was a large island, Ometepe, shaped like the number eight. She boasted two volcanoes, Concepción and Maderas, which sat on opposite ends of her land. Two giants in quiet contemplation.

After lunch, we walked along narrow cobblestone roads which wound through the city. All paths converged at the majestic Granada Cathedral, sitting stoically in the center of town. Her yellow and orange façade, shining bright, beckoned one and all. She was the crown jewel of this ancient town founded in 1524 by Spaniards, and rumored to be the oldest colonial town in Central America.

In 1855, an American named William Walker invaded and captured the city. That didn't sit well with the locals. They rose up and chased him out of Nicaragua. But William didn't go peacefully, he burned the city to the ground upon his exit. For William's final act, he returned and proclaimed himself President of Nicaragua. Willy would eventually find the tail end of Karma five years later, when he faced a firing squad in neighboring Honduras.

Later that night, I set out to explore Granada on my own. Craig was in the lobby, inflicting his dry humor on Kathleen from Florida and Tiffany from Louisiana.

"Keep him away from the alcohol!" I joked.

"Ha, Ha. How's the Spanish going?" he shot back.

I noticed Stephanie relaxing in a wicker rocking chair near the door as I made my way across the lobby.

"Where are you headed?" she asked, flashing her big smile.

"Exploring," I said.

"Well aren't you the brave one."

I beat my fists on my chest like a gorilla and walked out into the humid Nicaraguan night.

Children on bikes carried plastic bags filled with rice and vegetables, skinny dogs chasing after. Soccer balls bounced from one side of the road to the other. Couples held hands and whispered in each other's ears, as Salsa music drifted from open windows. The streets were alive! I reached down and smacked a mosquito having dinner on my ankle.

Granada appeared to be calm and tranquil, but I still had a sense of fear, being unable to gauge my safety level. I moved my head from side to side as I crossed small bridges and walked past dark corners.

I found a bar on the lake and ordered a beer. Kira and I had exchanged addresses the morning I left for Miami, and I was excited to tell her all about Granada, Craig, and the scorching heat. After pulling out a pen and sheet of paper, I paused and marveled at where I was. The warm air, now comfortable, hung suspended throughout the town. And the moon, heavy and full, bounced her bright light off the water's edge and onto my empty page. My future was unwritten, vague and out of focus. But, for now, I was right where I was supposed to be.

* * *

"I hear you're from California?"

I looked up from my breakfast the next morning and found Jason hovering above. He was tall and a little on the pudgy side with short brown hair, traces of gray coming in on the sides.

"Yeah, San Diego," I said. "What about you?"

"Northern California—Napa Valley." A waiter came by and handed him a plate of rice, beans and a glob of white, dried out cheese.

"That cheese looks nasty," I said, as Jason sat down next to me. "What's it called?"

"Guajada!" a voice called out. The guy who'd asked if I went to San Diego State pulled up a chair next to Jason. I hoped he wouldn't remember me, thinking I probably came across rude that night in Miami.

"Yo," he said, "What's going on?"

"Not much, I'm Kevin," I said.

"Yeah, I saw you at the bar in Miami."

"Oh really?" I said, acting dumb.

"I'm Mitch." We shook hands. He was lean and wiry with short brown hair parted on the side and a pointy nose. The patchy stubble on his chin contrasted with his serious, business-like eyes.

"Where are you from?" I asked, twirling my fork in the bean and rice mixture on my plate.

"Los Angeles, but I lived in China for the last year." I was learning that most of the other volunteers had already either lived abroad or traveled extensively.

"I'll take your cheese," Jason said, grabbing it from my plate.

"Did you guys take your Chloroquine yet?" Mitch asked.

"No, why?" I asked.

"I took it last night and had this crazy dream I was hunting pigs with a spear while men chased me through the jungle with machetes. I woke up sweating my ass off."

"Dude, you were sweating your ass off because of the thousand-degree weather here," Jason said. He had a funny way of curling his lips and revealing his two front teeth as he readied his next joke. The court jester's "tell."

"What's up with the nurse saying we'll be kicked out if we don't take our pills?" I asked.

"How are we going to get kicked out?" Jason said. "We're volunteers, not employees."

I hadn't taken my Malaria pills yet. Not out of fear of experiencing bizarre dreams—I'd always been partial to mind-altering experiences—but rather from sheer laziness.

"Hey," I said, pushing back my untouched plate of food, "I found a cool bar down by the lake…" I took a last sip of coffee and stood, ready to leave. "You guys want to grab a beer later?"

The three of us seemed to click, maybe it was a California thing…

"Yeah!" they both said.

Or maybe we all just liked to drink.

* * *

Later that night, as Jason, Mitch and I walked past a row of bars and restaurants on the lake, we heard a familiar voice.

"Good evening," Diego said. He was sitting alone on a patio, sipping a drink and working on paperwork.

"Diego!" we shouted and walked over to his table.

"Have you guys tried the local rum yet?"

"No," we said.

"Flor de Caña, best rum in the world!"

I'd been wondering about the dark rum I'd seen in all the bars and restaurants. Diego ordered a bottle. The waiter rushed off, returning a short time later with a tray on his shoulder loaded with Coca-Cola, soda water, a bucket of ice and tongs, sliced limes and Flor de Caña - Gran Reserva. He spread it all out on the table and said, "Salud!"

We filled our glasses with ice and then poured in the dark rum, topping it with a splash of Coke. We squeezed sliced lime over the top and twirled it with our index finger.

"Now this is how you drink rum," Diego said, holding his glass in the air and saying, "Nica libre…"

We clinked glasses and shouted, "Nica libre!" The rum was as smooth as velvet flowing down my throat.

"Now I need to get back to the hotel," Diego said. "You guys be careful." He bundled up his paperwork and went off to pay his tab, leaving us with the bottle.

We polished it off in no time at all and promptly ordered another. An hour later, we were skipping down the cobblestone streets towards the music we heard blaring in the distance.

"There," Mitch said, pointing to a pair of speakers tied to a tree limb. Past the tree was a sketchy looking Ferris Wheel in desperate need of a fresh coat of paint. Yellow blinking lights—half burnt out—spun in circles along the spokes, as passenger cars ferried children up into the dark sky.

Nearby, men wearing Guayabera shirts (formal dress shirts worn untucked) beat small mallets on a wooden instrument called a Marimba, as boys danced in circles around pretty girls wearing flowing green and blue dresses, which they held out to their sides, creating a vibrant, rippling effect. The boys, wearing puffy white shirts with red bows at their neck, kicked their knees high into the air, black knickers and red sashes fluttering in the breeze, then dipped low and bowed to their partners, their arms outstretched, straw hats snug atop their neatly combed hair.

"Holy shit," I hollered. "Look over there!"

Men on giant stilts walked through the crowds wearing colorful masks painted with rosy red cheeks, large mustaches and piercing blue eyes. They waved to the children and tipped oversized hats stuffed with yellow, red and purple flowers.

The smell of meat and corn on the cob roasting over a wood fire pierced my nose, and a thin blanket of smoke fell over the crowd. Jason spotted a beer shack and got in line.

"I wonder what's going on over there?" I pointed to a large tent, with a steady flow of men going in and out.

"That's where they kill the gringo's!" Jason said.

After we bought beer, Jason and Mitch walked back towards the Ferris Wheel while I snuck off to the tent. I lifted the canvas and ducked inside, just as a man spun a giant wheel. It reminded me of an upright Wheel of Fortune. The spectators shouted and pounded their palms on a long counter as it went around in circles. Other men were sitting at tables nearby drinking rum and playing cards. A few were slumped over. I smiled, remembering Craig and his face-plant in the Miami bar. I was in a Nicaraguan casino.

"Quiero jugar," I said to the man at the wheel. The men standing along the counter all turned and stared. Several began to chuckle and then the whole bar roared with laughter.

"Dele, dele, dele Chele," the man behind the counter said.

"Huh?" I asked, looking from him to the big spinning contraption. I handed over a fistful of money and grabbed the wheel. The men grew silent as I rocked it up a few notches and then cranked down, spinning the wheel as hard as I could. A loud roar went up from the crowd.

"Chele, chele, chele!" The men screamed as the wheel spun around and around. Click, click, click, click, click... click... click... click. The wheel slowed and landed on a strange Egyptian symbol.

"Gracias," I shouted over the noise and made my way back to the flap. But before I could duck under, several men pushed me back towards the counter. I got a sinking feeling in the pit of my stomach. Is this the killing gringo part?

"Te ganaste," the man said.

"Que?" I asked.

"Te ganaste," the man repeated, handing me a pile of Monopoly-looking money.

"I won?"

"Sí."

I'd won a whopping $9, but by the stack of bills they handed me, it felt like I'd just hit the lottery. I bought a round of beers for the men and ducked back under the flap. They were still hooting and hollering as I walked away.

Mitch and Jason were down the road chasing after a chicken. I sprinted over to get in on the fun.

* * *

The next day, Diego informed us we'd be living with Nicaraguan families for our three months of training. He divided us into five groups based on our Spanish ability. Each group would be going to a different town.

"You'll be living in Monimbo," he told me.

"Cool," I said, hoping Stephanie would be in my group.

He said it was an indigenous village which still retained elements of their pre-Columbian culture. "It's also where the Sandinista uprising began."

"Uprising?"

"Yes," he said, "the Revolution." Diego's background was in anthropology. He was a walking encyclopedia of Latin American history and culture.

I decided to read up on my newly adopted country. Ignorance is not bliss, it's just ignorance.

Like most history, Nicaragua's starts off in happier times; a peaceful land, inhabited by several tribes who lived off hunting, fishing, trade and agriculture.

Spain's quest for gold led them to conquer much of the land during the 1500's, decimating the natives in the process. They set up their own government and ruled over the territory for the next three hundred years, fighting off attempts by the Dutch, French and British pirates to take control.

Nicaragua gained its independence in 1821, but internal rivalries would fracture the country for the next few decades. Leading up to our good ol' friend, William Walker, declaring himself President of Nicaragua in 1856.

The U.S. would play an even more significant role in Nicaragua in the 1900's. But more on that later.

My week in Granada had come to an end. It was time to say goodbye to Craig, Mitch, Jason, Stephanie and the rest of my group. We'd become fast friends over the course of the week. I gave Stephanie a hug, holding on a tad longer than the others, "Take care," I said.

"You too. Have fun exploring," she replied.

"Stay away from the rum!" I told Craig while shaking his hand.

"Ha, Ha... tenga buen viaje!" Craig wished me safe travels, always eager to remind me of his superior Spanish skills. He was remaining in Granada with the advanced Spanish group.

A pretty volunteer named Elena climbed into the Peace Corps Land Cruiser as Diego and the driver loaded our bags into the back. We hadn't had much interaction over the past week.

"You nervous?" she asked, sliding into the seat next to me.

"I feel like I'm going to throw up."

"Me too," she said, fear flashing through her soft brown eyes as the truck started up and drove away.

"Don't worry, we'll be fine," was all I could offer up, as the Toyota bounced down the muddy road, closer and closer to Monimbo, my fear growing with each kilometer.

CHAPTER FIVE

RUNNING

I was drawing invisible circles with my finger on the dashboard when Mom touched me on the shoulder and pointed to a sign which read, "Welcome to Mississippi." My sisters were all asleep, heads resting on each other's shoulders.

It wasn't long after, she brought the Fiat to a stop. We'd driven far enough. Mom's "road" had taken us to Pascagoula, Mississippi.

I'm not sure if Grandma wired her some money, happy to have the chaos 2,000 miles away, or Mom knew somebody in town. But, somehow, she managed to move us into a small rural apartment, backed by a thicket of woods.

We got to know the neighbors, and on summer nights, we all gathered outside around picnic tables covered in newspapers, as a big, burly guy with a bushy beard and overalls dumped out a huge steel pot filled to the top with neon-red crawdads—freshly fished from the nearby river. A second pot was then dumped out, and steaming chunks of potatoes, corn and onions rolled down the table. Large saucers, filled to the brim with sweet melted butter, were passed down the line.

We cracked shells under the stars, butter squirting from our mouths with each bite of the juicy meat. Dipping foot long ears of corn into butter and nibbling on the edges. Adults drank bottles of beer and laughed at jokes I didn't understand.

After dinner, the kids snuck off. We ran around the fields behind the complex, a pumpkin moon lighting our path. We'd bite into mammoth-sized slices of watermelon and spit the seeds at enemy soldiers. War had broken out. The warm nights seemed to last forever.

I met my upstairs neighbor, Chip, at one of these cookouts. He was also 7, with spiky blonde hair and jagged teeth. He wore cut-off denim shorts and ripped up tennis shoes. I never saw him wear a shirt, even when we ran through the Greenbrier bushes pretending to be cowboys on the hunt for outlaws, making hand signals to move forward where we'd have a better angle to fire our imaginary rifles.

Chip had grown up in this rural land. He was much wilder and braver than me, but I tried desperately to never let him see me scared. A river ran behind the complex, and beyond the river, were the Sticks. At least that's what Mom and the neighbors called them.

Scary things lived in the Sticks—like ghosts, ghouls, murderers, and weirdos that kidnapped little boys. In San Diego, when people said, "you live in the sticks," it meant you lived far away from the city. In Mississippi, the Sticks were real sticks, Cypress and Sweetgum Trees growing in clusters near the river and pushing into broad swaths of land beyond.

"I dare you to cross the river and go into the Sticks." Chip taunted me one day as we ran along the riverbank.

"No way," I said. "I dare you back."

"You're just a pussy. What are you scared of… the ghost?"

"No, I'm not scared of anything!" I screamed.

"Well, go then."

I scratched my head and looked at the fast-moving water. Mom had told me a million times to never cross the river. I could still hear her saying the words, "I'll whoop your ass if I ever catch you in that damned river! The current will drag you to the bottom and drown you."

"I'll go if you go!" I cried, calling his bluff.

"Ok, let's go."

We walked—slow as molasses—to the river's edge, looked at each other for a moment and then stepped into the cold water.

"I'm really going to do it," I said, looking over at Chip and hoping he'd puss out and turn back. But he kept going.

I matched his every step, wading deeper into the chilly river. As the water flowed up to my waist, I began to shiver. I looked at Chip one last time as the water reached my chest, my teeth chattering uncontrollably. He wasn't turning back, and neither was I. I laid down in the icy water and let the current take me. The water chilled me to my bones. Suddenly, I was sucked downstream, moving fast. I kicked my legs and flailed my arms, swimming for my life.

A whirlpool grabbed me and spun me around like a rag doll. It sucked me under, like a great white shark pulling down his prey. I tumbled about, struggling to surface, swallowing mouthfuls of nasty river water. Blackness, my true fear, engulfed me. Air, air, I need air! I swung my arms frantically and kicked like a mule. My head finally popped out of the water and I gasped for air, my body shaking from exhaustion. My feet sank into the mud and I let out a deep sigh. I'd made it across. I crawled to the river's edge, panting heavily, and fell to the sand. I looked sideways. Chip was limping up the shore towards me.

"I told you I'm not a pussy!" I shouted, spitting out muddy Pascagoula river water.

"You ready to go into the Sticks?" he shouted back.

"Let's go!" I said, rolling on my back and wondering how I'd gotten myself into this mess.

We stepped into a thicket behind the river and wove in and out of lifeless Cypress and Loblolly Pines, moving deeper and deeper into the spooky woods. We wandered for hours, spitting and cussing, breaking off branches and using them as rifles. We slowed and scanned the area when we noticed an old ashen cabin with a caved-in roof and crumbling chimney up ahead. It appeared to have been abandoned a hundred years ago.

A creaking noise rang out from the splintered wraparound porch, freezing us in our tracks. We looked into each other's panicked eyes, then turned slowly back towards the house. A clump of sedge grass blocked our view. We tiptoed around, my heart beating fast. I got a better view and was able to make out an object on the porch—an old, crumbling rocking chair.

Then, the creaking started up again. I looked closer, my heart now racing inside my chest. The chair was rocking back and forth—not a soul in sight! I began trembling and looked at Chip. His face was white with terror.

Without saying a word, we turned and ran, sprinting through trees and bushes for the next twenty minutes, until we fell to the ground in complete exhaustion.

"What the fuck was that?" Chip asked between gasps of air.

"The fucking ghost!" I screamed, struggling to catch my breath.

"Shit!"

"It had to be a ghost. There was no wind or anybody around."

"Let's get out of here!"

"Ok, which way is back?"

We stood and looked from one direction to the other. It all seemed exactly the same, trees as far as the eye could see. After some debate, we picked a course and set off— wandering aimlessly for the next hour.

"Stop!" I finally shouted, holding out my arm. "We're going in circles."

We sat on the ground and drew maps in the dirt with twigs. Chip looked at me with big frightened eyes. I realized it was up to me to get us home. I turned away from his gaze and bit down on my lip, wiping away a tear with the back of my hand.

"Let's go!" I said in my deepest voice, pulling him up by his arm. I led us through the trees, weaving in and out, stopping only occasionally to search for something familiar.

"Wait," I said, stopping suddenly. "Did you hear that?"

"What?"

"Shhhh…"

We tilted our heads and listened intently.

"Those are people's voices!" Chip screamed.

"Let's go!" We ran off in the direction of the voices, our spirits lifted. But the sounds disappeared, and there was silence. We came to a halt and waited, lions ready to pounce, listening.

"Kevin! Kevin! Kevin!" Mom's voice was reverberating off the tree trunks from far away. We bolted towards it, running for several minutes until we poked our heads through some shrubs and came into a clearing.

It was dusk now, sunlight fading fast. We sprinted across a patch of sand and down the riverbank. Relief flooded over me as I spotted Mom and Chip's mom standing on the other side of the river, until I moved closer and was able to make out what they were saying.

"Where in the fuck were you?"

"You know you're not allowed to cross that God Damn river!"

"Get over here now! You're going to get the whooping of your life!"

Mom was red as a tomato and screaming bloody murder. Chip's mom had a belt in her hand, hanging menacingly by the side of her leg. Chip and I looked at each other, then back over our shoulders. We gave each other a questioning look. Should we run again?

Fear of the ghost rocking away in the Mississippi Sticks, outweighed any beating we were about to get. We waded into the frigid water and began swimming back—back to the ass whooping awaiting us on the other side of the river.

Mom grounded me the whole next day. But towards sunset, she'd grown tired of me running around the apartment like a wild animal.

"Ok mister, you can play on the front porch. But under no circumstances are you to move more than ten feet from the front door. You read me?"

"Loud and clear."

Outside, I put my arms out to the side and ran in circles, pretending I was an airplane. Making engine noises with my lips and looking up to the clouds. When I lowered my gaze, I caught a glimpse of Chip staring down at me from his upstairs window. I waved up to him, but his face was scrunched-up in anger. He must've gotten a worse licking than me. I went back to making airplane circles, happy for my newly found freedom.

Suddenly, a tremendous crash rang out, and glass rained down from Chip's window—narrowly missing me. Chip stared down at me with empty eyes, his fist covered in blood and poking through broken shards of glass. He had punched out his living room window! His mom let out a blood-curdling scream, rushed to his side and pulled him back.

Within minutes, adults were running up and down Chip's stairs, screaming and carrying on. Mom came out and grabbed me. Glass crunched under our feet as she rushed me into the apartment.

"Don't go back out there," she said.

Sirens rang out, blaring louder and louder as they approached the complex. Mom turned her back and I snuck out the front door. Red lights flashed off the apartment walls and scratchy voices echoed from walky-talkies, as men ran up and down the stairs. I knew I should go back inside before mom caught me, but I felt glued to the floor.

Chip came down the stairs lying on a stretcher. His arm was in the air, a bloody towel wrapped around it.

"Hey Chip," I said as they rushed him past. "You'll be alright." But I'm not sure if he heard me.

Mom told me later that night that Chip had nerve damage and the doctors had to put over eighty stitches in his hand and arm. She told me not to worry, though, because he was going to be just fine.

But I wasn't worried, I already knew he'd be fine, Chip wasn't no fucking pussy!

I never saw Chip again. Next day, mom piled us into the Fiat and headed back West.

CHAPTER SIX

MONIMBO

"Don't worry, you'll be fine," Diego said as we pulled up to my new home in Monimbo, echoing the hollow words I'd given to Elena an hour earlier. I flashed my sad, puppy dog eyes hoping he might take me back to Granada and the safety of the hotel, but he just set my bags on the sidewalk, shook my hand and drove away.

Taking a deep breath, I turned and faced the house. It sat on a small hill surrounded by trees. A pretty, blonde Spanish lady with green eyes smiled from an opened doorway. Next to her, a big, Mayan warrior wore no smile at all. He had shoulder-length jet-black hair and eyes to match. It appeared he'd been chiseled out of solid muscle. Between them, stood a dark-skinned boy with a smile so wide I could count every single one of his teeth, molars included.

I made my way into the living room where a naked baby swung lazily inside a woven hammock, sound asleep. The family motioned for me to sit in a bright-orange plastic chair. I looked around at my new digs; a brick house, neat and clean, with red tile floors. Not bad, definitely not the hut in the jungle I'd envisioned months before.

"Hola, me llamo Yolanda," the Spanish lady said. She pointed to the buff Mayan dude, "Osmar," and then to the boy, "Luis." She walked to the hammock and gave it a nudge. "Y ella se llama Maria."

I smiled and shook their hands. Osmar walked off without a word. Yolanda motioned for me to back up with her hand. I paused for a moment, confused, and then began walking backward.

"No, no, no. Ven, ven!" she said with a smile, coming towards me and grabbing my hand. Evidently, waving your hand forward—like when you tell your buddy to go long for a pass in football—meant "come forward" in Nicaragua. I grabbed my bags and followed her down a hallway into my new room. There was a small bed tucked in the corner and a dresser against the back wall. A window with a wood door looked out to a big tree and the street below. It was perfect.

I set my bags on the bed and returned to my chair in the living room. A rather pathetic attempt at communication ensued, with lots of nodding and smiling, and the realization that all my years of Spanish had been one giant exercise in futility.

As I pondered the depths of my ignorance, a sudden urge to pee shook me from my depression. Yolanda was talking up a storm. I didn't want to be rude, so I held it in. Luis sat nearby, staring at me intently as I crossed and uncrossed my legs. I continued to nod and smile for minutes which seemed like hours, not understanding a word.

"El tiene 12 años," (He's 12 years old) she said, pointing to Luis.

"Que bueno," I said, my eyes crossing. It was now or never. Either I asked to use the bathroom, or they were about to see the gringo piss himself.

"Baño, baño, quiero baño," I said, flashing the same puppy eyes I'd given Diego a short time earlier.

"Letrina?" she asked.

"Baño," I repeated

"Letrina?"

"No, baño!"

The back-and-forth went on for several moments until she finally said, "El baño, oh sí, sí, la letrina."

She motioned to Luis, who sprang to his feet, grabbed my hand and led me out the back door. We walked down a dirt trail that ended at a shack constructed of scraps of wood and old weathered planks. Luis, still smiling from ear to ear, pointed his little finger to the structure and said, "Letrina."

The stench of piss and shit overwhelmed me as I stepped inside. I covered my nose with my shirt and crept towards a two-foot-high cement slab with a hole in the top. It looked like a cement pyramid sliced in half. Flies buzzed around my head as I dragged my feet closer and closer to the edge of hell. Shutting one eye, I peeked down into the hole and discovered a horror show playing out just ten feet below; starring roaches the size of cats, a lake of piss and a colossal mountain of shit. I unzipped my fly and pissed on the underworld—while gagging, holding my shirt over my nose and swatting away pterodactyl-sized flies.

When I finished my circus act, I rushed outside and gulped fresh air for a minute straight, making a mental note to always bring matches and a bandana to the "letrina."

* * *

"Cock-a-doo, Cock-a-doo…"

I was rudely awakened at three, four and five o'clock in the morning, courtesy of the ugliest, stupidest rooster in Nicaragua. The orange and gray monstrosity lived in the avocado tree outside my window. I initially named him "Big Ben," but quickly changed that to the more fitting, "Fucker."

"Fucker" made valiant attempts to crow just as deeply and loudly as the other roosters in the neighborhood, but sadly, he could never quite match up, lacking the ability to sing the final "doodle doo." His inadequacies, and, frankly, a lack of self-esteem led him to overreach his lot in life, resulting in murderous shrills on an hourly basis that rattled me from my deep, malaria-pill-induced nightmares.

Flinging open my window, I returned his greeting, "Shut up Fucker, and get a real crow!"

I mumbled more profanities as I stumbled out of the house and down the dirt path to three wooden walls and a sheet of plastic. Welcome to the shower. But first I needed to go further down the trail to the well, where I lowered a plastic bucket, tied to a rope, twenty feet down and filled it with water. Pulling it back up, hand over and hand, I dumped the water into a five-gallon bucket and repeated the process eight more times. Then, I half-carried, half-dragged, the heavy bucket back up the trail to the shower.

There I squatted, naked, dumping bowls of ice-cold water over my head, trembling and groggy from the Chloroquine. I lathered up my body and attempted to wash away the sleep and booze, rationing the water so I had enough to thoroughly rinse, knowing that if I didn't, I'd spend the rest of the day covered in a thin film of soap. I was often unable to clean all the cracks and crevices on my body—no pun intended— during my "bucket-bath."

Chickens and pigs roamed freely as I made my way along the dirt path leading to Elena's house, just a stone's throw from mine, where we'd be studying Spanish for the next three months.

Elena was already sitting in a wicker rocking chair waiting for class to begin when I entered. "Hola," I said with a smile as I made my way to the chair next to her. The living room had the same red tile floors as mine. Large sheets of construction paper were taped to the walls, containing

Spanish verbs and nouns written in red ink, and a white-board stood at the front of the room, eager to showcase my ignorance.

"Hola, qué tal?" she said with a big smile, her dark-brown hair resting on her shoulders. I picked up a slight accent.

Where are you from?" I asked.

"Long Island."

"Nice. Do you like your Nicaraguan family?"

"They're really sweet. How about you?" Her eyes were wide and friendly.

"They're nice," I said, pulling out my pen and notebook and rocking back in my chair. "Well, the mom and son are nice, I'm not too sure about the dad."

Our teacher, a tall man with curly black hair, walked in and began talking in Spanish as if we were bilingual. Elena and I gave each other worried looks.

"Wait, we don't speak Spanish!" I yelled out over his gibberish.

"No preocupa. Ya va a entender!" he said and went right on talking.

Apparently, we were going to learn Spanish through osmosis. I sunk lower in my chair, hoping he wouldn't call on me. Hard to hide when there are only two people in the class.

By noon, my brain was scattered and confused. I wanted to escape all things Spanish and return home for my lunch and a nap. As I gathered my belongings, Elena's Nica mom brought her a ceramic plate piled high with meat and vegetables, along with a glass of reddish-purple juice. I drooled at the sight. So far, I'd only been served beans and rice from my family.

Life settled into a rhythm over the next couple of weeks. Monimbo was home to craftsmen, cobblers, artisans, and musicians. The village, comprised of a couple hundred houses all squeezed together on one chunk of land and connected by dirt trails, had no roads except those lining the perimeter. The hardworking village was on full display as I walked to and from class each day. Next door, a short, wiry fellow chiseled teak and mahogany on his patio, creating beautiful marimbas and guitarras. Behind us, an old sun-weathered man rubbed fragrant oils into leather saddles and boots as he worked underneath a mango tree. The village seamstresses were on my path, pedaling old-time sewing machines out on their porches, as they made colorful dresses worn by young girls who performed the traditional folkloric dances at town festivals.

Spanish classes were Monday through Friday from 8-5, with an hour off for lunch. Taught entirely in Spanish, they kicked my ass. Adding to my frustration, Elena was picking up the language much faster than me. As I was struggling through verb conjugations, she was having full-on conversations with the teacher, making me feel inept. We would sometimes hang out after class and complain about the heat and mosquitos or talk about being homesick. It was nice having somebody who could relate to what I was going through.

Osmar turned out to be quite the asshole. His first act of assholeism manifested itself in the form of my nightly dinners. The Peace Corps gave the families a monthly allotment to purchase our food and necessities. Osmar had calculated, that by feeding me only the basic staples needed to survive, he could squirrel away the bulk of the money. Now, beans and rice are the staple diet in Nicaragua—I get that. But beans and rice only? Can a brother get a slice of bread? Some avocado, vegetables, or a tiny slice of meat? No!

Lunch and dinner were always the same—day after excruciating day—beans and rice served on a bright-orange plastic plate. I learned to hate the color, associating it with misery. I even came to hate the fruit, and all things orange.

To Osmar's credit, the bland beans were always piled sky high. I wasn't going to die of starvation, maybe just monotony… or gas! Occasionally, the beans and rice were mixed together, with garlic added. This slightly tastier combo, known as Gallo Pinto or "spotted rooster," was a favorite dish eaten by almost all Nicaraguans. And while I enjoyed the diversity, in the end, it was still beans and rice.

I craved veggies, meat, pasta, chicken and cheese. My Malaria nightmares turned to food fantasies; of me biting into Big Macs and dipping salty fries into ketchup, or, of lettuce and cheese falling from my lips, as I shoved Taco Supremes into my mouth.

The pounds began falling off even faster than they had during my high school wrestling days. I carved extra holes in my belt to keep my pants up. The nurse made me get on the scale every time I saw her. "You're losing weight too quickly," she would say, adjusting the scale with one hand and priming a needle in the other. "Now bend over."

One night, as I was shoveling the millionth spoonful of beans into my mouth, Osmar began to speak. I nearly fell off my chair, having only heard him talk a few times. He went on and on about some foreigner, named Frans, who'd lived with them prior to me. He barked something to Luis, who ran into the living room and brought back an old picture of a tall blonde man standing with the family on the front porch.

From what I could make out, Frans had come to Monimbo from

Germany for a two-month research program studying a nearby volcano. My ears perked up. "Volcano?" I asked. But Osmar was too busy talking about the great Frans.

Osmar motioned for me to follow him into the living room, where he lifted his tree-trunk sized arm and pointed to a shelf on the wall. There, sitting like a prized trophy, was an unopened bottle of booze with a shiny red ribbon tied around its neck. Franz had given it to him as a going away gift.

Breakfast was somewhat better. Yolanda served a variety of pastries and delicious coffee. She would sit outside with me each morning as we muddled through a conversation, the village bathed in the smell of tortillas grilling on open flames. Yolanda worked hard around the house all day, washing clothes by hand on a cement slab and ironing each piece of clothing, down to the socks and underwear.

"I'll do that," I said one day when I saw her chopping firewood outside by the adobe oven. I could barely pick up the long axe. I raised it above my head and let it come crashing down, missing the log entirely. Worried I'd chop off my foot, she grabbed the axe from my hands and shooed me away, my career as a woodchopper ending before it began.

She mopped the red tile floors over and over throughout the day, waging battle against the unrelenting dust that blew in from open doors and windows.

Osmar was a shoemaker. From sunup till sundown, he pounded and molded leather into beautiful, sturdy school shoes for the local kids. Each Friday, he mysteriously disappeared. And each Monday, he reappeared, hammering away in his little shed.

One morning, as I drank coffee and nibbled on a fresh pastry, my curiosity got the better of me. "Where does Osmar go each weekend?"

"Oh, he goes to his novia's house," Yolanda said without skipping a beat.

Wait… what? Did I hear that correctly? Novia means girlfriend, right? I cleared my throat and asked, "Doesn't it bother you that he has a novia?"

"No," she said. "Why should it, she's my best friend."

She explained how many husbands in Monimbo had girlfriends. I tried telling her, in my garbled Spanish, how women in my country wouldn't like that. She seemed confused, so I just smiled and nodded. But then she said something about "the war," and I sat up in my chair.

"The Revolution?" I asked.

Her face hardened. I'd used the word "Revolución" which carried much deeper significance than "guerra" or "war." But I was curious, especially after Diego had told me about the uprising beginning in Monimbo. So I asked her to tell me about the war.

She looked around, making sure nobody was near, and began talking in a whispered tone. She told me how years ago the people had grown weary of the corruption and oppression of Samoza and his family, who'd been in power for over fifty years. A local boy was murdered during a protest, which rallied the neighborhood into a resistance against the National Guard. Heavily armed soldiers entered the village, but Monimbo fended them off for seven days using only machetes, Molotov Cocktails, and a few rifles.

Samoza sent in more troops and tanks. Helicopters flew over and dropped bombs from the air, killing hundreds of men, women, and children, and nearly destroyed the village. The insurrection was the first spark, lighting a powder keg of discontent throughout the country. This anger was sharpened and weaponized through the Sandinistas.

I felt a new sense of pride living in Monimbo, knowing I was amongst a group of rebels who'd stood up to tyranny. I no longer ducked my head from the people's stares as I walked the trail to Elena's house, smiling and waving, instead, as they toiled away in their shops. It was only later, when I learned how the U.S. had become mixed up in the conflict that I wondered how they could embrace me the way they did.

"It's so hot," Elena said, as we worked through all the verb conjugations of "ir." There were as many, if not more than beans in Monimbo.

"I know," I said, wiping sweat from my forehead.

Elena's family had a relatively large house by Nicaraguan standards. Half the house had been converted into a small store called a "Pulpería," which sold a variety of snacks, chips, grains, rice, beans, oil and the one product that could bring me out of my despair, Coca-Cola. I was so jealous. She could literally eat chips and drink soda whenever she wanted, while I was faced with a never-ending platter of beans blocks away. The inequity bothered me.

She continued outpacing me in Spanish. It was of little comfort when I learned she'd grown up with a Spanish-speaking parent. I hated feeling inferior, so much so that I even took the drastic step of studying Spanish in the evening, after eight long hours in class.

She fanned herself with a worksheet, "and these mosquitoes are driving me insane."

"Me too."

The teacher was blabbing away, "Yo soy, tú eres, el es, nosotros somos, vosotros vais, ellos son." We happened to be in one of the two countries in the world that still used the "vosotros" form of "you." Just one more thing to add to the list of "shit I don't know."

"I hate the food here," Elena said, pulling me out of my hypnosis.

"You hate the food? Are you kidding? I would kill for the food your mom feeds you."

"Yeah but she gives me way too much, and I'm gaining weight."

I wanted to gouge my eyes out. I tried telling Elena about my daily diet of beans, but she showed little empathy.

"I hate it here," she said.

I ground my teeth and forced my eyes to stay open and not roll up in their eyelids. "You just need to get out of the house."

"No, it's too hot."

"Ok," I looked up, the teacher was still going on and on, "estará, estarás, estarámos..." To be, or not to be. Will you be, or will you not be. Would you be, or would you not be. These are the questions... the questions Shakespeare would surely kill himself over if he was forced to learn them in Spanish!

"Do you want to hang out after class?" Elena asked, breaking me out of my trance again.

"I'm just going to go home and read," I lied. I was really heading to a little store that sold beer a block away. It had a table out front where I could write gibberish in my journal and dilute all the Spanish sloshing around in my brain.

It wasn't Elena per se, I just felt a need to walk solo, to soak up Nicaragua from my own unbiased vantage point. But, instead of just telling her that, which might have breached some weird code of ethics in my twisted mind, I stopped hanging out with her after class and listening to her problems. I was curt and dismissive, slowly pushing her away. We argued often, and as a result, she became incredibly homesick.

CHAPTER SEVEN

A ROCKY PATH

Imagine my surprise, sitting down for dinner one evening and finding the opaque eye of some round, bizarre-looking fish staring up at me. Osmar, the Mayan Warrior, must have been feeling generous that night, as the strange creature had replaced my usual glob of beans. I studied him curiously for a few moments, then proceeded to pick him up with my fingers and bite his fucking head off, ravenous for meat. It only took one bite to put his head away, eyeballs and all. Then I used my teeth like a beaver to scrape every last morsel from the bones. I moved on to the overcooked, greasy rice, which I wolfed down as well, using my fingers to capture any straggling grains. I then licked all the fish bones, one by one, for good measure. It wasn't a Big Mac, but it hit the spot.

Later that evening, as I sat outside drinking a rum and coke, warm tropical air swirling about, a familiar-looking lady approached.

"Hola, soy la mama de Elena."

"Buenas noches."

"Can you come by and talk to Elena? She hasn't left her room all day and stopped eating"

I sighed and drank a large swig of rum, "I'm not sure that's a good idea." I was buzzed and reluctant to go.

"Por favor, esta muy triste. Please, she's so sad."

I shifted uncomfortably in my chair, "No bueno."

"Por favor señor!" she pleaded, her face awash in distress.

I grunted and shook my head, "Ok, ya voy." After pulling on a shirt, I hiked down the trail, past the chickens and pigs, to her house.

"Hey Elena, it's Kevin," I said, knocking on her bedroom door.

"Go away!"

"Just let me in."

"No, just go away."

I thought about my glass of rum, and warm swirling winds waiting for me back at the top of the animal trail.

"Elena…"

"I said, go away. I don't want to talk to anyone."

"Oh, come on," I said, knocking harder and harder, "just let me in. Your mom is freaking out."

I heard some movement, and then the door flung open, "What do you want?" she said. She was wearing pajamas; purple silk shorts and a matching low-cut top which showed off her sizeable cleavage.

"I… uh… uh… just wanted to see how you're doing." *Eyes up Kev!*

She walked to her bed and sat down. "What do you care?"

"I do care. What's going on?"

"I miss my family!" She burst out crying the moment the words left her lips. Her pain hit me like a ton of bricks. I walked over and sat next to her, putting my arm around her shoulder.

"It's going to be ok. We just have to make it through training, and then everything will be different."

She continued crying. I pulled her closer, hugging her tight. We rocked back and forth. All of the loneliness and fear, bottled-up inside us since arriving in Nicaragua, began to fade. Our lips met. We kissed softly at first, and then more passionately, sinking into the bed. I became lost in the moment, transported from reality; chaos retreating at the speed of light. It was safe and warm. Can't I stay here just for a while? I opened my eyes and came crashing back to reality. "I'm sorry Elena," I said, springing from the bed. "This isn't right."

"Where are you going?"

"We can't do this, we're just lonely." No matter how much I craved affection, I knew it wouldn't be right. I heard her sobbing as I rushed from the room.

In Spanish class the next day, I leaned toward her and said, "Elena, I'm sorry about…."

"Don't worry about it," she said, moving her body away. "It's fine."

"Let's go up to the park tomorrow."

"No thanks," she said, pretending to scribble notes on a sheet of paper.

"Come on, it'll be fun."

"No!" she said firmly.

I didn't push it. We were both struggling to find our way in this new land, a place so very different from anything we'd ever known. And, just like I was searching for my path—often lost and lonely in a sea of green—it was up to Elena, and Elena alone, to do the same.

* * *

Monimbo was on the outskirts of a larger city called, Masaya. Early the next morning, I stuffed my journal into my backpack and set off to discover Masaya.

Adobe homes, painted in banana yellows, lime greens and blood reds lined the road. Large wrought iron gates and corrugated roofs gave the houses a rugged yet finished look. Skinny dogs and skittish chickens ran free, eating bits of trash on the rutted sidewalks. A short, stocky woman carried a giant plastic bowl, piled high with mangoes and papayas, atop her head. I marveled at her balancing skills as she passed by.

Turning a corner, the majestic Nuestra Señora de la Asunción Cathedral came into view, with its bell tower reigning over the city. While not as colorful and flashy as Granada's Cathedral, it was still an impressive sight. Entering Parque Central, I stopped to admire a water feature with massive Roman columns, an arched dome and cement swans in a pool of water. A nude woman stood on top, stretching her hands towards the heavens. A pose I knew all too well.

I was at the hub of this vibrant community, the epicenter being the Central Park (Parque Central) located on Main Street (Calle Central) with the Cathedral (El Catedral) towering over all. This same blueprint was copied throughout Nicaragua and most Central American cities.

A small outdoor café with wood tables caught my attention. I peeled off my backpack and plopped into an awaiting chair. A breeze blew in, swinging a Pepsi sign with the name Cafetín Flores painted in small green font. Cases of empty beer bottles were stacked next to a metal freezer with the word "Victoria" painted on the front. Below "Victoria" was a picture of a green beer bottle with condensation running down the label.

I waited several minutes for a waiter, but nobody came. I finally called out to a man behind the counter who looked at me strangely and then went about his business. I called out two more times before he finally came over.

"Que deseas?" he asked, his collared shirt unbuttoned to mid-chest, showing off a long, gold-chain necklace which appeared more yellow than gold.

I pointed to the freezer, "Victoria!"

"Cuatro Córdobas," he said, handing me an ice-cold beer. The exchange rate was 13-1, thirteen Nicaraguan Córdobas to one U.S. dollar. I liked the math. The Peace Corps had given me a modest stipend to buy odds and end while in training. By modest, I'm talking twenty bucks a week. John D. Rockefeller, I was not.

I noticed a pig walking nonchalantly through a group of boys shooting hoops on a run-down court. I smiled at the irony of a pig walking through a game of horse. The boys seemed oblivious to both the pig and the chuckling gringo.

The sun cranked up. Sweat poured off my head and rolled down my back. I moved to the other side of the table, catching shade from a giant Guanacaste tree, its massive branches, shooting up in all directions, screamed, "Climb me!" My beer screamed louder, "Drink me!"

"Otra!" I said holding up my empty beer.

My love affair with Victoria, la cerveza mas fina de Nicaragua (Nicaragua's finest beer) was sparked that day. A love affair that would only be rivaled by her sexy older sister, Flor de Caña - Gran Reserva— Nicaragua's finest rum.

No longer burdened with the responsibilities of life in America, I began thinking abstractly about my place in the world. Money, career, status: all the things I once thought so important, were fading away. Scaling the proverbial "corporate ladder" was now only a distant memory. My structure—My Order—was breaking off like a massive glacier and floating away. Yet, the small chunk of land I found myself standing on, felt solid, and seemed to be moving in the right direction.

I pulled out my journal and began a poem...

I've crossed the waters of azure blue,
and dipped my head in its vibrant hue
Sullen and shaken I thus emerged,
absent tears, my emptiness purged

The day slipped through my hands, and as if somebody had flicked a switch, the sun disappeared. Marimba music sparked to life, as if on cue, as people began whistling and singing in harmony. Chubby women, wearing oversized aprons, shoved tree limbs and branches into grills and lit them on fire. The aroma of smoke and charred oak spread through the park. A sizzle rang out with each chunk of beef and pork tossed on the blackened grates. My belly rumbled like a litter of lion cubs.

The court lights blinked to life, and a spirited game of 5-on-

5 basketball got underway with crowds filling the sidelines. Young girls moved in, giggling and turning red whenever their favorite player ran by and smiled their way. It was a magical setting.

With Victoria in hand, I cruised through the park salivating at all the colorful meats hissing on the grills, finally stopping at one with a wide variety. A portly lady, hacking through a slab of beef with a machete, paused her work and looked up. She pointed the tip of the blade toward me, and asked, "Que quieres?"

I pointed to a long strip of meat rubbed in red spices. I assumed it was pork, but it didn't matter. Hell, it could have been the pig wandering the basketball court earlier, for all I cared. She pulled the meat off the fire with her chubby fingers, fat oozing out the ends, and wrapped it in a plantain leaf.

I took a moment to admire the artwork before biting in. Grease sprayed the roof of my mouth, a good burn. Smoky fat and salty gristle mixed to perfection with the mild achiote seasoning. I chewed slowly, savoring the flavors, and washed it down with a swig of beer.

I could have hung out in Parque Central all night, but it was dark now—very dark—and I'd been gone all day. Leaving the bright lights behind, the town took on an ominous vibe. People appeared and disappeared into the shadows. Darkness was everywhere, except for the light spilling out from corner pulperías, revealing girls buying oil and rice for the night's dinner.

Old men sat on porches playing checkers in the moonlight, staring as I passed by. I tugged nervously at the straps on my backpack and picked up my pace. How had it become so dark? Why is there not one freaking street light in this city? A dog shot out of nowhere, barking and trailing me. I fake kicked, and he ran off.

The bright colors of the homes were no longer visible, making me lose my sense of direction. There were no street signs or landmarks, nothing distinctive to guide me home. I became disoriented, passing the same houses again and again. It all looked the same. Do I take a right here? A left at the statute? Should I cross at the empty lot? Is somebody going to spring out from the dark and stick a knife in the stupid gringo? What the hell am I even doing in Nicaragua?

I was beginning to panic when the dirt trail leading home appeared. I skipped up the path, brave once again. Everybody was in bed as I tiptoed to my room. Passing the kitchen table, I spotted my orange plate piled high with beans and smiled inside.

The heat was unbearable that night. I tossed and turned, sweat soaking my pillow. I devised an imaginary Misery Meter, pegging my current misery status somewhere between a seven and an eight. Swatting at kamikaze mosquitoes, I was suddenly jolted by loud screaming.

Osmar was going off on Yolanda. I leaned towards the voices, straining to understand the conversation, a sentence... a few words. Fucking Spanish! Shit was going down and I didn't need a Ph.D. in Español to figure that out. I rolled over and buried my head in my soggy pillow, raising my misery level to a solid nine. I conjured up a Caribbean Island with white sand beaches and coconut rum drinks—the image I'd envisioned when signing up for the Peace Corps. I strolled into the cool, blue sea as gentle waves lapped against my thighs...

POW! He hit her. She cried out in pain.

I wasn't in the fucking Caribbean. I was in a fucked-up situation. In fucked-up Monimbo. In Nica-fucking-ragua!

The powerlessness in her whimpers shot through me like a lightning bolt. That's it, last fucking straw, misery level TEN! I flew out of bed and rushed into the living room.

The buff Mayan God had morphed into an exploding volcano, puffing and screaming, spit flying, face as red as blood. Yolanda was crouched down, cowering in a corner. Osmar was towering over her, arms flailing. With his back to me, I saw my opening and sprinted towards him. I grabbed his thick neck and shoulders and wrestled him against the wall. His eyes were black with rage. Yolanda scooted out of the way.

He turned and tried to move towards her, but I applied more pressure, using my body to push him off balance, and wedging myself between them. My years of wrestling were paying off. With his back against the wall and my forearm on his neck, I was in the perfect position to punch him. My bicep tightened, and my fingers clenched into a fist. I wanted him to feel pain, wanted to inflict pain.

Yolanda pulled on my shoulders and pleaded with me not to hit him. I reached back and loaded up, ready to strike. But her voice pierced through my anger like an arrow. I slammed him into the wall, gave him my meanest glare and released my grip. Turning, I waited for the Mayan warrior's heavy fist to reign down on me, knowing it was going to hurt. But the punch never came, only the sound of the front door slamming as he made his exit.

My heart sank when I saw the nasty welt on Yolanda's eye. What the fuck! I suddenly remembered Osmar's prized bottle of booze and made a beeline for it. The bottle was glistening in the moonlight.

I snatched it from its dedicated shelf and ripped off the stupid, red ribbon. "Here's to you—you motherfucker!" I said, hoisting the bottle to the front door and chugging away.

Yolanda disappeared into her room while I sat in the dark, polishing off the bottle and wondering how I always seemed to wind up in these fucked-up situations. The "Peace" in Peace Corps was fading fast.

CHAPTER EIGHT

P51 MUSTANG

Mom said I swore like a sailor. My foul mouth wasn't something I acquired overnight, like reaching down and picking up a shiny penny. No, I worked hard to refine my craft. I suppose running and cussing like savages through the Mississippi Sticks helped form a solid foundation. But it was Mom who taught me how to sharpen my tongue into a deadly weapon.

After leaving Pascagoula, we returned to San Diego and moved in with my grandmother. Mom had fallen off the radar, disappeared. Grandma quickly realized what little hellions we'd become, and we were bounced from one relative to the next, eventually landing with my Uncle Mike in Long Beach. Evidently, caring for four wild children could be quite the challenge.

Uncle Mike was a devout Mormon, and I was not. You can see the problem. Even at the tender age of 8, I'd already acquired a healthy skepticism of organized religion. Forcing me to go to church was probably the worst thing you could do to me. I wanted to be Huck Finn floating on a raft down the Mississippi River. I would have taken a whooping with a belt, over being dragged into the antiseptic Mormon Church.

Everybody inside creeped me out, making me feel like I was in an episode of the Twilight Zone. Aliens masquerading as humans, the leader preaching to the lesser aliens as they sat silently in pews. Baby aliens were shuffled into back rooms and indoctrinated to the strange customs and norms. I'd tug at my collar, tight around my neck, and scratch at my itchy pants, watching the arms on a clock move in slow motion around Roman numerals. When it was finally time to leave, I was forced to smile and hug the other aliens.

My uncle tried his best to instill some manners and calm into our lives, but we were too far gone by then. Mormonism sure as hell wasn't going to save us. So after a long year battling for our souls, Uncle Mike grew weary and shipped us back to our grandma.

She owned a fourplex in University Heights, a sleepy neighborhood in central San Diego. She took her turn trying to rein us in, but we proved too wild. We knew it was only a matter of time before our well-worn suitcases made an appearance.

But then, like a phantom spirit searching for its soul, mom reappeared. She moved us into a two-bedroom apartment above grandma. We were all so happy to have our Mom back. We loved her dearly, flaws and all. She enrolled us at Alice Birney Elementary and walked us to and from school the entire first week. At night, we played Go Fish and Monopoly while she cooked four-course dinners.

She surprised me one day after school with a model. P51 Mustang was printed on the box above a picture of a WWII fighter plane. We carefully laid out all the parts and Mom showed me how to read the manual, check off the pieces and disassemble them from the plastic molds. On the parts that wouldn't pry loose, Mom used an X-Acto knife. My job was to sand down any jagged edges. "Smooth as butter," I'd always say, passing the pieces to her for inspection.

"Good job," she'd tell me with a smile. The smell of the glue made me dizzy. "Just a dab," she'd say, as I pinched the silver tube. I tried my best not to over glue the tiny pegs on the wings. After gluing the pieces, I'd squeeze them together until my muscles ached, then set them on the table and marvel at my work.

Night after night, we worked on the fighter plane. I loved reading through the instruction booklet, seeing all the parts and tools required. It was all so organized and official—everything in order. The best part, I had control over everything, except for the X-Acto knife, which was strictly off-limits.

I'd wait patiently for Mom to put away the dishes and have a smoke each night. I knew, almost to the minute, how long it took for her cigarette to burn to the end. And with each flick of her ashes, I was that much closer to working on the plane.

As the P51 neared completion, Mom took me to the craft store to pick out some paint. My three sisters had to stay home because this was a special mom and son trip. She guided me to the model paint section and pointed out all the different colors. It was so exciting. I imagined unscrewing the tin caps and smelling all the little jars. We found the green and blue paints listed in the instruction booklet, and then Mom said, "Now you need to add your own flair." She pointed to the wall of bottles. "Go on, pick your own special color."

I stared at all the different colors, analyzing my choices. I steered clear of the girly pinks and purples, and I also didn't want any boring grays or browns. My eyes suddenly widened, and I reached for Candy Apple Red.

"Great choice," Mom said.

Back home, I was bursting at the seams to work on the model. I tried playing with my army men, lining them against each other for a major battle, but my mind kept racing back to the P51 Mustang and the Candy Apple Red paint.

Mom sensed my angst. "I have to run some errands, but we'll work on it later tonight."

The minute she stepped out the door, I snuck into her room and stared up at the model airplane, sitting ever so quietly on its shelf. I wanted to pull it down so badly, to put the final pieces together and add my red flair. I was a big boy after all. I could even handle the X-Acto knife. But, I didn't want to make Mom mad.

I struggled all night to keep my eyes open, waiting for her to return home, until the sandman snuck into my room and tossed a handful of sand in my eyes.

I raced home from school the next day, eager to get to work. But Mom was sound asleep, and I didn't dare wake her. When she finally did wake, hours later, I overheard her say to my oldest sister, "Don't wait up for me, I have things to take care of."

Stephanie caught me in Mom's room later that night and yelled, "You're not supposed to be in there!" I gave her my dirtiest glare as I walked by.

Weeks passed, with Mom going out all night and sleeping all day. My oldest sisters, Stephanie and Michelle, were back in charge, making sure I went to school and ate my dinner. I growled like a rabid dog at their every command and order—I could take care of myself!

Late one night, as we slept, Mom came into our room crying and smelling of booze and cigarettes. We woke up scared, wondering what was happening. She pulled my sisters to her and began sobbing, "I love you guys so much. I'm a lousy mother. I'm so sorry."

My sisters latched on, crying and hugging tight—not wanting to let her go. "We love you too," they said through tears and sobs. "It's ok, we understand."

I rolled over and faced the wall, avoiding eye contact. She tugged on my shoulder and pleaded for me to hug her. But I clenched my arms to my side and kept my nose on the wall. I didn't understand. I didn't understand why she always left us, I didn't understand why I didn't have a normal mom and dad, and I didn't understand why I couldn't finish my motherfucking model!

I peeked into Mom's room early the next morning. She was gone. The P51 Mustang screamed, "Pick me up!" I rolled a desk chair over and pulled it down. I flew it through the air, making machine gun noises while dive-bombing imaginary battleships. Setting it back on the shelf, I noticed the Candy Apple Red paint.

I looked back towards the door. The coast was clear. Using all my strength, I twisted off the cap and held the paint to my nose. The smells made my nose tingle. I closed my eyes and took another deep whiff, breathing in the fumes. I became dizzy and grabbed the corner of the desk. My head was spinning on my shoulders like in the movie, The Exorcist. When my mind cleared, I put everything away quickly—before I got in trouble—and went into the living room.

Mom was asleep on the couch, sprawled out on her back. She had one foot on the ground and one foot hanging over the back of the sofa, toes pointing up to the popcorn ceilings. I sat on the carpet in front of her, slithering like a snake, hoping to get her attention.

I glanced over from time to time, looking for signs of life. I moved closer, searching her face for movement or breathing. A bottle of liquor, less than a quarter full, was beside the couch. I hated that fucking liquor. Using my best spy moves, I quietly picked up the bottle and tiptoed into the kitchen. Standing over the sink, I unscrewed the cap and dumped the stinky liquid down the drain, slowly, to mask the glugging sound it made coming out. The stench traveled up and hit my nose, reminding me of the cement glue. I wondered how she could drink that poison every night.

I filled the empty bottle with water up to the quarter mark, tiptoed back into the living room and set it back by the couch.

Then I noticed a pack of Mom's cigarettes on the coffee table. I pulled out the last five cigarettes, broke them in half and tossed them in the trash. If Mom couldn't save herself, I'd have to do it for her.

She still hadn't moved, and I was getting scared. I put my hand near her mouth and felt for breathing. When I didn't feel anything, my heart dropped. She was dead!

Then her hand fell to the side of the couch, grazing the bottle. She sat straight up, the bottle now in her hand. "Kevin!" she screamed, "What are you doing?"

"Just playing," I said. My heart was racing. Mom had just arisen from the dead, and I was hoping she'd be in one of her good moods. My stomach tied in knots when she twisted off the cap and took three long gulps. Her face turned Candy Apple Red, and she jumped off the couch. I was terrified as she leaped over the coffee table and lifted me into the air with one hand. She used her free hand to smack my bare legs over and over. I tried desperately to shield my ass and thighs with my hands, but she pulled them away each time.

"No mommy, no mommy, please stop mommy. Mommy I'm sorry, mommy…"

"You fucking little shit. What the fuck did you do with my vodka you ungrateful little shit!"

Mom beat me until her hand grew tired. My sisters didn't dare come out of the room. When she finally let go of my wrist, I fell into a heap at her feet, sobbing and writhing in pain. Mom was breathing hard and sat back down on the couch to catch her breath. My heart felt like it would explode when I saw her reaching for her cigarettes. She grabbed the empty pack of cigarettes and liquor bottle and stomped into the kitchen.

"God Damn It!" she screamed, tossing the empty bottle and pack of cigarettes in the trash. I froze, petrified, as she ran towards me, broken cigarettes in hand. She shoved them in my face and rubbed them on my cheeks. I tried crawling away, but she reached down and whacked me several more times. I finally just curled into a ball and closed my eyes.

My sisters ran out when they heard Mom slam the front door. No doubt off to the local bar. "What did you do?" they screamed.

I pushed them all aside and ran into Mom's room. Through my tears, I spotted the P-51 Mustang, jumped up and pulled it off the shelf. I spun it around in my hand, taking one last look at all my hard work, and then threw it with all my strength against the wall—smashing it to bits. "Fuck you bitch!"

* * *

Mom continued to slip, disappearing for days at a time, leaving my ten and eleven-year-old sisters to care for Kerry and me. They did their best, but they had learned to parent from Mom, so if we acted up or got sassy, we got smacked. Order quickly dissolved, replaced by Authoritative Chaos.

One night, as my sisters chased me around the apartment, there was a knock at the front door. We all froze and quieted down as Stephanie opened the door.

"Yes, grandma?"

"Where the hell is your mom?"

"Um… she's at the store," Stephanie said. But grandma knew better, and she was fed up with us screaming and fighting ten feet above her head.

"That's it," she said. "I'm calling your dad."

"Our dad!" we all shouted. He hadn't been in our lives in years. In fact, all we really knew about him, was from what our mom had told us: that he was an asshole who didn't pay his child support.

So, later that night, there was a second knock on our door. And this time, in walked my dad. I peeked at him from the opening in the hallway. He was a big, muscular guy. He saw me and motioned for me to come. I walked slowly towards him, staring at his curly blondish-red hair and big green eyes.

He reached down and picked me off the ground like I was a feather. The stubble from his beard brushed against my cheek. It was prickly like a cactus. I breathed in his aftershave and liked it. We filled our suitcases and left with him. I wouldn't see Mom for the next two years.

CHAPTER NINE

MOUTH OF HELL

Luis was a mellow boy with a big laugh and an even bigger heart. He worked hard around the house cooking, cleaning and looking after the baby. When he wasn't helping his mom, he was usually in the shed helping his dad make shoes. Luis rarely kicked a soccer ball around or shot marbles in the dirt like the other boys in the neighborhood.

One evening, as he was busy mopping the floors, I tapped him on the shoulder, "Luis, you want to go hiking with me to the Masaya Volcano?"

His eyes opened wide. "Sí! Sí!" he said.

We went together to ask Yolanda. She was outside, stirring the beans and adjusting the burning wood underneath.

"Buenas noches," I said with a smile.

"Buenas noches," she said, looking from me to Luis and then back.

"Can Luis go hiking with me tomorrow?"

Her eyes lit up, but then panic flashed across them. She stopped stirring the beans and set the large spoon down. "I'll have to ask his dad first," she said, marching off towards the shed, eyes straight ahead, as if headed to the gallows.

Osmar had only recently returned home after spending nearly two weeks away after the night of hell. The house had become so calm and tranquil in his absence, that when I saw him lurking around one day, my stomach began churning and I nearly puked. Thankfully, he kept a low profile, and I rarely saw him. He never said a word about his missing bottle of booze, and I took comfort each time I passed the empty shelf. It had become symbolic to me. My attempt at restoring order to the universe— pushing back against the chaos that was forever nipping at my toes.

Ten minutes later, Yolanda rushed back into the living room. "Sí, Luis can go!"

She put an ancient-looking iron into the hot coals. When it glowed orange and began to smoke, she set about ironing all the clothes Luis would wear on our hike, including his underwear and socks.

My feathered alarm clock, "Fucker," woke me at the crack of dawn. The sun was blood-orange and blurry like a mirage. I poured a cup of coffee and walked to the porch. Smoldering wood and the morning dew produced a rich, smoky aroma that hung over Monimbo like a warm blanket. I breathed in deeply, a drug addict getting his fix.

Yolanda wrapped tortillas and leftover rice in banana leaves, filled a jug with water and stuffed them into a backpack, along with extra clothes and a towel. "Cuídate – Be careful," she said to Luis, and then gave him a big motherly hug.

The morning was especially humid, the soggy stuff that keeps you in a constant lather. I slapped at a mosquito feeding on my neck. Instant death. Luis grinned as I rolled the little vampire into a ball and wiped my blood-streaked fingers on my shorts. He seemed immune to the heat and mosquitoes as we settled into our five-kilometer hike to the base of the volcano.

"Luis, I'm appointing you Vice President of the Monimbo Hiking Club."

He squinted his eyes, confused. I'm pretty sure he thought that I was a big idiot.

"How do you like school?" I asked.

"Bien."

"You like your profesoras?"

"Sí"

"You like making shoes with your father?"

"Sí."

Luis didn't seem all that interested in having any in-depth conversations, so we put our heads down and soldiered on.

I became drenched. So much so, that I could've wrung out my t-shirt and filled my canteen. The mosquitoes finally relented just as we arrived at Masaya and Nindirí, two live volcanoes which had erupted nineteen times over the past five hundred years. I was hoping today wouldn't be twenty.

A flock of Blackbirds swirled overhead as we made our way to the foot of the volcano. A wind kicked up, lifting the birds upward. They tucked in their bodies and flew towards the sun, climbing higher and higher, until they appeared to be a mere splattering of dots on the horizon. We arrived at the path leading up the volcano and prepared to make our ascent. I looked over at Luis who was staring up at the sky.

"Tienes miedo – Scared?" I asked.

Before he could answer, the birds dove from the sky and flew straight at us, a black cloud barreling down. We braced and waited for them to smash into our faces. But, just feet away, they changed course and flew off towards the volcano. Demon spirits in search of souls.

Luis looked like he had just seen the devil, but he puffed out his little chest and exclaimed, "Yo no tengo miedo!"

We followed the demon birds up a wide trail which wrapped around the volcano. The higher we climbed, the steeper the path became, to the point we were almost walking vertically. We were careful not to fall, fearing we might roll all the way back to the bottom. Poor Luis had his head down and was dragging his feet. For the first time, he was sweating as much as me.

I nudged him on his shoulder. "Descanso hombre - Break."

We wiped sweat from our eyes and gulped down water. Luis scarfed down his rolled-up tortillas with rice, as I wondered how he managed to keep such a calm, happy view on life with such a cold father. The sun was blazing, ninety-five degrees easy. I figured we'd made it about two-thirds of the way up when I noticed a man about my age and a boy hiking toward us. "Hey, are you American?" he called out in perfect English as they approached.

Whoa, hold up! I'd been in Nicaragua for four weeks at that point, and apart from with my fellow volunteers, hadn't spoken English to any other person. In fact, I hadn't even seen another American since leaving the States.

"Yes, yes, yes, I'm American!" If I had an American flag, I would've hoisted it in the air right there and waved it from side to side.

"I'm Rick, and this is Yadir." He pointed to a teenage boy who appeared to be Nicaraguan.

"I'm Kevin, and this is Luis." We all shook hands. Luis packed away his food, and we began hiking as a group.

"Dude, where are you from? How long have you been here? What are you doing in Nicaragua?" I fired off questions like an overeager teenager.

"I work for Pepsi," he said, turning to Yadir and rattling something out in perfect Spanish. Yadir turned and walked back down the volcano.

"Hey, where is he…"

"He'll be back," Rick said. "How long have you been down here?"

"Just over a month," I said, then deepened my voice an octave, "I'm in the Peace Corps."

"Peace Corps, oh wow, that's cool. I've been down here about two years. I'm Vice President of Marketing."

Rick lived in the capital, Managua, and traveled around the country selling Pepsi concentrate to independent distributors, who mixed it with soda water and bottled it.

"Is that why Pepsi tastes so different down here?" I asked.

"Yeah. Everybody thinks we ship bottles of soda around the world. Could you imagine how many ships we'd need to do that?"

"Hey, did you know Spanish before you got here?"

"No, I learned it here. I couldn't speak a lick when I arrived."

The sun was beating down, sweat burning my eyes. I became dizzy and morphed into a giant sponge, the yellow porous kind that people use to wash their cars. I was plunged into a bucket of cold water, emerging full and dripping wet. Only to be wrung out moments later, leaving me parched and bone dry.

"Kevin... Kevin... Kevin..." I looked up. Rick was shaking me roughly. "Are you alright, man?" I tried translating his words into English but grew confused. Wait, he is speaking English?

"Sit down man, drink some water."

"Yeah, I need to rest a minute." I sat down in the dirt. Luis sat next to me and gave me his water jug. As I drank, I took a quick analysis of my situation.

A. You're very hot.

B. You're extremely thirsty.

C. You're slightly stupid.

D, or is it E? It's 100 degrees, the humidity is 95% and you're hiking a volcano at noon.

Diagnosis: You're overheated, and stupid!

Then, a Toyota Camry came driving up the volcano. Shit, I'm hallucinating again. It pulled up alongside us and stopped. The tinted window lowered, and there was Yadir, in the driver's seat, motioning for us to get in. I scrunched my eyes, confused, and looked back down our path. We'd been hiking up a road this whole time.

"Screw this," Rick said. "I'm driving the rest of the way. Come on, I've got A.C."

I looked from the Toyota to the volcano's peak, and then back to Rick. "No way man, I'm hiking the rest of the way." Hearing the words leave my mouth gave me a boost of adrenaline.

"Come on man, you almost passed out a minute ago!"

"I gotta do it," I said. I wasn't in Nicaragua to find shortcuts. I hadn't upended my whole life to take the easy route at the first opportunity. I'd come to this country to slog it out, to find out who I was and what I was made of. I was here to find my essence, my core.

"Suit yourself," said Rick, climbing into the Camry.

Luis stared at me as he drove off as if I was the dumbest gringo in the world.

"Vamanos," I said.

An hour later, we reached the summit. Luis and I turned and looked out at the grandeur of Nicaragua, unbridled and pure. Green stretching as far as the eye could see, rolling and dipping, emptying into lakes and lagoons. Luis's smile returned as he gazed out at his country. We gave each other powerful high fives and turned back towards the volcano.

Fifty feet down the slope was a shack. Inside, a woman stood next to a pile of coconuts, machete in hand. Rick and Yadir were sitting on stools shaded by a palm frond roof, sipping from straws sticking out of two coconuts.

Rick make a clicking noise with his mouth and then a shishing noise, which caught the attention of the coconut lady. "Dos más," he called out as we approached. The woman grabbed two coconuts from the pile and began whacking at the husk with her machete. I winced, waiting for her fingers to come flying off. She carved out holes, stuck in straws and held them out. Reaching for my coconut, I counted her fingers, and was relieved to find them all intact.

"Wait till you see the volcano!" Rick hollered.

"You mean this isn't the volcano?"

"No, over there," he said, pointing to a strip of land sloping up with a plume of steam just beyond. "That's La Boca De Infierno, The Mouth of Hell."

My eyes lit up, "Mouth of Hell?" My strength was coming back. There was something therapeutic—mystical—in the coconut water, quenching my thirst like nothing I'd ever drunk before.

"Otro coco!" I yelled.

After gorging ourselves on coconut water, we walked the last hundred feet to the rim. Rick led us down a trail to a ledge which protruded out over the volcano. We bunched together and crept out, ever so slowly. Reaching the edge, we planted our feet, craned our necks forward and looked down. The crater, a thousand feet below, was hissing and spitting, steam rising from the center. I quickly stepped back and took a deep breath.

Then I curled my feet, wedging them into the rock like an anchor, and moved forward. Staring into the pit, into the bowels of hell, I became mesmerized by the bright orange fire sizzling at the bottom. It was like an ancient dragon, buried alive, huffing and puffing just below the rubble. Our noses crinkled from the sulfur filling the air.

Rick broke the silence, "You know 500 years ago they tossed virgins and children into the volcano to appease the Gods."

Luis took a step back from the edge. I envisioned Osmar, with his muscular arms, dragging terrified girls to this very ledge as they struggled to escape. He'd scream, "I give this virgin to you as a gift. Spare Monimbo your wrath!" Then toss the girl over, her arms and legs flailing as she plummeted into the Mouth of Hell, the mouth of the dragon; La Boca de Infierno!

"You want to check out some secret caves?" Rick asked, pulling me out of my daydream. Secret caves? Are you kidding me?

"Hell yeah!" I said.

Rick went to the car and returned with two flashlights. We walked to the other side of the volcano, down a hill and over a pile of craggy, igneous rock. Rick handed me one of the flashlights. "You're going to need this," he said as we moved through shrubs and over more porous, black rocks. When we reached the bottom, a cavern appeared with plumes of hot vapor billowing from the entrance. Rick and Yadir went inside without any hesitation.

I flipped on the flashlight and poked my head inside. It was dark and musty. Luis moved closer to me. Sulfur burned my nose as we hopped over a stream running down the middle of the cave. I ran my fingers along the slimy, bumpy walls. It felt like a reptile's body slit down the middle and turned inside out. The hairs on my arm stood up.

As we followed the curvatures of the cave, the sunlight, pouring in from the entrance, dimmed with each twist and with each turn, until the last wisp of light slid into the slimy walls and disappeared altogether. Flashlights were now our only weapon from the blackness surrounding us.

Our feet sank into murky pools of water as we maneuvered deeper into the cave. Rocks lining our path became so large, we had to hold each other's flashlights and take turns climbing over the slimy mounds.

Luis clutched the corner of my T-shirt and walked within inches of my side. "Estás bien?" I asked, pointing the flashlight in his eyes. He squinted and nodded yes. I gave him a pat on his back. With water now up to our ankles, we continued moving forward, even as the walls narrowed and the ceiling dipped, forcing us to stoop.

We crawled around a corner, the air dense—our breathing labored—and came into a vast cavern. I stood up and breathed in. A disgusting stench overpowered me. I shined my light on the ground, illuminating mounds of dark, slimy gunk.

"Oh nasty, what's that shit?" I asked Rick.

"Look up," he whispered.

I lifted my flashlight to the ceiling. There, hanging upside down by their claws were tens of thousands of bats. I was standing in a gigantic pile of bat shit—Guano—just feet below the little vampires! It was the thing of nightmares.

Then, the entire ceiling began to move. Either the light from my flashlight or my girlish screams had agitated the bats, awakened the dormant dragon. And with each beat of his heart, each flutter of his scales, a bat unclenched his claws and flew down the dark corridor.

Within minutes, thousands of bats had released their claws and dropped from the ceiling, filling the cavern. They formed one large mass and flew in circles around us, wave after wave, flapping and buzzing just inches from our faces. Gusts of wind from their wings blew across my cheeks and nose. My heart was racing. Rick shouted over the buzz, "Turn off your flashlight!"

"You're crazy!" I shouted. But I knew I was going to do it. My finger trembled as I switched off the light. Instant blackness. Luis dug his fingernails into my skin as I held my hand in front of my face, inches away. But, I couldn't see it. There were no shapes or shadows, no form or meaning. Nothing. I was in the void.

Disoriented and scared, I looked inward, searching for that self-preservation gene that had kicked in all those years ago in the Mississippi Sticks. My breathing calmed, and my heart slowed. My senses became hyper-acute. I smelled the sulfur and bat shit, heard the buzzing of the bats, felt the flutter of their wings. I put my hand on Luis's shoulder and stood tall, embracing the moment. Now you're living, Kev!

I turned on my flashlight. The last of the bats were flying off towards the cave's entrance. Rick motioned for us follow him further into the cave. The sulfur grew stronger with each step. Then my flashlight flickered and went out. I tried turning it on and off, but it was dead.

"Dude, my flashlight just died!"

"Don't worry, mine's still good," Rick said.

"Maybe we should head back," I said.

"No, It's all good..." But just as the words left his mouth, his flashlight flickered—along with my heart. "Yeah, maybe we should head back," he said softly.

Moments later his flashlight went out. He banged it against his palm, and it came back to life. Oh, thank God. Get me the hell out of this cave. We moved quickly, my heart beating like a bongo drum inside my chest. Luis held on even tighter.

Climbing down the backside of a boulder, Rick's light flickered again. The hairs on my neck stood up. Oh please, almighty flashlight lord, do not extinguish your light. I grabbed the back of Rick's shirt and formed a chain, his flashlight lighting a narrow path at our feet.

My feet slipped out from under me, and I landed hard on my ass—smearing bat shit on my arms and legs.

"Oh shit," Rick said, extending his hand. "Are you alright?"

As I reached for his hand, the light blinded me momentarily and went out. Pitch-blackness!

I began searching for Rick's shoes, feeling around the floor like a blind man. I heard him banging the flashlight against his palm. The flashlight Gods had denied my prayers. My hopes of surviving La Boca de Infierno were looking bleak. I felt Rick's shoe and pantomimed my way up. Luis had miraculously kept his grip on me during my fall. We were essentially one person now.

Our four-man chain continued feeling our way through the cave, blackness ripping into our psyche and reducing us to our core. We slid our hands along the slimy walls, climbing over rocks and inching forward, all in complete darkness.

Turning a corner, a ray of sunlight peeked down the corridor. The void was no more. Luis loosened his death grip. We were going to live!

Rick asked if we wanted a ride to Masaya. I'd had enough adventure for one day and accepted his offer. Rick suggested we get a beer. I thought a cold beer sounded like heaven, so we stopped at an outdoor cantina with a straw roof near our house. My first beer disappeared like a magic act.

To Rick's dismay, Luis wasn't a big Pepsi fan. He ordered an icy Coca-Cola instead, drinking it almost as fast as I'd drank my beer. "Otra?" I asked, but Luis wanted to walk home the last few blocks.

"Hey Luis, great job today!" I wanted to give him a bear hug and tell him what a great kid I thought he was. But a high five seemed more appropriate. He chuckled as I raised my hand, revealing dried bat shit and cave slime smeared all down my arm. He gave my hand a hard slap and headed home.

"You have to try the Conchas Negras," Rick said, tossing back a rum and coke. He made the clicking and shishing noise again, and the waiter came right over and took his order.

"What's that noise you keep making?" I asked.

He chuckled, "That's how you get somebody's attention down here."

"Oh wow, no wonder everybody keeps ignoring me. It seems kind of rude."

"Wait till you learn all the hand signals and facial expressions. If you want to point to something, just act like you're blowing it a kiss."

The waiter brought over a bowl of black clams mixed with tomato, onion, cilantro and lime. I spread it over crackers and washed it down with Victoria. It was the perfect combo for my first volcano and bat cave adventure.

Rick looked to the sky, "It's going to rain soon."

"What? You're crazy!" It was a completely sunny day, not a cloud in the sky.

"Oh, it's going to rain alright," he said. "And it's going to rain hard. I give it a half an hour."

Sure enough, thirty minutes later, the skies opened up, and it poured down for forty minutes straight. It seemed like all the rain in the world was dumping on Masaya. Roads turned into rivers, front yards to lakes. Cars looked like boats as they plowed through water halfway up their doors.

"Holy shit!"

"Don't worry," Rick said, lighting a cigar. "It'll be sunny again soon."

"You're insane." I was beginning to wonder if Masaya would even still exist after this Noah's Ark rain.

But, two beers later, the clouds blew away, and the sun came out of hiding, bringing the heat and humidity with it. You could almost see the rainwater being sucked back into the sky. The rivers and lakes all disappeared, and the roads were soon bone dry. Nicaragua truly is a magical place.

Rick drove me home. My day of mythical rains and bat cave exploration had come to an end. I'd managed to escape chaos, if for only just a day, and now it was time to return to the realities of my living situation, Elena, and the Peace Corps. It felt like a punch in the gut as I watched Rick drive away, a sense of abandonment I knew only too well.

Luis was crashed out on the floor as I walked inside. The little guy hadn't even made it to bed. I wrapped a blanket around him and went to my room. No longer afraid of the dark.

CHAPTER TEN

THE FEVER

Elena and I were grinding out past perfect verb conjugations when the Peace Corps Landcruiser pulled up to our little Spanish outpost, aka Elena's living room. Diego climbed out, sporting his trademark blue jeans and t-shirt, his Panama hat cocked to the side. Missing, was his usual smile.

"Kevin, walk with me."

Oh shit, the dreaded walk! Elena turned away, and I knew something was up.

Diego and I made our way up the cobblestone street, stopping just shy of the neighborhood whorehouse. Diego kicked up a clod of dirt with his shoe and sighed, "Elena has made a complaint about you."

"A… what?"

"She says that you've been acting mean, yelling at her or something."

"Are you kidding me? What are we in fifth fucking grade?"

"Well, were you yelling at her?"

"We argue all the time. Mostly about how she's picking up Spanish so much faster than me. But no, I've never yelled at her, maybe raised my voice, but I do that with everybody."

"So, what is she talking about?"

"Who knows! Maybe she's mad because I told her to stop complaining about every fucking thing under the sun. Or, because I told her to get out of her room and go see Nicaragua instead of saying she hated it all the time. Or maybe she's just mad because I've been ignoring her for the last two weeks."

I made myself calm down before I blurted out something I might regret. I didn't want to divulge anything about the night we had kissed, or about Osmar and my living situation—or anything else for that matter. Diego was a cool guy, but he wasn't my shrink. I'd been dealing with my problems, on my own, for my entire life, and saw no reason to upend that tried-and-true philosophy.

"Look," Diego said, "you have to be civil to her."

"I am, she's completely overreacting."

"That may be true, but you need to lay low for a while."

"Fine!" I said, deciding at that moment to keep the Peace Corps at arm's length. Events were conspiring against me, whirlwinds of disorder spinning about. I'd lay low all right. I'd lay so low, they'd think I was another white stripe on the Pan-American Highway; A coffin, six feet below the ground. Sadly, the Peace Corps was just another bureaucracy—warts and all.

* * *

I was awakened from a deep, tropical slumber by the moans of Osmar. I sat up in bed, tense, straining my ears. Oh please, not again. No, he seemed to be in some sort of pain, his moans growing louder. I rolled onto my side and pressed my pillow against my ears. Then he screamed out. I squeezed the pillow tighter, but he continued to moan, on and on, throughout the night. Good lord man, stop being such a pussy. The big Mayan God had turned out to be a big baby.

I crawled out of bed tired and cranky the next morning. "Que pasó anoche?" I asked Yolanda as she handed me a pastry.

"La Fiebre – Fever," was all she said. Oh man, all that whining for a little fever?

I didn't say a word to Elena during class. We still had almost two months of training left. Two months before I'd be free from the petty arguments, Spanish lessons, and Osmar. I could hardly wait for the day I'd pack up and move to a new city. The day I'd be on my own again—free of constraints. But for now, I needed to keep my nose to the grindstone. Low profile!

The next night I found myself cutting into a four-inch-thick rib-eye steak, dipping it in A1 sauce, and shoving it in my mouth. As I bit down, excruciating pain shot through my head, waking me from my surreal, (bordering on orgasmic), food-fantasy dream. I sat up in bed and opened one eye, fearing my brain might gush out my eye sockets if I opened them both. My skull was throbbing. I wanted to drill a hole in my forehead, like in the movie Phantasm, and let the blood rush out. Sweat was dripping from my every pore, and I broke out in hives.

My arms and legs itched mercilessly, regardless of how hard I scratched. I dug my fingernails into my skin, so deep that I bore holes which oozed puss and blood, staining my sheets red as I thrashed from side to side. My body turned lobster red and hot to the touch, even as I lay curled in a ball, shivering with chills.

"La Fiebre!" Yolanda said as she wiped my brow with a wet cloth. It was now my turn to moan, and moan I did! Ten times louder than Osmar. I wanted all Monimbo to know the gringo had The Fever.

Yolanda crushed leaves and seeds with a mortar and pestle and rubbed the paste into my forehead. The oily salve smelled like rotten fish and peppermint, making me dry heave. My head was in the jaws of a vise—the devil cranking on the handle. I was dying.

Yolanda sent Luis to the farmacía and continued massaging my head. He returned with a little red pill which she placed on the tip of my tongue. I gagged, but then swallowed it, and disappeared into the universe, floating gently—weightlessly—through the dark matter of space, where order prevailed and chaos vanished into the vacuum of primordial black holes.

When I woke, confusion set in. Where am I? What happened to me? As my mind cleared, and the throbbing returned, reality sunk in. I was messed up—and a billion miles from home. Yolanda became so worried, she walked up to the telephone office and called the Peace Corps. So Nurse Samantha sent an ambulance to Monimbo, right? Wrong! She told Yolanda to put me on a bus for Managua—two hours away.

Yolanda and Luis helped me into a cab and rode with me to the bus station. Once there, they guided me down the aisle of the bus and into a seat, wrapped a blanket around my shoulders and gave me a hug goodbye. I saw the worry on their faces as the bus rumbled to life and rolled away. I put my head on the seat in front and closed my eyes.

The driver shook my shoulder. "Ya estamos!" I lifted my head and recognized the haggard Managua bus terminal. After staggering off the empty bus, I made my way to a row of taxis, where men lay on their hoods staring at me blankly. A young guy, wearing a Yankees cap, ran over and put his arm around me, and helped me into the back of his cab. I mumbled directions to the Peace Corps office and leaned my head against the window.

The office, which looked like an ordinary 1950's bungalow-style house, sat in a tree-lined residential neighborhood. If not for the Peace Corps sign out front, you wouldn't even know it was an office.

The taxi driver helped me to the front gate, draped the blanket around me, and drove off. I walked, hunched over, into the building and to the nurse's office. After rapping on the door several times with no answer, I sunk into a chair outside her office and waited—moaning in pain. The secretary, a friendly Nicaraguan lady, came over and handed me a glass of water.

"The nurse will be here soon," she said. "What time is your appointment?"

"Eleven," I grunted. We looked at the clock hanging on the back wall. It read 11:15 a.m.

I put my head in my hands and tried to forget about the sledgehammer banging away on my skull, glancing periodically up at the clock, and fighting back the tears, as one agonizing hour after another passed.

Then, Samantha came flying past me. "I'll be right with you," she said, holding up a finger and rushing into her office. I looked over at the wall. The clock read 1:40 p.m. Two hours and forty minutes late, according to my rapidly melting brain.

She poked her head out. "Come in." I gripped my aching head and went inside. "Sit up here," she said, pointing to the examination table. Had she even bothered changing that stupid white paper from the last patient? I had tried being friendly with Samantha, to give her the benefit of the doubt, but she'd always been so cold and impersonal shoving needles into my body.

She was a New Yorker, married to a Nicaraguan businessman. A lot of us were under the impression that she was pissed off at having to live in a third world country, doling out medical advice and giving vaccines to whiny, privileged college kids.

She shined a light into my ears and nose and listened to my heart. Then, after pulling a thermometer from my mouth, she said, "You'll be fine. You have a temperature, but it'll drop."

"But…"

"You're still in training, right?"

"Yes, but…"

"Go back to…" She looked down at her chart. "Monimbo. Your Nicaraguan family will take care of you."

"But I can barely walk, and my head feels like…"

"Oh, and drink plenty of liquids." It was apparent she was in a rush, and I was an unwanted distraction.

"I can't hold down liquids," I said. "I keep dry heaving."

"Drink orange juice."

"Orange juice?" I wanted to slap her, but I didn't have the energy. I squeezed my head in my hands. "I feel like I'm dying."

"Don't exaggerate," she said flippantly. "You just have a little bug."

She walked back to the door and held it open. I cussed her up and down, under my breath, as I passed. Calm down Kev, low profile. Be a white stripe! I held my tongue, but there was no way in hell I was going back to Monimbo. If I was going to drop, I was going drop right there in Managua for the whole fucking world to see. My friends would all be coming to the capitol the next day for training.

I staggered around in a foggy haze for the next two hours—head throbbing, body aching—searching for the cheap, crappy backpacker motels known as hospedajes. I somehow managed to find the illustrious Hospedaje Santos, aka the shithole of Managua. Their motto, "Where backpackers come for the three R's: rats, roaches and raw sewage."

I gave the owner twenty-five Córdobas ($2), stumbled past stained sheets drying on a clothesline, and found my door. Shoving a key in a small lock, I fiddled with it until it opened, revealing a dirty, stinky room. Once inside, I slid the inside latch closed and crawled into the lumpy mattress. I moaned in agony for the rest of the day, dry heaving every time I placed a drop of water on my tongue. I was in serious trouble.

"Kev, it's Mitch, you all right in there?"

I opened my eyes, confused. I tried shouting, but my mouth was too dry. "Mitch..." I muttered, but he was walking away. I closed my eyes and nodded off.

"Hey, Kevin... you ok?" Craig was knocking on my door. I tried to answer but couldn't. "I'm going to leave some juice outside your door."

The owner must have been telling people from my group how sick I was when they checked in, as there were more and more knocks throughout the day.

"Unlock the door," I heard Stephanie say at one point, but I was too groggy and lightheaded to move, so I fell back asleep.

When I finally opened my eyes, I was plummeting down a dark shaft, my arms flailing above me. I reached out to stop my descent, but there was nothing to grasp onto. Down and down I fell, waiting to splat. "Kevin..." a voice called out. My body froze, and I was no longer descending. "Kevin..." it called again. I recognized the voice, it was Mom. She was banging on the walls. The clatter echoed throughout the shaft, propelling me upwards. It grew louder, lifting me higher. Mom was all around me now.

"Kevin!" I awoke. Somebody was banging on my door.

"Kevin, open the door!" It was Diego.

He banged harder. "Open the damn door!" I tried to speak, but my mouth was too dry and crusty, and I couldn't form words.

"Kevin, open this fucking door. NOW!"

Something finally clicked, and the direness of my situation became clear. I flung my body off the bed and attempted to crawl but couldn't get to my knees. I stretched out my arms and dug my fingernails into the cement floor, clawing my way to the door. I swung up my hand and grabbed the latch with my fingertips, trying to slide it open. But my fingers slid off.

"Open the door!" Diego screamed, pounding so hard I thought his fist might come through the door.

I closed my eyes and took a deep breath. Then, with a last burst of energy, I reached up high, slid open the cold metal latch and then slid back down with my back against the door.

"Help me! Help me! Help me! I don't want to die!" I mouthed, slapping my hand on the door. Diego forced the door open, pushing me to the side, where I lay in a crumpled heap.

Moments later, I felt several hands hoisting me off the ground and into the air. Diego and several volunteers carried me above their heads—like a prizefighter—down the corridor and out the hospedaje. They laid me in the back of the Landcruiser and raced to the hospital as I faded in and out of consciousness. At some point, I began dry heaving and rolled on my stomach. I pushed open the door and stuck out my head as cars whizzed by.

"Shut the fucking door!" Diego screamed as he zipped in and out of traffic. I pulled the door shut and closed my eyes.

When I came to, I was on a cold gurney being rushed inside a hospital. People stared down at me, shining lights in my eyes and shouting. A surge of pain shot up my arm as the nurse crammed a six-inch needle into the back of my hand. I closed my eyes and faded away.

"Despierta!" I opened my eyes. A man in a white coat was shaking me, while bone-crushing pain shot through my head. "Como se llama?" I was confused, but then I saw his stethoscope.

"Se llama Kevin," a voice said. My eyes moved from the doctor to Diego, who was standing next to him. The doctor asked me several rapid-fire questions in Spanish. I looked to Diego for the translation.

"When's the last time you urinated?" Diego asked. But I was too groggy and confused to understand.

"Kevin, when's the last time you urinated?" he repeated.

I played back my last few days of hell. It all seemed like a big blur. My head and muscles ached so badly I could barely think. "Two or three days ago," I finally said.

The pain was too much. I grabbed my head and reached for the doctor's sleeve. "Cabeza, Cabeza!" Couldn't he see my head was about to explode? The doctor said something to the nurse, who grabbed a vial of liquid and shot the contents into my IV.

A warm, tingling sensation began to grow inside my toes, inching its way up my legs, through my stomach and onwards to my chest. But then it stopped. My upper and lower extremities had fallen into a peaceful, euphoric state, but my brain was trying to worm its way out of my ears.

I grabbed the doctor's wrist, applying the same death grip Luis had used on me while in the bat cave. "Cabeza, Cabeza, Ayudame!"

He signaled to the nurse, who grabbed another vial of liquid magic and pumped it into my I.V. The warm tingling traveled the same route, from my toes to my chest. But then it moved into to my head, and sloshed around inside my cranium, releasing all the pain I'd been enduring for so long.

I moved my head from side to side, testing whether the pain was just hiding. When it didn't reappear, I took my first deep breath in days. I was going to live.

The nurse wheeled me into a private room and checked my vitals every fifteen minutes. As she switched out the third bag of saline attached to my IV pole, I began to wonder where all that liquid was going inside my body. After the fifth bag, I became concerned. That fluid must be piling up somewhere.

Evidently, the nurse shared my concerns, because she kept telling me to go pee. But I had no desire to go. Something had to be wrong. My body wasn't a magic thermos. Six, seven…

I watched in horror as the saline dripped down, flowed through the tube, and into the needle sticking in my vein. Eight, nine…

"Usted tiene que orinar ahoritita! - You have to pee right now!" she demanded, holding saline bag number ten in her hand. "Si usted no orina, tengo que usar un cateter."

Wait… Hold everything! I know my Spanish sucks, but did she just say something about a catheter? It sounded an awfully lot like the English word. Also, what's a catheter again? Is that where they stick something in my…

I pointed to my penis. When the nurse nodded yes, I jumped out of bed and wheeled my IV into the bathroom. And there I stood, for the next twenty minutes, staring into the toilet as if it held the meaning of life. But, no matter how hard I tried, nothing would come out. I turned on the sink and listened to it splash. But still, nothing.

I sulked back to bed, a defeated man. Like a snorkeler, whose mask is beginning to fill, I could taste the saline in my mouth. My stomach sank when I saw my pretty nurse carrying a glass tube, a rubber hose, and a bucket. I was in a horror movie, gagged and bound to a chair, while my torturer pulled pliers from a black bag.

I whimpered as she pulled my hospital gown to the side. Saline was about to trickle out my ears at any moment. I gripped the metal rails of the bed and arched my back as she inserted the catheter. My face grimaced and contorted as she pushed it in further. The pain was excruciating. As I was squirming my way into the farthest corner of the bed, I began to wonder just how in the fuck I ended up with a glass rod being shoved in my dick.

Eyes glazing over, I heard a stream of urine gush into the bucket held by my nurse. It sounded like a fire hose spraying down a burning building. Our eyes met for a moment, causing me to blush. I continued peeing, and her expression soon turned to shock as the bucket rapidly filled. Then, my pee began spilling over the side and onto my hospital gown, soaking through to my stomach. The nurse told me to hold the bucket and ran off. I moved, causing the warm pee to slosh from side to side, and spill between my legs. It seeped along the bottom of my legs and up my butt crack.

The nurse came running back with a fresh bucket and quickly switched it out. As she carried it away, the urine splashed over the sides and spilled onto the floor with every step.

We stared at each other in wonder as bucket number two hit the halfway mark. A huge sense of relief came over us when I finally stopped going. But then, unbelievably, I started up again. I looked for ways to disappear into my bed. My face felt flush, and my ears were itching. The bucket hit the two-thirds mark, and I stopped. This time for good.

My embarrassment would only grow as she gave me the first sponge bath of my life. I could no longer look in her eyes.

Diego stopped by later to check on me. "How you feeling?"

"Better," I said, turning down the volume on the TV.

"You have Dengue Fever."

"Ah… So that's what The Fever is…"

"What?" Diego asked with a puzzled expression.

"Oh, nothing."

"The doctor said you were severely dehydrated and in grave condition."

"Good thing I didn't listen to Samantha and go back to Monimbo!"

"I'm meeting with her tomorrow. I'm just glad we got you to the hospital when we did."

"When the hell is training going to be over?"

"Soon. Just hang in there."

I looked up at the bag of saline still dripping into my veins. "Have you figured out where I'll be living after training?"

"Not yet."

I turned slightly so he couldn't see my eyes, the bridge of my nose now burning. "Hey Diego, thank you…"

"Don't worry about it," he said patting my shoulder. "Just get better."

I spent the next two days watching cable TV in an air-conditioned hospital room—relaxed and pain-free. I nearly cried when they told me I was ok to leave.

CHAPTER ELEVEN

FIGHTING BACK

After my two-day stint at Hospital Bautista, I felt like a new man. The doctors told me I needed to rest, that my body was exhausted, but I felt good. So, when Nica 6 traveled to Rivas, a coastal town near Costa Rica, to blow off some steam, I was right there with them.

The moon puffed up fat and bright as we gathered in Parque Central to share our tales of woe, her beam moving to the sound of our voices. We passed around a bottle of rum and buried away our anxieties, if for only one night.

Our happiness spread like 'The Fever.' We sang and danced and built human pyramids. Safe inside our temporary world. Spanish, training, mosquitoes, the Peace Corps… all faded away. We had crested the volcano and were looking out on our lives and futures. We were young, alive and free!

Jason put the rum to his lips and chugged away. We all yelled, "Stop!" and reached for the bottle. He gave a sinister chuckle and took off running like an Olympic sprinter. We all gave chase, laughing hysterically. I spotted Stephanie from the corner of my eye and changed course. Her eyes grew wide as I neared, and she took off for the swings. I cornered her at the merry-go-round. We hunched over, gasping for air and laughing uncontrollably. When I caught my breath, I took a step forward. She faked one way and ran off the other. I chased her down, grabbing her near the seesaw. We fell to the ground, laughing, as sand filled our hair and mouths. I rolled on top of her and stared down.

"Asshole," she said, spitting sand from her lips.

"Brat," I replied, pouring a handful of sand onto her chin.

"Why don't you go chase Kathy or Susan?"

"Because I want to chase you, genius." I pushed a strand of hair from her eyes and kissed her lightly on her lips. Before she could say a word, I jumped up and pulled her to her feet. We ran back to the group, now huddled on a bench singing AC/DC's *Highway to Hell.*

The booze proved to be too much for my Dengue-weakened body. I passed out on the cement floor of my hotel room, using my arm as a pillow. When I arose from my semi-comatose stupor, I had excruciating pains shooting up and down my arm.

We all looked like death warmed over as we waited for breakfast the next morning. The waiter plopped down a plate of rice and beans, aka Gallo Pinto. He even threw in a chunk of salty, Guajada cheese. My stomach did a back flip. I pushed the plate away and rubbed my burning arm. Why was I always so stupid?

Stephanie invited us to her training town, San Juan de Oriente, for their annual Fiesta Patronal celebration happening the following weekend. Through bloodshot eyes, we all readily agreed to meet.

A discussion arose of where everybody wanted to live after training. It seemed we'd all been eyeing the map of Nicaragua, sketching out our favorite areas. I was still hoping to live in a shack on the beach, but ultimately Diego would make that decision.

The food provided little comfort for our collective hangover, and we decided to head back to our Nica families a day early. Our safe, temporary world had dissolved, like the tide washing away a sand castle. A tide of Flor de Caña Rum in our case!

"See you soon, genius," I whispered, hugging Stephanie goodbye.

"Ok, asshole." She flashed her smile, and a jolt ran through my body as if I was jamming a fork into an electrical outlet.

* * *

Walking to Spanish class on Monday morning, I dreamed of plunging my arm into a bucket of ice water. The pain had worsened over the last two days. Initially, just my thumb and forefinger burned, but now my entire arm felt like it was on fire. To add to my misery, I was slowly losing control over my hand

An hour into class, it became utterly limp, flopping around like a dead fish. Scared to death and unable to take the pain any longer, I shouted out, "I have to go to Managua!" to nobody in particular, walked out the door and headed to the bus station.

Two hours later, I was face-to-face with my dear friend, Samantha, who was now keeping regular office hours. She was unusually nice, as she pricked and prodded my arm. "You need to see a specialist, but it looks like you have nerve damage."

I shifted nervously on the exam table. "Nerve damage?"

"Yes," she said. "The slang term for what you have is drunk-man's disease or Saturday Night Palsy."

My face became flush and my eyes fell to my feet.

She lifted my hand in the air. "It's often caused by people drinking too much and passing out on hard surfaces, like a sidewalk, with their arm above their head…" She let go of my hand and watched it flop down like a dead weight. "pinching off their radial nerve."

Seeing problems on my horizon, I quickly blamed my zombie arm on my Dengue Fever. It was her turn to look at her feet.

A specialist fitted me with a cast, which kept my wrist propped up at a ninety-degree angle, and wrote out a prescription for something called, Diazepam, which I figured was the Nicaraguan version of Motrin.

Word spread about our drunken night in Rivas, and Nica 6 was pulled into the Peace Corps office and given a written quiz on our alcohol consumption. How many alcoholic beverages do you drink in a week? Do you ever drink alone? Do you ever drink to the point of passing out? When's the last time you drank?

I'm not stupid, I lied my ass off. You'd have thought I only drank on New Year's or my birthday from my results. Low profile.

Jason, on the other hand, fessed up to every beer he'd ever had in his life. Why yes, I do drink alone. As a matter of fact, I did drink last night. Do I drink alcohol three or more times a week? Well, there are seven days in a week, right?

Jason aced the test. His reward: a scholarship to Alcohol University, where he attended a weekly class on the perils of alcohol consumption. Smart guy!

* * *

"Bull dicks!" Mitch yelled, pointing to two men hitting each other with long, sword-type weapons.

We'd arrived in San Juan de Oriente for the Fiesta Patronal. Locals believed that Saints watched over the cities and towns of Nicaragua, protecting them from evil. Each village had their own Patron Saint, and on their birthdays, a party was given in their honor. The celebrations often lasted all weekend. Tonight, we partied in honor of John the Baptist – San Juan!

"Hijue Gran Puta!" people hollered, forming a circle around the two combatants. I moved to the front for a better view of the men swinging the strange-looking swords like drunken pirates. They hit each other's arms and legs with a fury, leaving deep welts and bloody gashes. Then, a dark-skinned man hit his opponent squarely on his head, sending him crashing to the ground. He stood over him and continued beating him, showing no mercy, as bystanders egged him on. Somebody finally jumped in between the two, and the melee was over. It was a frightening scene.

Two more men moved into the circle and prepared for battle. I noticed Mitch standing next to me and nudged his arm. "Dude, this is insane."

"I know," he said, handing me a flask of rum. "Did you know those black sticks are really bull penises, picha de toro?"

"No way!" I said as the two men began beating the shit out of each other.

"Yeah, we talked to some guys earlier who were working on some. They said they dry and stretch them for over a year, rub oil into them and mold them into swords. All to fight for a few nights every year."

"What the hell for?"

"Who knows," Mitch said. "There's a rumor the fights are reenactments of a William Walker sword fight. But nobody really knows, and they've been doing it for longer than anybody can remember."

"Crazy. Let's get out here."

We found Stephanie, Jason and Susan and moved away from the madness. The streets were filling up quickly. I chugged down some rum and handed the flask to Jason. I'd taken my first Diazepam pill earlier, hoping to dull the intense pain in my arm, but it had barely registered. A few boys ran by and threw lighted firecrackers at our feet. We jumped back as they popped off. "Hey, you little shits," Jason hollered after them. Then, suddenly, a loud explosion rang out, and we all ducked.

"What the fuck was that?" I asked, crouching next to Jason.

"An M80."

"Are you sure, that sounded like dynamite?"

"Yes."

We bunched closer together and moved down the block, where several men were mounting horses and trotting up to a line drawn in the dirt road. Somebody shouted, "Dele, dele, dele!" and the horses took off, kicking up dirt and galloping away. As they rounded the corner, their hooves clacked loudly, now racing over cobblestones. The crowds waved their straw hats in the air, hooting and hollering. Rounding the third turn, and back on dirt, one of the horses slid out and rolled on the ground, throwing his rider down the road. A hush rose up from the crowd, as we looked on in horror, expecting the worse. But then, through a cloud of dust, we saw them spring up to their feet.

"YEAH!" I screamed, pumping my fist. The jockey climbed back on his horse and galloped off at full speed.

We all grew tense as the riders came flying down the road in front of us. They pulled on their horses' manes and angled them towards a house with a live chicken nailed to the door.

Leaning almost sideways off their horses, they reached out to grab the chicken, one hand still holding tight to the mane. Feathers flew everywhere, but the chicken remained, its eyes now wide with terror.

As the riders made another loop around the block, I worked my way over to Stephanie.

"I win," I said, grabbing the back of her shirt.

She turned around, smiled and said, "Ha, ha."

The horses came barreling down the road again. The lead rider reached out and grabbed the chicken, ripping him from the door. He struggled to fly away, but the man held tight. His feet still dangled from the nail, the white door now streaked red with blood.

The other riders lifted the winner onto their shoulders and paraded him through the streets as he held the bloody chicken high in the air. I pulled Stephanie into the crowd and gave her a long, deep kiss, squeezing our bodies together.

Our group ended up in a bar later that night, clanking beers and toasting to the end of training, which was approaching rapidly. We vowed to visit each other once we'd settled into our permanent sites. Sadness came over me, knowing I'd be leaving all my new friends soon. We'd spent nearly every weekend together since arriving in Nicaragua, becoming each other's support system, just as they had told us we would back in Miami. And now, within a few short weeks, we'd be dispersed throughout the breadth of Nicaragua, entirely on our own, a frightening prospect.

We were getting a little tipsy and decided walking was the best remedy. We came upon a group of men climbing, or rather attempting to climb, a metal pole greased with the fat and innards of a dead chicken lashed to the top. The men, covered in grease and fat, tried in vain to claim their prize, slipping and sliding and falling each time.

I nudged Stephanie towards the pole, "Go for it!"

She laughed and pointed to a group of young boys chasing after a giant pig. They jumped on his back and attempted to corral him, but he slipped away each time—having been greased in lard from snout to tail. "They love their animal fat!" she joked.

I took a swig of rum and passed her the bottle. "Just another Friday night in Nicaragua," I said. We laughed, realizing that this was now our new normal.

Stephanie and I found ourselves in bed later that night, kissing and holding each other, the stresses of our world disappearing. The pain in my arm soon faded, and with it, went the chaos. I pulled her in close as she wrapped her legs around me. But as I began to take off her clothes, she grabbed my hand. "No, we can't do it here."

"Why not?"

"My family will hear us." I hadn't even realized we were at her training house.

"I'll be quiet," I said, pushing my pelvis into her and chewing on her earlobe.

She arched her back and sighed, "No Kevin, we can't."

My body trembled, "I want you so bad."

"Not here."

I rolled over and moaned.

"You'll live."

"I doubt it," I pouted.

* * *

Diego popped into Masaya one day, and we drove into town for a beer. "How's your arm?"

"Good," I lied. The pain was ungodly, forcing me to double up on the Diazepam pills, even though they made me feel a little loopy.

"How are things with Elena?"

"Fine. Just laying low." I'd learned from an early age to take care of myself and deal with my problems on my own. Seeking help from others always seemed to make things worse.

Training was coming to an end, and I figured the real reason for his visit was to tell me where my site would be. I'd given up any hope of living on the beach in paradise since most business volunteers were placed in big cities.

"Everything good with your…"

"Oh, come on man, just tell me where I'm gonna live for Christ's sake!"

He smiled and tugged on his hat, "I've picked a great site for you. You're going to be living in Estelí, a big city in the northern mountains of

Nicaragua."

He went on to describe a bustling commercial city surrounded by tobacco fields and coffee plantations. "It has a cool climate all year round," he said, "pretty girls and lots of restaurants and bars."

"Can I leave now?" I joked.

"You can't leave now, but you're all going on site visits this weekend. You'll be able to check out your towns and meet your counterparts."

A few days later, I boarded a bus for Estelí, my future home, but I wasn't alone. Diego had sent a teacher with each volunteer. God forbid we miss an opportunity to study Spanish.

Miguel and I settled into our seats for the four-hour journey north along the Pan-American Highway. My arm felt like it was in boiling water. The pain seemed to grow with each day. Miguel told me all about his life in Nicaragua. He was from Granada and loved teaching Spanish and working for the Peace Corps. "There aren't a lot of opportunities for Nicaraguans," he said. I nodded and reached for another Diazepam.

Our bus sputtered, and I heard the grinding of gears, as we climbed higher and higher into the Segovia Mountains. "Que es?" I asked Miguel, pointing to a swath of land covered in plants as far as the eye could see.

"Tobaco," he said. "to make puros – cigars."

The temperature dropped, and a gust of cold air blew across my face, the first in months. It felt like a drop of heaven. Miguel told me Estelí's temperature averaged eighty-five degrees year-round, a godsend from the one-hundred-degree sauna of Monimbo.

As we reached the mountain's crest and began our descent, I got my first peek of Estelí snuggled in the valley below. Surrounded by lush trees and rolling mountains, she seemed at peace. We coasted the rest of the way down, through hills and valleys, pulling into a bus station on the edge of town.

Taxicabs flew up and down the street, narrowly dodging oncoming cars and children on bikes. Vendors lined the sidewalks selling ceramics, food and clothing.

"Chele, chele comprame un faja, - Whitey, buy a belt!" hollered a lady on a stool, as we made our way up the main street.

Estelí had a fast-paced, exuberant energy, much different from the slow, almost neglected vibe of Monimbo. After checking in to our rooms, I switched into flip flops and headed to the lobby.

Miguel was sitting in a rocking chair watching the activity on the street. "I'm going to explore the city," I told him.

"I should go with you."

"No, I'll be ok."

"Wait, I'll show you around," he insisted.

I reluctantly agreed, and we walked around Estelí checking out different markets, parks and vendors. It was getting hot, and my arm felt like a three-alarm fire. "Look, Miguel," I finally said. "I'm going for a beer. I'll see you later."

"We shouldn't drink," he said with a straight face.

I almost fell over laughing, and for a split second, the pain in my arm disappeared.

"Thanks for the advice," I said in my butchered Spanish. "See you back at the hotel."

"Wait," he said as I walked off, "if you're going to drink, let's go to a bar I know a few blocks from the hotel."

"Fine, let's go!"

Can't a guy just get some booze to wash down a pill to erase the pain in his limp, murdered arm?

We went to a pool hall on the main drag, where Miguel taught me the bizarre rules of Nicaraguan billiards for the next two hours. The beers weren't smothering the fire in my arm, and I was getting tired. "Ya me voy," I said, hanging my cue on the wall.

"Por que, you don't like pool!" Miguel hollered loud enough for the whole bar to hear. He'd been hitting the beers pretty hard and taking shots of rum in between. A few men looked up from their games.

I told him whacking balls as hard as you can and hoping they go inside a pocket wasn't fun for me. "We call this 'slop pool' in the United States."

"Pinche puto Yankis!" he yelled, drinking another shot of rum and slamming the glass on the bar.

Now, my Spanish was far from being up to snuff—even in the swearing department—but by the way he slung out the word "Yankee," I knew it was time for me to leave. Dr. Jeckyll had arrived! I snuck out the door while he shouted for another drink.

Later that night, I was awoken by the sounds of yelling and banging into walls as Miguel made his way into the hotel. There was some back and forth with the owner, and then I heard his voice boom down the hallway, "Quiero una mujer!"

Wait! Did he just order a hooker? No, can't be. Not long after, I heard a woman's voice in his room, separated from mine by only a thin sheet of plywood. Then, for the next twenty minutes, I had the distinct pleasure of listening to Miguel grunt and moan as he banged some whore just feet from my head.

The sun was barely up when I heard a knock on my door. I struggled to open my eyes as more thumps echoed through the room. I rolled out of bed and threw on a pair of shorts. Sunlight poured in as I opened the door. There, standing like an archangel, with light radiating off his body, was Miguel.

"We need to start our lesson."

"Qué!" How was this guy even conscious? I drank half of what he did, and I could barely move.

"We need to start our lesson," he repeated.

"No," I said. "Go back to bed!"

"Diego said I have to give you a Spanish lesson on the trip."

"I'm not the Spanish police!" A pain shot through my arm, and I rubbed the outside of the cast. "Besides, I got a good enough lesson last night." I began to shut the door, but he stopped it with his foot.

"We have to do it now!"

Hungover and lethargic, I practiced Spanish pronouns for the next hour, rubbing my dead arm and wondering how Miguel was even still alive. After class, Miguel told me he had to return to Granada early for some reason and left. I crawled back into bed and dreamed I was surfing in warm water on perfect waves.

I made a solo exploration of Estelí when I woke. I was finally alone, back in my orderly world of solitude. The freedom felt amazing. Diego had been right about the cool climate and natural beauty surrounding the city. More importantly, he was right about all the pretty girls, they were everywhere—and were staring at me, just as much as I was staring at them.

I worked my way to the Cooperativa de Ahorro y Crédito, San Benito, the small Savings and Loan where I'd be working. I was excited to meet my counterpart, Ramón.

The bank was at the end of a long muddy road, on the outskirts of town, and within throwing distance of a maximum-security Penitentiary. The bank was made of cement blocks painted jungle green. As I entered, I noticed the teller wall separating the cashier from the customers was built of plywood, and propped up rather flimsily by a couple of 2x4's. If you wanted to rob the place, all you had to do was blow real hard. A plump lady with a welcoming smile sat behind Fort Knox.

"Hola, esta Ramón?" I asked.

"Sí, sí. Un momento," she said rushing off to the back.

Ramón came out and introduced himself. He was skinny as a rail, with deep lines in his face making him appear much older than he probably was. He gave me a brief tour of the building and then took me into his office. I sat in front of his desk, stacked three feet high with papers and folders, while he lit a cigarette.

"So, what do you think about La Cooperativa?" He had a heavy accent.

"Muy bien," I told him.

He took a long drag on his cigarette and eyed me curiously. "Where are you going to live?" His words came out as fast as a machine gun and were filled with so much slang, I could barely understand a word he said.

"I don't know yet."

He didn't smile or seem happy to see me in any way. After some more small talk, and me saying, "Que?" after every sentence, we sat and stared at each other for the next five minutes. The awkward silence ended when he stood up abruptly and motioned for me to follow.

He took me to a large warehouse being built behind the bank. I stared at the steel beams, fifty feet up, trying to understand how they related to the bank. Then, without warning, Ramón stuck out his hand and said, "Adios!" Apparently, our meeting was over.

I knocked on a few doors on the way back to my hotel, hoping to find a place to live for the future. There were no "for rent" signs or classified ads to help me. "Se alquila?" I'd ask. But the people would just stare at me as if I was from another planet.

I had mixed feelings on the bus ride back to Monimbo. Estelí was almost the polar opposite of a beach town, but the city in the mountains did have its charm, and the hills surrounding it would provide plenty of opportunities for exploring and finding peace and freedom. A sense of dread was mounting, however, each time I thought about working with Ramón, in the gloomy little bank by the prison, for the next two years.

* * *

I drank coffee on my patio the next morning, back safe and snug in Monimbo. Up the road, a boy whacked the rumps of cows with a switch, and yelled, "Oye!" each time they wandered off the trail to nip at strands of grass. The herd moved to the side when a Land Cruiser came flying up the road, kicking up dirt and barreling towards my house.

Diego popped his head out, deep lines wedged into his brow.

"Walk with me."

"Oh fuck, what now?" I said frowning.

I set my cup down and followed him up the road, walking briskly and searching my memory banks for my latest crime.

He finally stopped and turned around. "What happened on your trip?"

"Trip… you mean to Estelí?"

"Yes."

"Nothing!"

"Kevin, you have to tell me everything that happened in Estelí."

"Nothing happened!"

The normally calm and cool Diego was extremely anxious, which made me nervous, very nervous. Maybe they found out about Miguel and his hooker. But I wasn't going to snitch on him.

"Is it Miguel? Is he ok?"

"Kevin, for God's sake, just tell me what the hell happened!"

"Ok." I gave him a play by play of the entire trip, leaving out Miguel's drunken bar scene and the hooker.

"Are you sure that's all?" Diego asked, tugging on his mustache and pushing up his glasses.

"Yes," I said. "What the hell is going on?"

"Miguel told the other teachers that you got drunk in a bar and started yelling, 'Nicaragua sucks, U.S.A. is the best' in front of a group of Sandinistas."

"What!"

"And he said that you bought a hooker."

"That fucker!"

"Word got back to the Director, and he wants to send you home."

The blood drained from my face, and I felt my heart thumping in my chest. Whoosh, whoosh, whoosh. I was that scared little boy running through the woods of Mississippi. I was Yolanda cowering in the corner. I was every kid that had ever been bullied, and it was time to fight back. Fight or flight? I choose fight, motherfucker!

I spilled my guts to Diego, told him every sordid detail of my trip. But I didn't stop there, I went on, telling him about Elena, my Nica family, my food situation, my health, and all the fucking chaos I'd been dealing with since arriving in Nicaragua. A dam had exploded inside me. I could no longer fight the world on my own, I needed an ally.

Tears welled up in my eyes, but I fought them back. My nose burned, my arm throbbed, the pain was all around me. Diego's face grew softer, the lines disappearing from his brow. "I believe you, Kevin."

I looked down. "I can't catch a break down here."

"Don't worry, I'll take care of it." Then he grinned and said, "Just lay low."

"Maybe I should just bury myself in a fucking hole!"

He put his hand on my shoulder. "Don't worry, I know how to deal with these fucking bureaucrats!"

I looked up, surprised to hear this side of Diego, and felt an immediate bond to him. It was as if his words sparked a deep, resonating drumbeat inside me, propelling me forward.

CHAPTER TWELVE

DAD

As Mom knocked back vodka in some dive bar, my dad drove my sisters and me to his condo in Santee, a rural town east of San Diego.

He introduced us to his wife, Susan, and her eighteen-year-old son, Scott. We set our suitcases in the living room and looked around nervously at our new home. Scott was kicked out of his room to make space for the four of us. Banished to the living room, he hung curtains around the couch, and clipped on a sign that read, "Keep Out!"

Santee was much different than the busy streets of Central San Diego. Our neighbors owned horses and farm animals. The local boys drove little Kawasaki motorcycles, RM80's, through the hills surrounding the condominium complex.

Susan seemed nice at first. She was an Avon saleslady and always smelled nice and dressed pretty. She wore a different shade of lipstick each day that matched the bows and ribbons placed strategically in her wavy black hair. When the orders came in, she would sit in the living room and bundle up the merchandise; bottles of cologne in the shape of old fashion cars, bubble bath that looked like turtles and dinosaurs, eyeliners, and a hundred different perfumes.

My dad was always gone, off building a taxicab business. We might see him once a week, for an hour or so, and then he'd disappear again. When he did come home, Susan would scream and shout at him for not being around more, while my sisters and I played games in the room, pretending we couldn't hear it. But I heard it. I heard it all. I heard her screaming at the top of her lungs, "I didn't sign up to be a goddamn mother again!"

Susan grew angrier every day. She made disgusting dinners of peas and clumps of butter and served it with white bread. We weren't allowed to drink milk or water until we finished everything on our plate, telling us it would ruin our appetite. When I refused to eat the disgusting food, she smacked me on my bare legs. I jumped up from the table and ran, screaming, "I'm still not eating that shit!" as she chased me around the condo.

When school started, I was teased mercilessly for being the new kid. "Kevin Crumble Cake, Crummy Kevin." The other boys had grown up together their entire lives, and I was an outcast to them, an aberration. To escape their torment, and steer clear of Susan, I began hiking through the hills behind our condo. I liked the freedom, nobody could hurt me up there. I learned how to read the different trails and stay away from the rattlers and coyotes. When the sun dipped below the horizon, I'd reluctantly race back down the mountain to the condo.

Susan liked order in her life and felt she could achieve it through discipline. Discipline coming in the form of her hand, and eventually the belt, or any object within reach. Wooden hairbrushes being her favorite. She was too strong for me, so I was always running from her. I was fast and able to make a lot of close escapes out the front door. But if she cornered me in the kitchen, it was time to curl up in a ball and take a beating.

I showed her all the nifty cuss words I'd acquired on my travels, and she reciprocated by showing me her favorite bar of Avon soap, which she shoved in my mouth and ground over my teeth. Sometimes she'd give me a choice. Hold out my hand and make a fist, so she could smack my knuckles with a wooden spatula or drop my pants, so she could spank my bare ass with my dad's thick leather belt.

One day, a man from the Santee Boy's Club came to our school. He asked if any of us boys were interested in being stronger and faster. I couldn't raise my hand high enough. He passed around a brochure that said, "Wrestling Club." I figured if I could just get a little stronger, maybe I could finally stand up to Susan.

I joined the club and rode my bike to wrestling practice every single day. I was small but fast, and a quick learner. In just a few weeks' time, I was beating the other boys in the gym. On weekends, I'd get rides from my coaches, or my dad would send me in one of his cabs, to different tournaments where I'd wrestle boys from other towns.

One tournament, I made it to the finals against "Head-and-Arm" Howie. He'd been wrestling since he was four, and all the other boys called him a stud. He got his nickname from being a master at his favorite move, the Head and Arm, where you throw your opponent over your back. But, to do the move, you must first tie-up, or grab the neck and arm of your opponent.

"Don't tie-up, whatever you do," Coach told me. "If you do, he'll throw you right away."

"Ok," I replied, trying to calm myself down. The other wrestlers on the team slapped me on my back and wished me luck, all happy they didn't have to face Howie.

When the match started, I circled around, careful not to tie-up. Howie came at me, and I shot for his legs, but he got away. I'd learned to wrestle by tying-up, so it was throwing off my style. I figured if I already knew what move he'd try, I could counter it. So, I moved in close and grabbed the back of his neck. Howie grabbed my head as fast as a guillotine and flipped me in the air. I landed on my back with a thud and struggled to move. The ref slammed his hand on the mat and blew his whistle. Pinned!

I shook Howie's hand and took off to a dark corner of the gym, where I slumped to the ground and slammed my headgear against the floor. Coach came over and put his hand on my shoulder, "Why'd you tie-up?"

"I thought I could handle him!"

"Calm down, you'll get 'em next time kid."

I wiped away my tears as Coach walked away.

* * *

On Sunday, I decided to head up to my secret spot in the hills. Susan told me I had to be home by noon to help her around the house, but I got busy carving a spear with my buck knife and lost track of time. When I realized I was late, I sprinted down the mountain as fast as I could and tore into the house. Susan was standing in the kitchen, her face red as a tomato. She glared down at me, shooting daggers with her eyes. Then she planted her fists on her hips like an evil Wonder Woman.

"Where the hell have you been!" Spit shot out from the corners of her mouth, and she took a step closer, causing my body to tense up.

"I... I... I got lost."

"You got lost huh? Well, I'll teach you to never get lost again. Go out back and find me the biggest switch you can!"

"No Susan, I'm sorry, I'm sorry. I'll be good."

"And if you don't bring back the biggest switch..." her lips and nose twisted like an errant vine, contorting into a wicked grimace, "I'm gonna whip you twice as hard!"

I went out back and walked around the shrubs and bushes, moving from one patch of brush to the next, searching for the longest, fattest switch.

My breathing was hard and fast, almost to the point of hyperventilating. I began to cry, softly at first, but then louder, from a place deep inside me, moaning and sobbing uncontrollably. I was petrified, but I knew I had to calm myself down. I began telling myself, "it's gonna be ok, just breathe," over and over, until my breathing slowed. I looked around to gain my bearings and realized I was pretty far from the complex. In case Susan was watching, I pretended to measure the different reeds, looking for the longest.

When I neared the base of the mountain, I took off running. I ran hard and fast, up the steep path until my legs hurt and I could no longer breathe. I collapsed in the dirt and gasped for air. When my heart slowed, I looked down the mountain and all around. The hawks sailed overhead. I was safe again. She couldn't see me, nobody could see me.

I worked my way to my hideout and kept a lookout for the rest of the day. Nobody came looking for me. When it got dark, the crickets and beetles began to chirp and click. I became scared, knowing the coyotes and rattlers would be coming out to hunt soon. I decided to go back and face my punishment.

I raced into the condo expecting to enter a firestorm, but my dad was home, and everybody was worried about me. Susan fed me a big plate of spaghetti and even allowed me to drink milk with it. When I finished, they told my sisters and me to go into our room. They began arguing, even louder than usual, but I didn't care. I had a big smile plastered on my face, knowing I'd escaped Susan's switch.

A few weeks later, at a tournament in nearby El Cajon, I beat all the other wrestlers in my weight class, making it into the finals where I'd once again be squaring off with "Head and Arm" Howie.

"Don't tie-up with him! Remember what happened last time," Coach said.

I pulled on my headgear, jumped up and down, and slapped the sides of my head and bare legs. "Ok Coach."

The ref blew his whistle, and we circled each other. Howie shot for my legs, but I sprawled back, wrapping my arms around his head.

"Spin around, spin around," Coach yelled from the side. But, instead of spinning around and controlling Howie, I let him up. "Don't tie-up, don't tie-up," Coach hollered, as I moved in closer and our heads bumped. I reached up and grabbed the back of Howie's neck. "No, No!" Coach screamed.

Howie wrapped his fingers around the side of my neck and slid his hand to my elbow. Trap set. He shifted his hips and tried to rip off my head, but I ducked at the last second and felt his arm scrape against my face. I used his momentum to lift him off the ground and throw him to his back. He fought hard as I squeezed his head with every ounce of energy in my body. The ref's hand seemed to move in slow motion as he slammed it to the mat. I pinned "Head and Arm" Howie! The ref lifted my arm in victory as Coach and all the wrestlers from our team shouted. The people in the stands were all quiet, still in shock.

Later that evening, I stood on top of the award stand and received my gold medal. And then, when they announced the winner for Outstanding Wrestler of the Tournament, they called my name. Two girls handed me a giant trophy with a wrestler on top. I strolled around the gym in a happy daze, hoping my dad—and not one of his drivers—would pick me up so I could show off my awards.

People began filing out as I walked in circles looking for my dad or a driver. Nobody came. When the gym was almost empty, only a few stragglers remaining, I could no longer hold back my tears. A man and his son approached me, "Now why would a fellow like you be crying? You have a gold medal around your neck and a trophy just as tall as you are."

I whimpered, "I don't have anybody to take me home."

He kneeled in front of me. "Well, where the heck are your parents, little man?"

"I don't know," I said wiping snot off my face

"Your coach?"

"He left."

"Well settle down now," he said. "Let me just finish closing up the gym, and then Toby and I will give you a ride home." He pointed to his son who looked about a year younger than me.

As we pulled up to the condo, he said, "Now flick the porch lights on and off when you get inside, so I know you're safe."

"Ok, thanks, Mister!" I grabbed my trophy and raced inside. Everybody was either in their room or gone. I flicked the lights and went to bed.

The beatings got worse, and even though I had gotten faster and stronger through wrestling, I was still no match for Susan. My sisters and I had a meeting and decided our only option was to run away. We packed some clothes and essentials in backpacks and set off for the mountains, climbing up and along the ridge, and then working our way back down to Mission Gorge Road, the main drag of Santee.

We headed towards the Old Mission Dam. We planned to keep moving west, like frontiersmen. But then, our dad's blue cab came blazing down the road and screeched to a halt right in front of us. We scattered in all directions. Kerry and I jumped in a dumpster and covered ourselves with trash.

"Shhh, be quiet," I told her, but our dad threw open the lid and pulled us out. He marched us to his cab and put us in the back seat. "Don't move!" he growled. We felt like criminals about to be taken to jail. He managed to round up Stephanie and Michelle and drove back home.

"We're just going to keep running away!" my sisters yelled from the back seat. "We hate living there. Susan hits us every day."

When we got to the condo, he told us to get all our stuff together. Something had finally clicked. We pulled out our trusty suitcases and packed in record time. We stayed in motels until he was able to rent a house in Del Cerro, a suburban neighborhood in the center of San Diego. Once we settled in, he disappeared again—back to his business—leaving us to fend for ourselves.

We wouldn't see him for days, sometimes weeks. My older sisters were back in charge. It was summer, and we spent our days running around the neighborhood like wild dogs. At night, we'd occasionally have fistfights over whose turn it was to do the dishes or take out the trash.

"It's your turn to do the dishes."

"No, fuck you, it's yours!"

The fights often led to shit being broken around the house, like cabinets, toilets and electrical circuits. Soon, half-eaten apples, spilled cereal and empty cans of spaghetti-os and other trash piled up so high on the kitchen floor, that it became impossible to walk through. I'd crouch down and pretend to be Rolf Benirschke, field goal kicker for the San Diego Chargers. I'd take two steps forward and kick the trash bags, sending garbage flying into the air and splattering on the counters and walls.

The mountain of trash became so big that we had to call a meeting, where a truce was established, long enough to clean up the town dump. When we lifted the rotting bags from the mound, they ripped open, spilling millions of tiny white maggots onto the carpet, already sopping wet from the overflowing toilets. We nicknamed the hallway "the river." You had to remove your socks to cross "the river," and if you forgot, you'd spend the rest of the day sloshing around in mushy, sewage socks.

Kerry and I escaped the science experiment unfolding inside by climbing into a treehouse in the backyard. There was safety there. As if the branches created an invisible forcefield which protected us from the world. We talked in hushed tones, making plans to run away and live on the beach.

It was always me and Kerry, versus Stephanie and Michelle. Since we were the youngest, we lost all the battles. Our only salvation came from our secret hiding spot in the tree. During one especially bad fight, we raced out back, ready to climb to safety, only to find the tree split in half and toppled over. The treehouse was broken into a thousand pieces and strewn all about the yard. We lost yet another battle that day.

There was a park near our house. To get there, you had to walk up a hill and through a patch of dense trees. After the treehouse was destroyed, I spent my days alone, roaming through the trees and brush. I found a stream behind a clump of Oleanders and spent all my time there, away from the madness. But, inevitably, I had to go home.

The knock-down-drag-out fights became a daily occurrence. And when we weren't slapping and punching each other, my sisters got a big kick out of pinning me to the ground, kneeling on my outstretched arms and tickling me until I peed my pants. Even Kerry, my supposed ally, got in on the fun. We were wild animals, kids raising kids.

My dad showed up one day, out of the blue, and sat us all down. "Your mom wants to see you." I almost fell off my chair. I looked at my sisters' faces, all scrunched up as if he'd just told them a rocket ship was waiting out front to take them to Saturn. We hadn't seen Mom in years.

"I want to see her," Kerry said.

"Me too," Stephanie and Michelle said in harmony.

"I don't want to see that bitch!" I screamed. My dad leaped over the coffee table, grabbed me off my chair, and raised me into the air. "Watch your mouth!" I almost had a heart attack right there.

My sisters began taking trips on the weekends to stay with her, but I refused. I was just fine living my wild and carefree lifestyle, free from drunk raging moms and wicked step-monsters thrashing me with belts. I was perfectly content living as a savage.

"You should go visit Mom, she's better now," my sisters would say. "She's sorry for everything that happened before." But I wasn't buying it, I'd fallen for her shit before.

They cornered me one day and told me they were moving back with Mom and said I had to go too. I pushed them away and shouted, "Did you forget about all the shit she put us through!"

"She's different now, she's not drinking anymore," they said. But I'd already decided to continue living in the house on my own, they could do what they wanted. A couple days later, my dad made another rare appearance, asking me to go for a ride with him in his cab. I loved listening to the squawk of the radio and the dispatcher sending the drivers to different calls. I made him turn on the meter and watched the numbers roll around the dial, $3.00, $3.10, $3.20…

He bought me an ice cream as I continued watching the meter. "Listen Kev, you need to move back with your mom."

"No, I don't want to live with her. I want to live with you." My nose began to burn, and my eyes became blurry. $3.60, $3.70…

"I can't take care of you anymore."

"I can take care of myself!" $3.80…

"No, you guys need to stick together."

"But what about wrestling?" $3.90…

"I don't know, maybe they have a team where your mom lives."

I looked down at my ice cream, blurry through my tears, and took a lick. It tasted like broccoli. "When?"

"Tonight," he said. $4.00…

When he dropped me off, I ran as fast as I could to the creek, spitting and cussing the whole way. When I reached the edge of the water, I fell to my knees and cried. But I only allowed myself two minutes, then I dried my eyes, hiked back to the house and packed.

CHAPTER THIRTEEN

RIVER OF BLOOD

It was time to leave my adopted family. Diego had managed to save me from the wrath of the Director. I was losing track of all the beers I owed the guy. Miguel didn't get fired, and I guess that's just as well.

Luis and his mom waited in the living room, an assembly line of love. I kneeled in front of Luis and handed him my favorite walking stick. "You are now the official President of the Monimbo Hiking Club." I felt the power in his little arms as he squeezed my neck. I was going to miss him.

The big Mayan appeared. I stood and gave him a powerful handshake. His eyes widened when I handed him a brand new boombox. When I pointed to the empty shelf where the booze once sat, his scowl returned and he quickly walked away.

Tears rolled down Yolanda's cheeks as I wrapped my arms around her. She was stiff, her arms heavy by her sides. She put her head on my chest, and I felt the cold teardrops on my skin. I squeezed her tighter, and she draped her arms around my back, limp at first, but then her embrace grew stronger, the tension draining from her body. We'd been through so much together.

She'd cared for me like her own, showing empathy and kindness. She'd fought by my side as I battled Dengue Fever. I'd be forever grateful to both her and Luis, for loving a kid from San Diego as he struggled to find his way.

I slung my duffel bag over my shoulder and took one final look at my adopted Nicaraguan family, then turned and walked away.

It was time to be sworn-in, and we were all bursting with excitement. Unbelievably, the previous three months had only been a dress rehearsal.

Upon arriving at the President's Mansion in Managua, Nica 6 was ushered into a large ornate room, where we nibbled on cucumber sandwiches and mingled with the U.S. Ambassador, Diego, the Peace Corps Director and Caribbean Mike—my new Business Sector boss. The President of Nicaragua, Violeta Chamorro, entered the room and shook our hands. Then, we gathered as a group, faced the ambassador and swore the Oath of Office.

It was official, we were Peace Corps Volunteers. I waited my turn and took my picture with the President and the Ambassador. It was a proud moment, regardless of all the shit I'd endured to get there.

"Hey Diego," I said, as he passed by, "Can I talk with you for a minute?"

"Sure."

We walked to the side of the room, away from all the people and I began to sputter, "I wanted to… I just, well…" I'd rehearsed what I wanted to say in my head, but the words were coming out like vomit. "Diego, thank you for everything you did for me. I wouldn't have made it this far without you. I mean you literally saved my fucking life!"

"You don't have to thank me. You deserve this. Although I must admit, I did have my doubts whether you'd make it or not. You caught a lot of bad breaks."

"Is that what you call it?" I looked down at the cast on my arm and was reminded of the pain I'd been trying to ignore.

"Look, Kevin, sometimes you let your emotions get the best of you. But you're willing to fight for what you believe in, regardless of the consequences. Don't ever lose that."

"I'll try not to."

"Listen to that voice inside you, it won't steer you wrong."

"Thanks again, Diego."

"You're welcome. Good luck in Estelí."

The next morning, my new boss, Caribbean Mike, loaded me and my bags into his truck and drove north. As we passed by vegetable stands piled high with giant carrots and radishes, and began our ascent into the Segovia Mountains, I turned and asked him, "So am I the only volunteer getting a ride to his site?" All my friends were still in Managua, making final preparations before they boarded buses for towns spread throughout Nicaragua. Some were staying in the capital for a couple days for one last celebration before saying goodbye to each other.

Mike gripped the steering wheel with both hands as we bounced over a stretch of potholes. "The Director wanted to make sure you got situated in your new site."

"Just me?"

"Yes."

We pulled into Estelí and drove to the Parque Central. Mike helped me with my duffel bag, and we walked over and sat on a bench facing the Cathedral. My arm felt like it was inside a pot of water on a slow boil. I looked at the bags at my feet and wondered where I'd packed my Diazepam. Mike was a big, mellow Nicaraguan with a scruffy beard and wire glasses. He was from Puerto Cabeza on the Northern Caribbean coast and spoke perfect English.

We sat in silence for several minutes, watching people move up and down the busy streets. Mike scanned the park from side to side, pulled off his glasses and then cleared his throat. "You're going to be the first volunteer to live in Estelí since the Sandinista War."

"Really?"

"Yes," he said, cleaning his glasses on his shirt. "We feel it's safe now."

"Wait... It wasn't safe before?"

"No." He squinted and held his glasses up to the sun, looking for smudges. "We're just beginning to place volunteers in the North."

"Why wasn't it safe?"

"There was still some Contra activity going on."

"Contras?"

"Yes," Mike said, swatting at a mosquito buzzing around his ear. "There are still many dangerous areas, but we feel Estelí is safe now."

"Dangerous areas?" I felt my throat tighten.

"Now listen, this is important;" He turned and faced me with a serious expression on his face. "Don't ever talk politics in the city, or anywhere in the north for that matter. Many people still hate Americans here."

"Uh, ok."

"And try to stay out of the bars."

"Stay out of the bars!"

"Oh, and one last thing, don't ever walk in the mountains surrounding Estelí."

"Why can't I walk in the mountains?"

"Because there are still thousands of landmines planted up there from the war."

And with those final words of wisdom, Caribbean Mike shook my hand and drove away.

A million thoughts raced through my head as I sat there all alone on a bench in the middle of Estelí, with two bags at my feet containing everything I owned in the world. I was thirty pounds lighter, wearing a dirty, stinky cast over my nearly dead hand, and I had no home or anybody to turn to. A smile spread across my face, realizing how that night around a bonfire in Mexico, had led me to this very moment.

I crossed the street to a little café and bought myself a beer, content to be on my own again, like I'd been my entire life. I would soon break every one of Caribbean Mike's rules, but for now, I needed to find a home. So, I finished my beer, scooped up my bags and trudged through the city, knocking on doors and asking, "Se alquila? Se alquila?"

As the sun cranked up and the hours passed, I grew worried, wondering where I'd sleep for the night. The straps on my duffel bag dug into my shoulders, and the weight bogged me down, forcing me to stop and catch my breath. I sat down on the sidewalk, my arm throbbing in pain, and contemplated crying. But a nearby pulpería distracted me from my misery, and I dragged myself to it.

"Coca-Cola, por favor!"

The icy syrup tasted like heaven. I made small talk with the owner. She seemed sweet, so I asked if I could leave my bags with her as I continued searching for a house to rent. She agreed, dragging the bags into her home. When she returned, she mentioned that her son had a house for rent just a block away. Shhh, is that fate banging on my door? She didn't have the key, but I could look at it from the outside.

I practically flew down the street. The house was solid, built from cement block. It had an iron gate and a thick, wood door. A ten-foot-high wall ran around what I assumed was a yard, due to the mango and orange tree branches hanging over the wall.

"Inodorno o letrina - toilet or outhouse?" I asked.

"Inodorno," she replied.

"I'll take it!" I said, right there on the spot, never even seeing the inside.

More than content with my progress, I left my bags with the lady and hopped a bus back to Managua to party with my friends, before they spread out around the country.

We spent the night moving through the streets of Managua. First, going to a wild baseball game where women walked up and down the aisles selling fried plantains and papaya slices, while their babies slept peacefully in slings on their backs—immune to the screaming fans and chaos all around.

From there, we made our way to a fancy bar with pool tables and air conditioning. We pretended to be important people, without a care in the world, joking and laughing for hours, wishing the night would last forever, not knowing when we'd ever see each other again.

"Anybody nervous about moving on?" Mitch asked, piercing our thin veil of invincibility. We were quiet for a moment, and then we laughed and threw back a shot of rum. But reality hung over us like a heavy cloud, and before we knew it, it was time to move on. It was time to put our thumbprint on Nicaragua.

Mitch headed south to Masaya. Jason went east to cattle country in Chontales. Craig had left the day before for Condega, a small town just north of Estelí. Fittingly, he would be the closest volunteer to me.

Stephanie was moving to Ciudad Darío, a town just off the Pan American Highway going north towards Estelí, which allowed us to share a bus for part of the ride. I'd written her a letter earlier that morning, telling her how much I liked her. I figured it was easier than chasing her around the playground like a nine-year-old.

I clutched the letter in my hand, flipping it nervously as we made small talk. My brain was doing back flips, calculating whether I should give it to her, or not. The bus pulled into her town and sputtered to a stop. I helped her with her bags, my heart screaming to give her the note. She gave me a big hug and began to make her way down the aisle. Now or never! I stood up and screamed, but nothing came out. I closed my sweaty hand around the letter and slumped back into my seat. Fucking pussy!

But as I watched her walking towards the sleepy town and her new life, my heart suddenly surged. I stood up and screamed through the window, "Stephanie!" as the bus rumbled back to life. She froze and looked at me with that same tense, nervous expression we'd shared while entering Nicaragua months before.

She began to walk back as the bus rolled forward, picking up speed as she came along the side. I reached out the window and dropped the letter. It fluttered down and landed in her hand as the bus drove off. "I wrote you a letter!" I shouted into the wind—just in case she couldn't figure it out by now.

She unfolded the note as we pulled onto the Pan American Highway, and as we sped away, she looked up from the letter and flashed her beautiful smile. I could barely breathe.

I practically ran from the bus station to the pulpería where I'd left my belongings, eager to begin my new life. After giving me my bags, the lady reached into her pocket and handed me a shiny new key. As I was leaving, I noticed a pharmacy next door and remembered the prescription in my pocket. My arm still burned like a grease fire, day in and day out, and I'd run out of pills. I bought thirty tablets and four beers and headed to my new home.

It was a simple house, comprised of a small living room and a bedroom, but it's best feature was the indoor bathroom. The owner had left me a little bed, a nightstand, and two wood chairs. I threw my bags in a corner, popped in a Bob Dylan cassette, and cracked a beer. Life was good.

The next morning, I woke at 7 a.m. and took a freezing cold shower. I may have had indoor plumbing, but I sure didn't have hot water. I shaved, dressed in my nicest clothes, and walked the two miles to the Cooperativa de Ahorro y Crédito, San Benito, arriving fifteen minutes before they opened their doors at 8 a.m.

It was apparent that nobody was expecting me, as the secretary hurriedly cleared stacks of files from an unused desk. I sat at my new desk and pulled out a notebook and pen. Ramón came out from his office and stood over me with a scowl, "Buenas, que quiere hacer?"

What do I want to do? The question caught me off guard. I assumed he would've had something lined up for me already. I muttered something about wanting to work with the "socios" or small businesses who had loans with them.

"Vamos a ver – We'll see," he said, and quickly walked away. I sat quietly at my desk, sipping coffee and rubbing my burning arm for the rest of the morning as everybody stared at the strange new creature. I wanted to stand up and dance the jitterbug for all the curious onlookers.

When lunch rolled around, I speed-walked home, stopping at a tortilla stand across the street from my house where a lady mashed dough under a tin roof all day. She sold four piping hot tortillas with a dollop of cream for one Córdoba - roughly ten cents. Caddy corner from her, a vegetable stand sold avocados, green onions, peppers, and squash. A half block up, a butcher and his sons carved sides of pork and beef in the morning, selling the meat for around a dollar a pound. I could walk fifty feet in any direction and get whatever I needed.

I gobbled down the tortillas and made myself a cucumber and tomato sandwich; then I sat down and rested for a moment. But then, it was time to return to work. I jogged all the way back to the bank, arriving at 1 p.m. on the dot, and then proceeded to sit around and do nothing once again. The monotony was only broken by the cute secretary making her afternoon rounds of sweet coffee and fruit pastries. By 2:30, I was nodding off. I peeked into Ramón's office and told him I needed to take care of some personal business. His nose scrunched up and deep canyons appeared on his face. He took a long drag on his cigarette and exhaled slowly, then he waved his hand dismissively and said, "Esta bien."

As I pushed open the bank doors, the sun hit my face and I felt a rush like I'd just busted out of jail. The Peace Corps had given me an extra month's stipend to set up my household, and I headed to the local bicycle shop and bought a new mountain bike for $100. It felt amazing riding through town with the wind blowing through my hair. HONK! HONK!! I almost fell off my new bike as one taxi driver after another banged on their horns and flew by me, missing me by inches.

I used the rest of the money to buy dishes and a small propane stove. Our stipend was roughly $200 per month, and although that seemed like a paltry sum of money, I learned to think of it in terms of córdobas, the local currency, as opposed to U.S. dollars. Receiving 2600 córdobas per month, sounded much more pleasing to the ear. My rent was 600, beers were 5, and a sit-down dinner ran around 25 córdobas. The math worked.

It turned out, my house was actually a large house split right down the middle by 1/8" sheets of plywood. A young woman and her baby lived on the other side of the razor-thin wall, allowing me to hear everything that happened on her side just as clearly as if she was in my own house. It also meant that she could listen to everything that happened on my side just as clearly.

She told me the owner had cut the house in half the day I returned to Managua to be with my friends. I don't think the house had ever been for rent. I believe the enterprising old woman hatched the plan the minute the 'rich gringo' crawled into her pulpería, in a desperate search for Coca-Cola and housing.

I arrived at work around 8:30 the next morning. Ramón made a little joke about me being late and disappeared into his office. Once again, I sat at my desk doing nothing, growing increasingly alarmed that this might be my future for the next two years.

The Peace Corps in Nicaragua had sought out different Savings and Loans for the business volunteers to work within, thinking that this would be a means for us to seguey into working with the small businesses that took out loans from them. Working at the grassroots level, being the true aim of the Peace Corps.

The Savings and Loans took on the volunteers because: A. We were free labor to them, and B. It looked good to have a gringo or foreigner working within the business.

Now, the counterpart role is meant to be just that: a partner or guide who helps you in your new job, showing you areas where you could be of service. The counterpart is a local person, who works where you work, and often helps you settle into your new community, assisting the volunteer in finding housing and adjusting to his or her new environment.

I'm sure a lot of volunteers have great experiences with their counterparts and with their jobs, but for whatever reason, Ramón seemed to have little interest in being either my counterpart or my guide. So, after organizing my desk for the tenth time, I'd had enough, and found an empty chair in front of one of the accountants and sat down.

"Hola, Yo soy Kevin."

"Buenas, soy Jonny."

"Jonny?"

"Sí."

"Come on man... really?"

"Sí!"

After a brief, confusing conversation, I determined that either his dad was a big John Wayne fan, or he wanted me to wear a cowboy hat and call myself "The Duke." Jonny was very patient with my ever-evolving Spanish, still rough at that point, and he was curious about the U.S., asking about American football, Hollywood, Disneyland, and most importantly, American women. I gave him a rundown on the good ol' U.S. of A, teaching him all that I knew about the different subjects, and all that I didn't know about American women. He reciprocated, telling me about the local Perdomo cigar factory, and about the favorite bars and restaurants in town, including one that sold exotic meats like monkey, snake, and iguana.

"Oh, and you should check out the waterfall," he said.

"Waterfall?"

"Yes, it's in the mountains outside of town."

"Hey Jonny, what does Estelí mean in Spanish?"

"It's not a Spanish word. It's a Nahuatl word meaning river of blood."

"River of blood! Why is it called that?"

"There's a river that runs along the edge of town filled with red obsidian rocks. Some say these rocks turn the river red. Others say it's due to a battle between good and evil that took place long ago."

"Cool," I said. Then I looked around the bank. Everybody's heads were buried in ledgers, busily working. "Hey Jonny, what would you say the main problem is with the bank?"

Jonny looked up, his eyes wide. He glanced over his shoulders, slowly, and began to speak in a hushed tone, "The bank isn't doing well."

He went on, giving me a synopsis of the Savings and Loan. Their principal operation was making loans to small businesses, setting them up on payment schedules, which they serviced, and providing savings accounts. Jonny leaned in close and whispered, "The default rate is 28%." OUCH! That meant that over a quarter of their loans were failing. Or, put simply, not being paid back. I didn't need to be some fancy business guru—although I fancied myself one—to realize there was a major problem going on here at the San Benito Cooperative. Strangely, nobody seemed alarmed.

After lunch, I headed back to work with a plan. I'd devote half my day to working with the bank, and the other half to working with the small business owners (socios) who had outstanding loans. I asked Jonny for a list of the businesses he thought could use my help and then I ran the plan past Ramón.

"Why do you want to bother the businesses?" he asked with his usual scowl.

"I don't want to bother them, I want to help them."

He grabbed a stack of folders and grumbled, "Let me think about it."

I went back to my desk and twiddled my thumbs for most of the day. By 3 o'clock I'd had enough, and marched back to Ramón's office.

"So?" I asked standing in his doorway, my head bouncing up and down like a chicken.

He looked up from a ledger, rubbed his eyes, and put a cigarette in his mouth. Then he leaned back in his chair and stared at me without saying a word. As he reached for his lighter, I saw my opportunity.

"Ok great, I'll see you tomorrow." I raced out of the bank before he could utter a word, and then rode my bike like the wind to my first potential client, a tire repair shop.

"Hola, soy Kevin," I said to a man covered in grease and lying under an old Datsun pickup.

"Que querés vos?" he shouted while banging on a rim with a tire iron.

I reached down to shake his hand, but he shook his head, "no" showing me that it was caked in grease.

"If you ever need any help with your business, I'm available," I told him. "I work with the Cooperativa San Benito."

"Bueno," he said, eyeing me strangely.

"Oh," I said, as he started banging away on the rim, "and my services are free."

From the tire shop, I rode to a business that rented Nintendo machines by the hour. Located in a little room off the main house, the owner had ten TV's hooked up to Nintendo machines.

As one kid after another wandered in and shoved Donkey Kong and Frogger cartridges into the machines, I began my spiel. Occasionally, one of the kids would grab a bag of chips from the wall and hand the owner a coin. He seemed suspicious of me at first, but became more receptive after I mentioned the free part. I told him I'd be back in a week to follow up and set off to visit three more businesses. All with mixed results.

On my way home, I stopped at an old cement bridge just a stone's throw from my house. Women washed their clothes and bathed in the river flowing underneath. Shirts and pants were spread out on the boulders lining the shore, drying in the warm sun. I thought about Stephanie and the letter I'd given her, wondering what she was thinking. Had I misread the situation? I thought about Kira, who I'd had been writing letters to since that last night in San Diego. Was there something there? I thought about Mom and my life back in the States.

Children, wearing only their underwear, lathered their bodies with soap and jumped off the boulders into the river. I had traveled so far, both mentally and physically. Where would my journey lead me next? I marveled at the smooth red rocks radiating from below the water, giving it a reddish appearance. This was my home now, Estelí—the River of Blood.

CHAPTER FOURTEEN

CRAIG

I slept in, rolling into the Cooperativa San Benito at 9:30 in the morning, just in time for morning coffee and pastries. Ramón poked his head out and asked to see him in his office.

As I sat across from him, separated only by a desk, he leaned forward, and spoke in his gravelly smoker's voice, "Office hours are eight to twelve and one to five." Then he leaned back, clasped his hands behind his head and said, "You understand?"

I looked around his shabby little office, at the folders scattered around his desk and the twisted cigarette butts in his ashtray, my anger simmering. A slow boil, but heating up. Low profile.

I bit down on my lip and stood to leave. Moving towards the door, I stopped and turned back. "Just what do you expect me to do here all day?" His eyebrows furrowed into knots of confusion, gears smashing and grinding behind his dull, muddy eyes. Before he could divine an answer, I blurted out, "I want to look at the books and figure out why the default rate is so high."

His face turned red, and he screamed, "That's the accountant's job!"

I went back to my desk and gulped down my coffee. I looked around the bank, there were no computers, only stacks of ledger books piled on every desk and flat space available. Everything was entered manually. I really was in the time of the woolly mammoth.

"Sup Jonny?"

"All cool," he replied. I'd been teaching him a little California lingo.

"Can you teach me your accounting system?"

"No problem, bro!"

Jonny and I spent the next two weeks going over debits and credits, as I suffered through flashbacks of my dreaded college accounting classes.

He showed me how to enter loan payments and make saving withdrawals into the corresponding ledgers.

I continued working with the Nintendo owner in the afternoon, devising a coupon book where every fourth hour the children got one free hour of play. They would often play two to three hours more than usual just to get the free hour. He got so busy he had to buy more TVs and Nintendo's. I added a bootmaker and wrecking company to my clientele. We came up with different marketing strategies to promote and grow their businesses.

Ramón stayed out of my way for the most part, and we fell into a peaceful coexistence. I think he was secretly happy not having to deal with me every afternoon. Jonny and I kept our morning accounting classes under wraps, not wanting to upset the tyrant.

I hadn't heard back from Stephanie, no reply to the letter I'd given to her. In fact, I hadn't heard from any volunteers. I wasn't worried though, figuring they were all busy settling into their new sites.

The fireball inside my arm had dulled slightly, but the embers that remained were driving me insane. I took two Diazepam's every night to help me sleep. It worked somewhat, but I discovered that if I popped three or four pills instead, and drank them down with three or four beers, it worked even better.

One night, I was out of beer and washed the pills down with rum. As I sat in my favorite chair, looking at the sky through my window, I thought about how we were all just fuzzy dots on a pretty blue sphere—slowly revolving around a star.

They say our universe goes on forever, that it's infinite. An explosion, or rather an expansion, happened fourteen billion years ago. From nothing, something. And now, we are all living within this ever-expanding world, tumbling through life, searching for purpose. Order within chaos, the lines blurred.

I woke up slumped over and slobbering, reggae music blasting—flesh burning from a lit cigar dangling between my fingers. Tile floors and cement walls were all that prevented the house from burning down.

The doctor who had treated my hand and arm had given me the name of a health center where I was to go for therapy. My hand still had no movement, it just hung there like a dead weight, flopping from side to side when I moved my arm. It was a disturbing sight, and kept me in a constant state of fear, wondering if it would ever come back to life.

As I walked into the Centro de Salud (Health Center) for the first time, it reminded me of a horror movie. The lighting was low, and the walls were dingy. A lady at the front desk took me to a back area after showing her my paperwork from my doctor in Managua. An old man was attempting to walk between two parallel bars as I sat down at a table.

"Hola," said a pretty young therapist. Her nose scrunched up when she saw the dirty cast on my arm. After some brief paperwork, she grabbed a pair of medical scissors and began cutting off my stinky cast. "So how do you like Nicaragua?" she asked. A poof of putrid air rose up as she cracked open the cast—like opening the lid of a sarcophagus. She cleaned my mummy arm with alcohol and said, "Lift your thumb." I stared at my hand, trying to will it to move, but it just hung there lifeless.

"Can you move your meñique?" I tried moving my pinky, using telekinesis and other magical powers, but it was all futile. She replaced the cast with a removable Velcro brace and told me to come back in two days.

Three days a week, the pretty therapist rubbed salve into my fingers and arm, while I shifted uncomfortably in my chair trying to hide my erection. Thankfully, she kept her eyes on my hand. After the massage, she'd have me perform different hand and wrist exercises to awaken the nerves.

I enjoyed my visits, no longer noticing the cracked paint and dim lighting, but seeing, instead, how clean they kept the place and how friendly the staff was; All so dedicated to their jobs and possessing an endless supply of enthusiasm. I marveled at how all these services were provided to me for free, in the poorest country in the Western Hemisphere, while I'd been unable to afford health insurance for most of my life while living in the richest country on the planet.

I studied my Spanish books at night and practiced what I'd learned with the locals as I purchased fruit, vegetables and tortillas. I began making inroads into the complicated culture of the hard-working people, learning their slang words, hand and mouth gestures and different folktales.

I read voraciously. Learning about transcendentalism and communing with nature through Thoreau, and about the dark, sinister side of the world from Poe. Michener took me around the world, showing me the evolution of mankind, while Steinbeck guided me through the struggles of the early 20th century in America. I rode a riverboat down the Mississippi with Twain, as he unveiled a more innocent time in the late 19th century, and hopped on freight trains with Jack Kerouac and drank cheap wine as we crisscrossed the U.S. These authors, and others, became my buddies, helping me to adjust to my new home and keeping my loneliness at bay.

The mountains surrounding Estelí produced gentle breezes, which rolled past the trees and swept across the city, creating cool, comfortable nights. My body finally stopped its endless sweating and acclimated, and although the mosquitoes were less vicious in the cooler climate, I still slept underneath a mosquito net. Occasionally, a bloodsucker would sneak in, and I'd wake up in misery, my body looking like a horror version of Connect the Dots.

On weekends, I liked to walk up to the Central Plaza and watch the city in action. I would buy vigorón—boiled yucca with cabbage, lime, and bits of fried pig wrapped in a banana leaf—and eat it on a bench, as merchants hawked their handmade crafts and couples snuck kisses under the cover of trees. Shoeshine boys worked fast, snapping their towels and dipping them into tins of black paste, polishing leather cowboy boots for one córdoba. When they made their quota for the day, they packed away their tools in wooden boxes and ran to the food shack, where a hard-working lady sold them tamales and fried cheese.

The Cathedral in front of the park was dedicated to "Nuestra Señora del Rosario," the Patron Saint of Estelí. The church was a hub for Estelí's devout Catholics. The Museum of the Sandinista Revolution was across the way. It was run by families of Sandinistas soldiers who'd been killed during the war. Many of the buildings around the park were still riddled with pockmarks and gouges from mortar and tank artillery. Civil War had ripped through Estelí, right in the center of town, less than 20 years ago, and it still had the battle scars to prove it. It was a moving sight.

"Hoy vago. Que hecho?" I greeted Jonny early Monday morning, throwing out the Nica slang he'd been teaching me

"No hay de que," he replied.

We dove back into the exciting world of debits and credits, analyzing the loans for problems. After a couple of weeks, I still wasn't getting the big picture of why the default rate was so high. It was almost lunchtime, and I was getting hungry and frustrated, but just as I was about to take off for home, Jonny tensed up and pushed a few files towards me. Ones I hadn't seen before.

"Que es?" I asked.

"Mire adentro – look inside," he replied.

Flipping through them, I quickly realized that each file represented a different loan in default—significant default. From what I could deduce: the loans had been opened, a few payments had been made, initially, and then all payments suddenly stopped. They all had the same pattern. When I got to the fourth file, I recognized the name of the borrower typed on the tab and nearly froze. Ramón!

I looked at Jonny, my eyes open wide and then looked towards Ramón's office, as if to ask, "Our Ramón?" Jonny nodded yes. The picture was suddenly clear. Ramón was loaning money to himself and not paying it back. Not only that, several Directors on the Cooperative's Board, and their friends, also had outstanding loans. They were using the Savings and Loans as their personal fucking piggy bank.

Jonny, who'd apparently been biding his time and waiting to see if he could trust me before spilling the beans, now spoke in whispers and gave me the rundown. They'd been making loans to themselves for years. Whenever the bank was teetering on bankruptcy, foreign aid came in from outside countries. They gave the bank large chunks of money, thinking the money was being lent to small businesses in a developing country. Cash from countries like Germany or the Netherlands would arrive in large chunks, upwards of $100,000, and keep the bank in operation.

Only a portion of the aid was being used to help small businesses. I surmised the giant warehouse being constructed out back was probably a side business used to store products they were purchasing with the money. Just then Ramón walked by and saw the pile of files in front of us.

"I told you I didn't want you working on the ledgers! That's for the accountants."

"Hmm," I uttered.

He turned to Jonny. "If you show him the files again, you're fired. Now get back to work!"

Turning back to me he said, "I don't want you working with any of the small businesses anymore. You can work here in the afternoon like everybody else."

My face and neck became hot. I wanted to lash out. I stared at the thick lines on his face, knowing I was looking at a thief. "Is that all?" I asked.

"Sí."

"Pasa buen día," I said with a smile, walking out the bank mid-morning and hopping on my bike. As I began to ride home, I saw Jonny staring at me through an open shutter, remembered the waterfall he had told me about and set off to find it.

I rode towards the edge of town, where the buses entered, and past a police checkpoint shack. I turned onto a dirt road, riding my bike fast and hard, wind whipping through my hair, flush with adrenaline. The path wound like a snake up into the mountains. I pulled over to ask for directions and took off my shirt, letting the sun beat down on my face and body.

The higher I climbed, the freer I felt—like when I was a boy, hiding in the mountains, far from my stepmother. Thick tree branches arched over either side of the road, creating a dark green tunnel. The songs of birds from high atop their perches propelled me forward, pushing me to pedal harder. When I reached a blue house, I opened a barbed wire gate and rode past. It felt like I was trespassing, but nobody came out. I maneuvered down a path for two hundred yards until it narrowed and forced me to walk my bike. When it closed in even further, I had to carry my bike over my shoulder. I began to hear water cascading in the distance. It grew louder with each step. I was near.

I poked my head through a clump of bushes and was blown away by the sight of a vast lagoon, surrounded by flowers and plants growing from the craggy cliffs forming a semi-circle around it. Water, gushing over a ledge, eighty feet above, crashed into the center, creating a magnificent waterfall.

I stripped down to my boxers and waded into the frigid water, so cold it took my breath away, washing away my sweat and anger. As I neared the fall, I looked skyward, to the water pouring over the cliffs. I moved closer, feeling the water hit my head, soft at first, but then it came pounding down so hard that I became frightened, and swam towards the shore.

Something inside made me turn back, and as I neared the fall, I dove down and swam hard, popping up directly under the crashing water. It felt like a thousand wooden spoons were smacking me over my head, but I stayed in the same spot, treading water and ignoring the pain. I felt powerful and free, I felt like me!

I dove and swam through the thunder and explosions sending shockwaves through my limbs. When I surfaced, I spotted a ledge, twenty feet up, and swam to a rock just below it. Cramming my foot into a nook, I pulled myself up and climbed to the top of the rock, where I slipped on a patch of moss and nearly fell off the side. The rock protruded out from the cliff, forcing me to dangle over the water as I maneuvered around it. I hugged the cliff and sidestepped the rest of the way to the ledge.

I took a deep breath, letting the moist crisp air fill my lungs as I looked out at the lagoon below. The waterfall was crashing just feet away, the spray and mist washing over my face. The cliffs trembled under the power of the water. I was standing on a rock next to the waterfall that rose another sixty feet above me.

My heart was racing like a stallion as I prepared to jump. Even here, I was twenty or thirty feet above the lagoon. I dug my foot into the cliff and felt a sharp pang in my stomach. I crouched and leaned forward. Taking one last look at the waterfall next to me, I pushed off, kicking my legs in the air as I sailed down and splashed into the lagoon. What a fucking rush!

I looked to the top of the cliffs, where the waterfall began and tried to calculate the height. It had to be a good eighty feet up. Now that would be a jump! I scanned the cliffs, looking for a path up, but there was none. You'd need a rope to get to the top. I felt a sense of relief. My heart fluttered just thinking about jumping from way up there.

I swam back to shore and lay in the sand, staring up at the red and yellow Bromeliads growing on the cliffs. I was buried in a deep hole in the center of the Earth. Suddenly, I was floating upwards towards the sky, passing the cliffs and the waterfall. Higher and higher I climbed until I had reached the edge of the clouds. I looked back down and saw myself lying in the sand far below. Am I just a mere grain of sand? A speck of dust floating through the infiniteness of space? Do I matter?

* * *

I didn't bother going back to work that day. Fuck Ramón. It was Friday, so I had the weekend to figure out what I was going to do. A door in my bedroom led to the backyard where mango, orange and lime trees provided plenty of fruit for my rum drinks, and shade to wash my clothes on a cement washboard.

Several older women had knocked on my door recently, asking if I needed somebody to wash my clothes and clean my house. I found this strange, having always washed my own clothes and taken care of myself. But, the culture was different here, and after gouging holes in the few clothes I owned while washing them by hand, I readily agreed to the next woman who knocked.

Josefina was busy slapping and pounding my boxers into submission, while I sipped rum and fresh mango juice, scribbling out a letter to Kira. Her 6-year-old daughter snuck up beside me and stared inquisitively at the strange gringo. She sprinted off in laughter every time I talked to her in English.

There was a knock on my door. A man from the post office handed me an envelope from Kira. I tore it open, surprised the letter had found my house. I had given her my new address in Estelí, but had been wondering whether mail would actually arrive due to my unusual address. There were no street signs or addresses in Estelí, or Nicaragua for that matter. My official address was, "From the banks, three and a half blocks to the river. Estelí, Nicaragua. Central America." Miraculously, I had her letter in my hand. She wrote that she was coming to visit with my best friend, Stevie and their cousin, Amy.

"Yee-haw!" I shouted, waving the letter in the air and kicking up my legs. The people passing by just stared, growing accustomed to the crazy gringo.

I rubbed my arm. My dance had awakened the dull, steady fire inside. Wiping a bead of sweat from my brow, I thought about popping a Diazepam, but then I spotted a white guy walking down my road, and nearly fell over from shock. A trail of children tagged behind his loud, red and white striped shirt. It was as if a circus clown had arrived to perform tricks for the neighborhood. I laughed out loud, amused by the sight, but then it struck me, this must be how Nicaraguans view me: as an oddity—a minority. I looked at the man again, noticing how white his skin was. He seemed out of place even to me, like a bright neon sign bouncing down the road. Where's Waldo in a sea of brown people.

When he got closer, I realized it was Craig and doubled over in laughter, watching his big, familiar grin come into view. Happiness flooded over me. It was great to see my friend.

"Oy Kebin," he joked.

"What the hell?"

"Como he estado?" Still flaunting his Spanish skills.

"Dude, what are you doing here?"

"I got bored of Condega and wanted to see a real city."

"Well, bienvenidos a Estelí!"

"Gracias, now what's good to eat around here?"

"The tortilla shack!" We crossed the street. "Cuatro tortillas con crema, por favor," I asked the lady.

Without even looking up, the short, plump lady wiped her hands on her apron and grabbed a handful of masa, mashed out four patties and tossed them on the grill. She gave them a final pat and shifted a chunk of smoldering wood underneath.

"You're going to love these."

"I better or I'm going home."

When they puffed up and began to smoke, she grabbed them with her sooty fingertips, slapped a spoonful of cream in the center and folded them in half. She placed them on a banana leaf and handed them to Craig who was smiling from ear to ear.

"How's Condega?" I asked, watching him shove one tortilla after another into his mouth.

"Boring," he replied, cream now smeared on the sides of his mouth, "Guess what?"

"What?"

"I live in the bank!"

"You live in the... what?" I burst out laughing.

"The bank!" Craig said laughing. "I live in the bank. There wasn't any other place to live."

"Well, at least you have a short commute."

I showed him around my house and backyard. We decided to make a homemade dinner and headed for the market near the edge of Estelí. Craig was impressed by the variety of stores and restaurants as he lived in a much smaller town.

The market was sprawling, an explosion of color in every direction. You could easily get lost in the maze of stalls and vendors. People shouted at us to buy their papayas and star fruits. We bought onions, peppers, tomatoes, cheese and bread.

Back at my house, we prepared tomato sauce and toasted the bread, making our own version of pizza. Craig talked about his travels around the world. My little jaunts to Mexico paled in comparison to his. He told me about living on a cruise ship for several months during college and traveling around the world.

"It's called Semester at Sea," he said, his eyes lighting up as he told me about all the different ports and adventures he had.

"What are you some sort of rich kid or something?" I could have only dreamed about something like that during college.

"No, not at all. I worked and saved up. I also got some financial aid and a loan."

"Wow, that's really cool. I'm impressed."

"Thanks."

"So, how's your job going?"

Craig told me he wasn't doing much work at his bank either. His counterpart was a nice guy, an older man, but his town was so small, the bank didn't have much business, and there weren't many small businesses to help.

My arm was beginning to burn, so I grabbed a beer and pulled two Diazepams from the little bag the pharmacy gave me.

"What are those?" Craig asked.

"I don't know, they're for my arm. I think it's like a strong type of aspirin or something, Diazepam."

Craig began to laugh. "That's Valium."

"No way!"

"Yes, way."

"Oh man, no wonder I keep passing out all the fucking time."

"You're a mess," Craig laughed. "What's going on with your job?"

"Dude, my counterpart is ripping off the bank!"

"What?"

I gave him a rundown of everything I'd discovered.

"Man, you have all the luck. What are you going to do?"

"I don't know. Any advice?"

"Yeah, give me another slice of poor man pizza."

Craig and I spent the next two days exploring Estelí and eating out at cheap restaurants and street vendors. I showed him my newly discovered waterfall, and we joked about all the difficulties we were having adjusting to life in our new towns. I came to enjoy his companionship and dry sense of humor.

After he'd shoved the last of his clothes in his backpack and stood to leave, I reached out to shake his hand, "Have fun sleeping in the bank."

"Ha, ha. Don't O.D."

"I'll try not to."

"If you get bored, you know where to find me." Craig walked up the street towards the bus station. As he turned the corner and vanished from sight, I felt a sense of sorrow.

I went to my backyard and laid down in my hammock. Looking up at the fruit ripening on the trees, I thought about Stephanie and Kira and about how my life had become so very different. Craig had helped put things in perspective, reminding me to laugh and find joy in the absurd. I still didn't know what to do about Ramón and my work situation, but I wasn't going to let it bring me down any longer.

I felt my arm begin to tingle. It was alive! I moved my pinky and then my thumb; they were coming out of hibernation, along with my spirits. Perhaps I could make it down here in the dense foliage of Nicaragua. I'd been through a lot already, and still had a long haul in front of me, but I was coming into a clearing and finally able to see the sky.

CHAPTER FIFTEEN

SEX, DRUGS & METAL

Mom had made some significant changes in her life. She'd been remarried, to an older man named Mac, and moved to a little house in an alley in the rough-and-tumble, blue-collar neighborhood of Normal Heights. More importantly, she'd given up the bottle. Mom wanted a do-over.

As I walked down the main drag of Adams Avenue for my first day of 5th grade, wearing my Santee Wrestling Club jacket which I rarely took off, I was shocked by the morning bustle and cement landscape, so much different from the rural Santee I'd grown accustomed to. Instead of sauntering past chickens and horses on the way to school, I passed honking cars and banging steel doors as business owners opened their hardware stores and antique shops.

John Adams Elementary was a big melting pot. I was hesitant at first of all the black and brown kids, having had only limited interactions with them to that point. That, coupled with the fact that my impressions were all skewed by movies and TV which portrayed them as fighters and thugs, made for some intense first days. I quickly learned their lingo, and my gutter mouth shocked even the hardest amongst them, but, for some reason, whether culturally or economically or something else, the environment led the kids to form a pecking order, of which I (being the new white kid) was at the very fucking bottom.

"Nice fucking jacket, what are you some kind of fag wrestler or something?" said a stocky kid as I walked on the playground my second week of school.

"Fuck you!" I said and wrestled him to the ground. Once on top, I gave him a quick few jabs to the nose and then let him go. But it wasn't until I'd had my fourth or fifth after-school fistfight, proving I wasn't a "bitch" or "punk-ass motherfucker," that I earned my stripes, "street cred" is what we call it in da' hood. My wrestling days came in handy. I could throw a punch, but even better, if they got too close, I'd pull a "head-and-arm-Howie" on their ass and be on top of them before they could blink, and if you've never been in a fight, basically, if you can get the top position, you're going to win. Unless, of course, you're a "punk-ass bitch," in which case you're gonna' get your ass kicked, "you fuckin' whitey!"

While I was busy fighting or "scrappin" through my first month of 5th grade—eventually learning to make friends with kids of all colors by looking past their exteriors—Mom was home playing June Cleaver. She cooked four-course meals and helped us with our homework each night. After, my sisters and I would all pile into the living room to watch Little House on the Prairie and Silver Spoons, while Mom crocheted or read books. Life, with all its twists and turns, had become somewhat stable for the first time in my life.

My dad disappeared from my life again, and although I was used to it, it still stung. Before moving in with him, I hadn't thought much about him. And, although we rarely saw him during the two years we lived in Santee and Del Cerro, I had seen enough of him to realize I loved and missed him.

I tried to be a good kid, at least in the beginning, but I was always hesitant, waiting for the chaos to return. A wildness burned inside me—bred from my unstable, parentless youth—and fueled by an inner-loneliness I could neither define, nor overcome.

As a result, I began acting out, defying "Mom's rules." How could she expect me to be home by five, when I was used to coming and going as I pleased. I felt confined, trapped. No longer able to run and hide in the mountains, slip off into the "Sticks" of Mississippi, or release my anger on a wrestling mat (turns out there were no wrestling teams in the inner-city), Mom and I had major battles. Screaming, profanity-laced fights that the entire neighborhood had the pleasure of listening to.

And, after a couple of years, Mom finally had enough, moving me into the musty garage across the patio from our house. She nailed an old parachute to the rafters so termite shit wouldn't fall on me when I slept. She needed a break from me, just as much as I needed one from her. At night, I would shiver and wrap blankets tight around my body, staring contently at my parachute ceiling. It was a piece of the mountains, a slice of Mississippi: a chunk of freedom.

I received two gifts on my fourteenth birthday that would last a lifetime. The first was from my sister, Michelle, a 45-rpm record: Ozzy Osbourne's, *Flying High Again*.

"Ozzy's coming in concert," she told me excitedly, "You'll like him."

I remember putting the little plastic spindle inside the record and watching the disc drop. Hearing the whooshing of the needle as it passed over the vinyl, until it reached the grooves, and began playing the deep bass and heavy guitar riffs. I bobbed my head up and down to the music—as if possessed—feeling the energy and power. I looked around to see if anybody was near, feeling like I was breaking the rules. I liked the intensity, and turned it up even louder, moved my head faster. I played the record over and over. Embracing my introduction to heavy metal.

The garage—my new room—had two windows, one looking out to the patio and house, and the other facing the neighbor's garage, a mere two feet away. Late one night, I peeked through the curtains, making sure all the lights in the house were off, opened the window facing the neighbor's garage, and climbed onto the window sill. I'd calculated the odds earlier that evening, determining that sneaking out through the window posed far less risk than trying to cross the patio.

I was now faced with the task of squeezing my body between two narrow walls and maneuvering ten feet to the alley. I sucked in my stomach and slid down between the two walls, holding my arms straight up above my head. The space was so tight I could barely breathe. Once my feet touched the ground, I moved my hands sideways along the wall like a mime.

Inch by inch, I moved, until my head poked into the alley, and I was able to release my belly and all the air stored in my lungs. I took a deep breath and moved quickly away from the house, walking like a burglar in a bank vault so as not to make a sound. I rounded the corner and worked my way along the broken sidewalks of Adams Avenue, cautious to avoid cops. I ducked inside business alcoves and hid behind cars whenever I saw the outline of a siren or the shadow of a shotgun sticking up behind the windshield.

I hurried past the arcade, closed now, where I spent long days playing Donkey Kong and Missile Command while peeking at girls when they weren't looking my way. I passed by dive bars, smelling of stale beer and cigarettes, and my old elementary school, gated and locked for the night.

When I saw the bright lights of the Kensington Theater, *The Ken*, my heart finally stopped racing. The marquis was lit up like the sun, "ROCKY HORROR at MIDNIGHT." I passed by the energetic crowds milling about, many dressed in black leather vests and maid's outfits, and crossed the street to the park. Beth and Jim were sitting on the swings smoking a cigarette.

Jim looked up when he saw me and blew out a cloud of smoke, "Happy Birthday man!"

"Thanks, bro," I said, grabbing the chain on his swing and pulling him forward. "What's up?"

"Not much. Just got here." He brushed his long, stringy-blond hair from his eyes and took a drag on his cig. Jim and I had been friends since elementary school, growing up in the same neighborhood, and able to relate to all the shit that it entailed.

"It's your birthday?" Beth asked. She'd been staring at me since I arrived.

"Yep."

"Oh wow, Happy Birthday!" We'd met a few times before, but she didn't go to Jim and I's junior high. She was wearing tight blue jeans and checkered Vans. Her dirty-blonde fell just past her shoulders.

"Thanks," I said. "Have you guys seen any pigs tonight?"

"A car went by earlier that looked like a cop, but I'm not positive," Jim said.

Beth grabbed the cigarette from Jim's fingers and took a long drag, staring at me the entire time. She blew the smoke my way and asked, "So what do you want for your birthday?"

Just then, a cop car came rolling up the street. "COP!" I cried out and ran towards the library. Jim and Beth jumped off the swings and followed my path. We ducked under the benches lining the perimeter of the building. A searchlight lit up the park and moved back and forth along the grass and across the swings, as we crouched down and moved further under the bench.

Beth scooted closer to me and put her hand on my leg. My face got flush, and I got an instant erection. My heart was racing. I wasn't sure if I was more scared of the cops or Beth's hand on my thigh. The searchlight flashed across the library, coming within a few feet of us. We were silent, nobody moved, not even an inch. Waiting. We heard his engine rev up, and he sped away.

"Holy shit, that was close!" Jim said.

"Dude, let's get on the roof," I replied.

We climbed up a pine tree growing next to the library and crawled out on a thick branch that hung over the roof. We jumped on the roof and quickly ducked before any cars saw us, then walked, bent over, to the center of the building, sinking down behind an air-conditioning unit.

Jim pulled out his pipe and baggie and stuffed some pot into the bowl. Then he flicked his lighter and hit the pipe. A sweet, woodsy smell rose into the air. He took another hit and passed it to Beth. I stared at her boobs as she inhaled and quickly coughed. "Here," she said, giving me the pipe. I watched the fire being sucked into the bowl as I took a deep hit. The smoke burned my lungs, but I held it in. Beth put her hand back on my leg. I coughed loudly and blew out all the smoke.

"Shhh," said Jim, "You want to get us all thrown in juvie?"

I passed the pipe back to Jim as Beth slid her hand up my leg to my inner thigh. The night was dark, but I could see her smiling at me. I was hard as a rock. Jim was smoking away, oblivious to us. I put my hand on her leg and began inching my way towards her crotch. We were in our own secret world now. Jim passed the pipe around again, but I wasn't interested in smoking weed anymore. Beth was way more interesting than pot, heavy metal or anything else for that matter.

"Ok, let's go to Rocky Horror now," Jim said. As we headed back towards the tree, Beth grabbed my arm and held me back. I let Jim go ahead and watched as he climbed onto the branch and down the tree. Beth grabbed me by my shirt and pulled me close. I squeezed her tight against me and moved my hands down to her butt. She put her hand on my neck and pulled my head down slightly. "Let's go somewhere alone," she whispered in my ear.

"Ok," I said nervously. "What about Jim?"

"I'll tell him I have to go home."

"Alright," I said, helping her onto the branch. I couldn't take my eyes off her butt as she moved across the limb and down the tree. The pot was hitting me, making me feel both excited and horrified, like seeing a car crash.

"Hey Jim," Beth called, as we walked across the grass. He was just ahead of us. "I can't go to Rocky Horror tonight. I need to get home before my mom checks on me."

Jim swung around, "Since when does your mom check on you?"

"Since she caught me smoking pot last week. Kevin, can you walk me home?"

I tried to act surprised, "Uh... yeah, sure, ok... I guess." My acting skills sucked. I turned to Jim, who had a confused look on his face, "Sorry man, let's meet at the arcade tomorrow."

"Yeah, sure," he said. Jim and Beth were just friends, but I still felt bad about bailing on him and lying about it.

We gave each other a knuckle handshake and parted ways, Jim heading to Rocky Horror, and Beth and I pretending to walk to her house.

But, as soon as he disappeared into the Ken theater, we turned around and headed towards my garage, where I knew we could be alone.

You could only squeeze out the garage window, not in. So, we had to tiptoe ever so quietly across the patio. I turned to Beth and put my finger to my lip, then slowly turned the doorknob, my heart pounding, trying to not make a peep. The door opened, and we rushed inside. I'd just closed the door behind us when Beth grabbed my shirt and pulled me towards the bed. I fell on top of her, and we began kissing. She opened her mouth wide, and I pushed my tongue deep inside. She slid her hand over my jeans to my penis. I felt like I was going to explode as I pushed my hand up her shirt and under her bra. Beth tugged on the buttons of my Levi's, and with each button she snapped open, the blood coursed faster through my body. I yanked off her O.P. top and reached for her jeans.

That's when I received the second life-altering gift of my fourteenth birthday. I lost my virginity. Beth was caring and understanding as she guided me through, even helping me put on the rubber my mom had made me carry in my wallet. And, while it wasn't the grand, love-making experience I'd seen in the movies, I'd discovered a form of pleasure and closeness I never knew existed, and I wanted more. Much more!

* * *

Mom and I continued to battle. The wildness, once packed neatly away inside, began to emerge in full force. I grew my hair out and listened to heavy metal exclusively. Jim became my mentor, educating me on the finer aspects of the fast and loud music. Iron Maiden, Judas Priest, Motley Crüe, AC/DC: all subjects taught in Metal Guru Jim's advanced Metal Shop.

Smoking pot became a daily ritual. Junior High—hazy. A fog of smoke and metal, a constant search for weed, and places to smoke weed. Every morning I put on my 501 jeans and OP shirt and rolled down El Cajon Blvd. My tattered Vans pumping hard, pushing my Pine Design skateboard along cracked sidewalks and rutted asphalt, until I reached the racquetball courts of Wilson Jr. High. Here, a group of metal-heads and surfers, including yours truly, started each morning by getting nice and high before 1st period.

At lunch, we headed straight back to the racquetball courts for another round of smoking pot. In woodshop, we used scroll saws to make pipes from chunks of scrap wood, while our teacher read magazines in his office. We hid behind the drill press and tested our pipes, waving our hands in the air in a futile attempt to dissipate the sweet smoke. Amazingly, we never got caught. Perhaps because nobody really gave a shit about us inner-city juvenile delinquents.

Between periods, we huffed inhalants called Locker Room or Rush and nearly fell to the ground from the massive head rush it gave us. It reminded me of the time I had smelled the Candy Apple red paint from my model. After school, we'd go to a friend's apartment whose mom worked until 5 and smoked more. Then we'd roam the streets and see what we could get into, trying to stay off adults' radars. We were true latchkey kids.

Wilson was a tough school, surrounded by tough neighborhoods. At times, it felt more like a prison than a school. You had to choose a group or a "set." And the "sets" were broken up according to race. The whites were known as, "Stoners" or "Surfers." The blacks, "PBI" or "Playboys Incorporated." The Mexicans called themselves "Cholos" or "E.S.D." for East San Diego. And the Asians, many of whom had recently arrived from Vietnam, kept to themselves.

If you weren't in a "set," you became an outcast and had no protection from any of the groups. Being white and smoking pot all day, by default I was part of a "set."

Fights broke out every day, mainly at lunch, but it wasn't surprising to see a brawl break out in the hallways between periods. Just looking at somebody for too long, called "mad-dogging," was grounds for fighting, or "squabbing." "Yo bitch, why you mad-dogging me, you wanna squab motherfucker?"

And, if you backed away from the fight, or showed weakness, you were labeled as a "bitch" and became a target. At least once a week, a big fight would break out, involving twenty, thirty, forty people from different "sets," all brawling on the blacktop during lunch. I'd thought my fighting days were behind me, but I was wrong, they were just getting started. Forced from retirement, I began scrappin' with a fury. School officials chased after us, but we scattered into the crowds, making them powerless. They hired security guards and brought in the police, so the fights moved off campus. 3 o'clock behind the QuickMart became the new time and place to settle scores.

My grades dropped. I didn't give a shit about school. I had doubts about life in general. At night, I would lay in bed, high as a kite, thinking about how my life didn't seem real anymore, like I was living in a dream where nothing really mattered. I became worried, knowing I had to break free. But, it seemed almost impossible, I was addicted to pot and my whole world revolved around it. What would happen if I lost my friends, or worse, became an outcast? I doubted I could even summon enough power inside me to quit. I tried to stop several times and failed. I was weak and beaten down, foggy.

My buddies and I were riding our BMX bikes up to Devil's Peak to smoke pot. Devil's Peak was a chunk of dirt next to a canyon, scrubland really, with biking trails, but hidden away from people and houses. I was third in line behind Larry and John, jumping off curbs and riding down streets and alleyways. We entered an apartment complex and swerved left and right through a maze of narrow walkways.

We came to the end of a courtyard, where you could either go left or right. If you went right, you'd continue on to Devil's Peak. Larry went right and then John. But then, something inside me—deep in my core—screamed, "Go left, Go left! Go left!" For a fraction of a second, the fog lifted, and I felt awake for the first time in years. The strength I had once seeded and nurtured as a boy, to help me through those fucked-up days of being scared and alone, had grown and flourished and was now a part of me. I no longer wanted to live in a dream, I wanted to be present. I didn't say a word, I just veered left and never looked back.

I quit smoking pot that very day. In fact, I abandoned my old life altogether. I never hung around John, Larry, Jim or Beth again. I stopped going to the racquetball courts and Devil's Peak. It took the rest of the school year and the whole summer to clear my head. And when summer ended, I cut my hair.

CHAPTER SIXTEEN

CORN ISLAND

The Managua airport always surprised me by how clean and modern it appeared, while just outside men rolled down the Pan-American Highway in wooden carriages pulled by horses and oxen.

I jumped from my chair as Stevie, Kira, and Amy made their way through customs. After hugging each of them, I grabbed Kira by her hips and leaned in for a kiss. She seemed surprised, almost hesitant, but she kissed me back. Her letters had been a lifesaver; providing comfort when I was lonely, and a source of strength through the struggles of training. Seeing her now was intoxicating. It wiped away the pangs of rejection I'd been feeling after not hearing back from Stephanie.

We hailed a cab to Barrio Martha Quezada—the poor man's hotel row—and checked into the lovely Hospedaje Santos, where just two months earlier I'd nearly died.

"Nice digs," Stevie said, "Do they clean after every fourth or fifth guest?" We'd known each other since the seventh grade, although when we met, I could have never imagined that we'd one day be friends. I was stoned out of my mind, hair past my shoulders, wearing an Iron Maiden T-shirt. He was running around the gym putting up posters that read, "Stevie for Prez." He had short blonde hair, perfectly combed, and bright white teeth that glimmered inside his permanent smile.

"Slow down dude, you're making me dizzy," I said when he bumped into me.

"Hey," he replied, "Be sure to vote Stevie for 8th Grade President."

"Yeah, I'll be sure to do that," I said, but he was already running up to the stage and sitting down with the rest of the clones waiting to give their speeches.

He won the race that year, and our unlikely friendship spawned shortly after. Two polar opposites, each seeking something in the other, we found missing in ourselves.

At my going away party, he had vowed to come visit me in Nicaragua, but I never believed he would follow through. So, when Kira's letter arrived, saying that they were both coming, along with their cousin, I was ecstatic. And their visit couldn't have come at a better time. I needed a break from Ramón. Jonny had shone a light on the bank, and I still wasn't sure what to do with the information. I had told him I was traveling on "official" Peace Corps business and would be back in two weeks.

"So, what's first on the itinerary?" Stevie asked.

"I thought I'd show you guys…"

Kira came out of the room wearing denim shorts and a t-shirt, revealing her tight, compact body in a subtle, innocent way that drove me crazy!

"Show us what?" she asked with a grin, knowing I was staring at her like a cat eyeing a mouse.

"Uh… I was going to show you guys around Managua."

We spent the rest of the day looking at the different sites within Managua. An earthquake had destroyed much of the capital in 1972. Twenty plus years later, much of the city still lay in ruins with people living in the partially destroyed buildings. As we walked through the streets, an eerie feeling came over us. A six-story dilapidated building, with clothes hanging out to dry on the patio walls, was leaning so far to one side that we ran past it just in case it toppled over. The entire city had a feeling of what life would be like if a nuclear bomb were detonated over it.

Managua was sprawling, with no focal point. It seemed like one giant maze. We found our way to the Malecón, or walkway, on Lake Managua and were rewarded with spectacular views of the mountains and volcanoes surrounding the vast lake, forty miles long and 16 miles wide. I looked over at Kira staring out at the lake, she seemed so peaceful, "tranquilo" is how they described it here. That feeling you get when you're about to nod off while rocking in a hammock. I couldn't wait to tell her about all the crazy stories that had unfolded since my last letter to her.

The heat and humidity coming off the lake were so intense that not even the breeze coming off the lake and blowing the palm fronds straight back could alleviate our discomfort. "Let's get out of here," Stevie finally said.

Later that night we ate grilled chicken and steak at a popular "fritanga" or street vendor, and then sat around drinking beers and bullshitting on the Hospedaje's patio. "I still can't believe you guys are here," I said with a big grin on my face.

"I told you we were coming, man." Stevie wiped the rim of his beer with his hand, stuck his index finger in the bottle and pulled it out quickly—making a popping sound. All in perfect form, just as I'd taught him. The Peace Corp volunteer's preferred method of sterilizing bottles.

Kira jabbed me on my shoulder. "Yeah, have some faith in people." Amy was off chatting with a group of backpackers from the Netherlands.

"Ok, ok, my bad," I said, "I'm just glad you guys are here." After all the shit I'd been through since arriving in Nicaragua, it was just nice to have a moment where everything shitty in the world seemed to disappear, if for only just a while.

The conversation continued into the night until Kira finally stood up and said, "Well, I'm going to bed." I watched as she walked away, wanting desperately to chase after her. I tried waiting the obligatory five minutes, not wanting to be rude to Stevie or appear too desperate to Kira. When I couldn't take it any longer, I fake yawned and told Stevie, "Well, hey, I better get some sleep. We have a big day tomorrow."

"Ok, see you in the morning."

When he turned away, I ran to my room, dove into bed and latched onto Kira. As she turned towards me, an explosion of passion flooded my brain. I kissed her deeply and touched her body all over. The tension and stress living inside me, washing away. I was ravenous for her affection and wanted to be inside her. I pulled her close and began taking off her panties.

"No, Kevin."

"What's wrong?"

"Let's slow down."

"Slow down?" I tried to see her face in the dark.

"Yes. Let's not rush into anything."

"But we've already had sex," I said, thinking I was being rational.

"I know, but we rushed into it then."

I knew she was right, and this wasn't about me. We had rushed into it before, but I still felt rejection radiating through to my core. I tried suppressing it, but my body ached. My brief moment of happiness was gone. I was no longer, "tranquilo." We kissed a little more and fell asleep.

In the morning, we traveled to Masaya and walked through the sprawling market near the bus station where the local artisans sold their crafts. They bought colorful hammocks and pottery while I picked out a hand-carved wooden mask to send back to my mom.

We worked our way through the city towards Monimbo. As we approached my training home, Luis came running out and threw his arms around my neck as I kneeled in front of him. I introduced him to my friends, and then we went inside and met Yolanda. She sat us all down at the table and served up coffee and pastries in a matter of minutes. "Y Osmar?" I asked nervously. She smiled, "He is gone for the day." I think we were both relieved. She told us that Luis was doing well in school and that everything was going well at home. I hoped it was true.

From Masaya, we traveled to a small town called Catarina and marveled at the breathtaking view of Laguna Apoyo (lagoon), located at the bottom of a crater. Legend had it, a giant sea monster lived at the bottom of the deep murky water, surfacing only rarely to feed on children and adults who dared to swim within his home. We cinched the straps on our packs and began our hike to the bottom.

"Rumor has it," I said, looking from Kira to Amy, "that human-like monkeys live in the trees here and rape young women as they hike down the slopes."

"Bullshit!" Amy shouted, taking a step closer to the group.

"Hey, I'm just telling you what the locals say."

"That's just an old wives' tale," said Kira.

"Maybe," I said. "So why don't you and Amy go on up ahead, I'm sure you'll be fine."

Kira grinned at me, "You're a funny guy."

When we reached the edge of the lagoon, we stripped down to our bathing suits and waded into the cold water. I reached my hand out to Kira. "Don't be scared, I'll protect you." She batted it away and rolled her eyes. "Suit yourself," I said with a smirk, "just watch out for the sea monster."

Many people did actually die in the lagoon each year, but I attributed their deaths to the lagoon's conical shaped floor, which went from shallow to above-your-head deep, within just a few steps. Combine that with the fact that most Nicaraguans were poor swimmers, even before they got shitty drunk and waded into the lagoon. Not to mention the weird undertows and currents that existed. Add it all together, and you had a recipe for disaster. And, an evil, malevolent sea monster who swallowed up unsuspecting drunk, poor-swimming Nicaraguans, seemed much cooler than the obvious.

The bottom suddenly disappeared from underneath my toes, and I set off swimming. Small waves lapped against my face as I moved further into the lagoon. I goaded the others to follow, but they all stayed close to shore. I continued swimming, showing off my bravery with each kick and stroke. The water turned an inky black, and an incredibly foreboding sensation washed over me. I stopped swimming and looked back, realizing how far I was from the others.

For a split second, panic raced through my body. What if there really was something lurking in the water? And what about those strange undertows? I began swimming back to shore as fast as humanly possible, not daring to look behind me. As I got close, I saw Kira standing in water up to her waist. She had a gleam in her eye and an outstretched hand. "Don't be scared," she said. "I'll protect you."

Later that night, I handed Stevie a Perdomo cigar wrapped in dark brown tobacco leaves. "Best cigars in the world. And they make 'em a few blocks from my house."

"Nice!" said Stevie, passing it in front of his nose and taking a deep whiff of the earthy tobacco. "What's up with you and Kira?"

"I don't know man. I like her, but we just keep pushing each other's buttons."

"Oh great," he said, biting the end of the cigar. "Well, don't screw up our vacation."

"Anything for you, douchebag! By the way, you're supposed to use a poker, not bite the end of your cigar. Now you're gonna have little bits of tobacco floating around your mouth while you smoke."

He fired up the cigar, "Ok, Mr. cigar expert," and took a long draw, puffing several times. He exhaled and took a big gulp of Flor de Caña rum and coke. "Now this is the life."

"Nicaragua does have its perks."

Kira was asleep when I crawled into bed later that night. I didn't bother to wake her, curling into a ball and facing away, instead, where I suffered in silence for the rest of the night.

"Are you mad at me?" Kira asked, as we packed our clothes and prepared to leave the next morning.

I turned and looked into her eyes, wanting to explain how I had felt rejected that first night. How I wanted to be closer to her, mentally and physically. I wanted to tell her how much her letters had meant to me when I had felt so alone. But, "No," was all that came out.

"Well ok then," she said rolling her eyes and turning away.

We took a bus to Coyotepe, the old Samoza Prison. It was on top of a hill with a view of Masaya and the surrounding land. "Who was Samoza again?" asked Amy.

"He was President. He and his family ruled Nicaragua for almost fifty years until the Sandinistas overthrew them in 1979. This is where he kept his enemies."

"This place is creepy."

We made our way down into the dark, underground tunnels where the cells were located. You could barely see the cages where the prisoners once lived, sleeping for years and years on the cold rocky floors. The sun's position determined whether they received fifteen minutes of sunlight each day through narrow slits in the rock, or none at all. As we moved towards the center of the prison, an area where sunlight never penetrated, and the torture chambers were located, I put my arm around Kira. She quickly dipped her shoulder and moved away, walking even faster into Samoza's pitch-black torture chamber.

We arrived in Estelí later that day. I showed them the Parque Central and the market. Then we went to the restaurant Jonny had told me about that served exotic foods. It was located on a hill surrounded by trees and bushes on the edge of town. After ordering a round of beers, the waiter came over and I began talking to him about all the different animals we could order.

They all stared at me, waiting to hear the translation. "He said we could go around back and check out the animals," I finally said.

Stevie's eyes were wide in amazement. "Dude, just relax, we're just going to look at them."

"No, it's not that," he said, "I just can't get over how well you speak Spanish. It's like you're a native."

"Well shit, I spent enough time in class. But trust me, I still suck!"

We walked behind the restaurant and found rows upon rows of cages, some stacked two and three high, filled with every animal imaginable. Snakes, iguanas, monkeys, giant rats, beavers. It was like a mini zoo. Amy and Kira were grossed out by the whole thing and decided to stick with beer. It was hard to pick a monkey, iguana or any animal for that matter, having just seen them moving around in their cages. Stevie and I both ordered venison, the least exotic on the menu.

"Have fun eating Bambi," said a grinning Kira as I put a fork full of meat into my mouth.

We set out for the waterfall the next morning. The hike was long and hot. We kept our heads down and didn't talk much. Our only relief came from the intermittent shade from the Mango and Guanacaste trees cresting over the path. From the corner of my eye, I caught Kira taking off her shirt. She wore a white bikini top underneath. I looked around nervously, seeing if any houses were nearby, "Kira, what are you doing?"

"What?" She scrunched her eyes and nose and looked away.

"It's a bad idea to be walking around up here in a bikini top." I noticed a farmhouse up ahead in the distance.

"Nobody cares," she said, still looking away.

"Are you serious? This isn't California, it's Nicaragua."

"Oh really? Thanks for the update. What's the big deal anyway?"

"The big deal is that this is an extremely conservative country. Almost everybody that lives here is Catholic, and we're way up in the mountains, where there are basically no laws."

"Oh my god, I'm just wearing a bikini top, I'm not having sex in the woods."

"I know, but these men aren't used to seeing white women. Let alone white women in bikinis."

"Oh, give me a fucking break."

"Look, can you just put your shirt on until we get to the waterfall?" The mountains always spooked me. I'd heard of a man getting drunk and whacking his wife to death with a machete, and the police not finding her for weeks. The people all stuck together up here, meting out their own form of justice.

To my relief, Stevie finally jumped in. "Just wear it until we get there," he said.

Kira muttered a few more expletives, but put her shirt back on. Everybody was tired and cranky when we finally arrived at the blue house. I opened the barbed wire gate, and we walked past the house and down the narrow path. Poking our heads through the shrubs, the lagoon and waterfall came into view, looking even more amazing than the last time I'd seen it. Perhaps, sharing it with friends, added deeper and more complex layers of beauty to it.

"Wow," Amy said, as we stripped down to our bathing suits, "It's beautiful here."

"Dude," Stevie said. "Where's that ledge you jumped off?"

I pointed to the ledge as we waded into the icy water, refreshing after the long hike. Stevie and I swam towards the fall, while Kira and Amy swam the other way. Our relationship, or friendship, or whatever we had between us, was slowly ripping apart.

As we scaled the rocks and worked our way along the cliffs, I wondered why relationships had always been so difficult for me. We reached the ledge and looked out, taking in the beauty of the lagoon and the lush vegetation around it. Without a word, Stevie suddenly jumped, screaming, "Woooooo Hoooo!" all the way down.

I looked around one last time and spotted Kira sunbathing on a rock. She glanced up at me for a moment, then turned away. Was this chasm growing between us my fault? Was I pushing her away? I closed my eyes and jumped, weightless and free, wind rushing against my face, before splashing into the cold water.

From Estelí, we traveled East to the steep mountains of Matagalpa, and into a nearby cloud forest named Selva Negra, where coffee was king and grew like wild weeds throughout the region. Germans had settled here in the late 1800's on their way to California in search of gold. They planted the first coffee beans here and discovered the conditions to be perfect, in fact, golden! In the 1970's, a new group of Germans came to the area and built wooden chalets around a lake surrounded by a dense forest. It was so beautiful, Samoza ordered his bombers to spare the region from bombing runs during the Revolución.

The trails leading into the cloud forest beckoned us from the moment we arrived. Stevie and I woke at four thirty in the morning and hiked into the misty, dense underbrush. The plants and shrubs were all sopping wet from the low-hanging clouds, and we were quickly surrounded by massive trees in every direction. We leaped over a few small brooks, before coming to a stream, which required us to hop from boulder to boulder to cross. When we reached the other side, we pushed aside a clump of ferns eight feet high and stepped into an area filled with black and white butterflies circling blue orchids and red and purple bromeliads. I was pushing aside a group of giant plants when I heard a strange noise.

"Shhh," I said, stopping dead in my tracks, "Did you hear that?" We listened carefully and heard the grunts of monkeys in the distance.

We looked high above, into the canopy of fig trees, palms, and evergreens blocking out the sky. A family of howler monkeys was jumping up and down on a tree limb. I tapped Stevie on the shoulder and pointed, "Look!" The huffing and puffing became louder, and soon, hundreds of monkeys joined in the ruckus, grunting and screeching throughout the jungle. Birds began singing and whistling to each other, while insects clicked and buzzed. The forest was alive, and we had a front row seat!

After a few days exploring the area, Stevie, Kira and Amy headed off to the beach, while I returned to Estelí. Kira and I needed some time apart, and I wanted to check in on the businesses I'd been working with. I didn't bother telling Ramón I was back in town. I stayed close to home and finished setting up my house.

My zombie hand sprang to life while they were gone, the dead resurrected. With its rebirth, came a constant tingling sensation, a thousand needles and a thousand feathers, all working diligently to drive me mad, and even though the valium made me feel like a rock star—a drugged-out, slobbering rock star—I knew it was time to wean myself off the magic Diazepam pills. Adding another vice to my repertoire seemed self-defeating, even to me.

Stevie, Kira and Amy returned to Estelí a few days later. They only had one week left, and I was determined to give them a big send-off, one final grand adventure. We laid out a giant map of Nicaragua and studied it carefully, from one end to the other. Stevie pointed to a little speck of an island in the Caribbean. It looked perfect. We all smiled, even Kira, and raised our glasses of rum and mango juice into the air, "To Corn Island."

"Corn Island!" Clank, clank, clank.

* * *

Getting to Corn Island was going to be a significant undertaking. The first leg was a four-hour trip to Managua where we burned up most of the day hanging around the Peace Corps office, reading books and writing in journals, waiting for an 11 p.m. bus.

We arrived early at a small parking lot where several buses sat idle, gearing up for the overnight ride into the jungle.

I approached a man with a wad of cash in one hand and a ticket book in the other. "Cuatro boletos, por favor."

"Ya no," he said. "Estamos lleno."

"What did he say?" Stevie asked.

"Shit! He says they're sold out." Incredibly, after sitting around Managua for the entire day, we'd arrived late.

"Fuck!" Now what?" Stevie asked.

"I don't know, man. I guess we come back tomorrow."

The air went out of us all and we started to walk away, but then the ticket seller yelled out, "Todavía hay boletos por el pasillo."

"What'd he say?" Amy asked.

"I think he's saying he still has tickets for the passage or passageway."

"Passageway?" Kira asked. "What does that mean?"

"I'm not sure," I told them, "but it's either that or come back tomorrow. You guys decide."

They looked at each other and shrugged. "Let's just go. How bad can it be?" said Amy.

The ticket man hollered for everybody to board the bus, but as we walked up the stairs, he put his arm out and told us to wait with a small group of people off to the side. When the bus was full, he motioned that it was our turn. Our group climbed up the stairs and filed down the aisle. When we got to the back of the bus, everybody turned around, faced the front and sat down on our butts. Apparently, "pasillo" meant aisle, not passage. There were about twenty of us crammed down the center of the bus. We pulled our knees up to our chest, leaned back on the knees of the person behind us, and tried to get comfortable. It was going to be a long ride.

We bounced from side to side all night as we journeyed deep into the jungle, shifting our weight from one leg to the other, and attempting to stretch our cramped legs alongside the person in front of us. None of it worked, and we finally gave up and passed around a bottle of rum, swigging straight from the bottle, in hopes of forgetting our misery. It didn't work.

Twelve hours later we arrived in Rama, a small indigenous town carved into the jungle, and literally, at the end of the road. You couldn't get any closer to the Caribbean without a boat. After waiting several minutes for the blood to return to our legs, we hobbled off the bus. Kira gave me a little nudge on my arm, "Well, that was fun. What's next on the agenda?" Her sarcasm was actually a welcome relief from the silence she'd been giving me.

"A boat ride," I told her. "A loooong boat ride. You're gonna love it!"

Children tugged on our hands and tried pulling us down to the riverbank where panga boats, huddled side-by-side, bobbed up and down in the muddy water. The captains stood at the stern, one hand grasping the handle on the outboard, while the other waved frantically to the people from the bus, trying to lure them onboard for the ride to the Caribbean.

A shirtless boy with shaggy hair pleaded with us to take his father's boat. "Oy chele, vengan conmigo a mi lancha. Somos pobres. – Hey, whitey, come ride our boat. We're poor," he said.

"Oy moreñito, cuanto? Yo tambien soy pobre. Hey little brown boy, how much? I'm poor too."

Stevie looked on as I negotiated the price of the trip with the eight-year-old businessman, "Yo Kev, doesn't moreñito mean like little brownie or something like that?"

"Dude, I know, I tripped when I got here too. It's just how people refer to each other down here, by their characteristics, like shorty, fatty, or blondie. They call me gringo, whitey, skinny or cat man because of my blue eyes."

"Crazy," he said as we made our way to the river. We passed our backpacks to an old, skinny man with a cigarette hanging from his mouth. The boat only held two people, so we quickly negotiated for a second one and got Kira and Amy settled in. Stevie and I climbed back into the first boat and sat back, using our backpacks as cushions. The old man pulled the starter cord, and we took off on our jungle cruise down the Rio Escondido

(Hidden River). Destination: the city of Bluefields.

Our boats were fast, buzzing by each other, as we raced down the river. We reached out and tried to touch hands as the boats passed each other. Kira pulled her hand away at the last moment. The banks of the river were teeming with birds and animals. Raptors and vultures flew overhead, and while jaguars, cougars and pumas are rarely seen, they're known to prowl the dense brush and jungles here. Disneyland's jungle ride has nothing on Nicaragua.

"This is amazing," screamed Stevie over the roar of the engine. I pointed to a bird as big as a pterodactyl, imagining how Earth must have looked like 150 million years ago.

After four long hours, our boats raced out of the Rio Escondido—and Jurassic period—and into the mouth of the Caribbean, arriving in Bluefields, a bustling, sultry, port city on the edge of the blue waters. Boats were everywhere, along with pastel-colored houses on stilts and palm trees as far as the eye could see. The docks held a wide array of salty characters, all hustling and bustling and moving commerce. There were so many different ethnicities and languages being spoken within the market stalls, that it made my head spin.

Mesquite Indians sold monkeys, turtles and iguanas, while other dark-skinned indigenous men sold teak, mahogany and other hardwoods. Tall, black men blasted reggae from portable radios while whittling wood with machetes and small knives—selling their creations to the occasional backpackers. I felt like I'd walked into a Robert Louis Stevenson novel.

We dropped our backpacks in a nearby hospedaje—backpacker's motel—and set out to explore the fast-paced city of Bluefields named after the 17th-century Dutch pirate Henry Blufeldt who once called the area home. We ordered a round of beers in an outdoor cafe and listened to the people around us speaking Miskito, Creole, Spanish and other dialects and languages. It was a completely different world than what I'd experienced so far in Nicaragua.

We went to a reggae club later that evening. The music was loud and clanky. Tall, rough-looking Rastafari men kept asking the girls to dance. Most were polite when they declined, but one group became aggressive. "Oh my God, they won't take no for an answer," Kira said in my ear.

"Hey man," I said in my deepest voice, standing up and facing the men, "They don't want to dance, ok?" The men towered over me. I knew it could get ugly quick. Fortunately, they walked off laughing and joking in broken English. The whole scene was feeling sketchy, and I was relieved when Amy said. "I want to get out of here." As we jumped into a taxi and drove back to the hospedaje, Kira moved in closer to me and grabbed my hand.

After boarding a puddle jumper for the thirty-minute flight to Corn Island, I was surprised to see the pilot just a few rows ahead of us as we taxied down the gravel runway. The flight was turbulent, with only the slightest gust of wind pushing our plane around the sky. We all smiled and pointed when the island came into view. It was oval except for one small smidge of land sticking out.

"Dude, wouldn't that be crazy if we landed on that little patch of land?" Stevie said as he stared out the window.

"No way, there's not even a landing strip there, it's just dirt. We'll land in the center somewhere."

But the plane turned and flew straight towards the small patch of land, and we heard the landing gear being lowered.

"Oh shit, we're going to land on that strip of dirt," Kira yelled from across the aisle.

The pilot pointed the nose of the little plane downward and revved the engine. Through the windshield, I could see the dirt coming closer and closer, and just beyond, the Caribbean Sea. I didn't know how we could possibly stop in time.

We hit the dirt hard and bounced up. When we came down the second time, I heard the brakes squeal. Our heads were pushed back against our seats as the tires dug in. A cloud of dust kicked up as we raced down the strip, brakes grinding, turquoise sea getting closer and closer. The plane abruptly stopped, jerking us forward. A collective sigh rang out through the cabin, and several passengers made the sign of the cross. The plane sat twenty feet from the Caribbean in a plume of dirt. Welcome to Corn Island.

We found two cheap rooms on the water's edge for four dollars a night, and sprinted towards the blue waters, running past rows of palm trees and across sugar white sand, before finally diving into the sea. The sea I'd been dreaming about for so very long. Water so beautiful and colorful, it was as if God had melted down emeralds and sapphires to create it. The struggles I'd endured to get here had all been worth it—if for only this one brief moment in time.

We splashed water and twirled in circles. We were movie stars and millionaires. Kira, wearing a white bikini, cupped water in her hands and poured it over her head. It was as if she were a mirage, so beautiful and happy. We swam in the crystal-clear waters for hours, looking at the different fish and coral just feet from shore. Farther out, boats of all shapes and sizes floated lazily in the sea, a true tropical paradise.

When our arms grew weary from swimming, we ran up the beach and slid into the soft sand, squishing our fingers through the grains, as the sun beat down on our skin, rejuvenating our bodies and our souls. All life's bullshit faded away. Here was life… here was living.

We followed the trail of a boy as he ran up the beach, kicking up sand with his every step. He wrapped his arms around a palm tree—its trunk bending away from the sea from all the years of constant wind—and began to climb, pinching his little bare feet around the trunk and hopping higher and higher, until he had reached the crown. With his short brown arms, he shook the palm fronds with all his might, harder and harder, until coconuts began falling to the ground. Then he scurried down and wrapped as many as would fit in his shirt and ran off down the beach.

Kira and I laid down for a nap underneath a mosquito net, inside our room, still sandy from the beach and smelling like saltwater and rum. We had been distant for almost the entire trip, and now it all seemed so trivial as we lay there in paradise. I licked her salty neck and pushed inside her. We made love for the rest of the afternoon, as a fan blew cool air over our bodies and waves lapped just outside our room.

Later, the four of us set off to explore the island. After a couple hours, the sun and humidity became too much, and we turned back. We were on a deserted stretch of coast far from our hospedaje. Out of nowhere, the skies turned black, and the wind began whipping violently. A bright flash cut through the air and rain came pouring down. "Run!" I screamed, sprinting towards a row of palm trees blowing sideways by the strong winds.

We ran through a patch of trees, soaking wet and tripping over shrubbery as the rain beat down on our faces and thunder rumbled overhead. We stopped for a moment and tried to catch our breath, but lighting shot through the sky and exploded all around us. We took off running, faster this time, maneuvering through trees and breaking into a clearing.

A bamboo hut with a tin roof sat a hundred feet away, and we sprinted towards it, rain and wind now coming at us sideways, lashing at our faces. We flung open the door and raced inside, as a streak of lightning lit up the sky. A group of black men with long dreadlocks stood at a bar drinking rum and swaying their heads to bongos and steel drums. We'd entered a local Rastafarian bar. The melodic reggae music suddenly stopped, and all eyes were upon us, as we stood there like deer in a headlight, sopping wet and shaking. A tall man with a ring in his nose and dreadlocks down to his ass came over. "Wut dat' got u?"

We looked at each other, confused, ready to rush out.

"Hey mon, not dat u wirry."

"Sorry," Stevie finally blurted out, "We were just trying to get out of the storm." We took a step backward.

"No wirry, hit now, u get dat gud rum eh? Make dit good warm."

The bartender poured four shots of rum and slid them down the bar. "Up dat' now," said the man, motioning to the drinks. We grabbed the shot glasses, held them in the air, and poured them down our throats. The room exploded with clapping and yelling, and the reggae music sparked back to life, pulsating through the hut. We looked around at each other like we'd just discovered the New World, or sugar... or sex. Perhaps we had. We ordered another round for ourselves and our new host. Then we bunkered down and rode out the storm; dancing, drinking rum and talking Pidgin to Rasta dudes, in the reggae shack, in the middle of the fucking jungle. In the Caribbean!

* * *

We sat on a patio overlooking the water on our last night, eating lobster and fish and drinking cold beer. A small wall to the side had been built entirely from conch shells and reflected the purples and pinks coming off the Sea.

"Amazing trip," said Amy over the gentle crash of a wave.

Stevie held up his beer. "Best trip ever."

"I'd have to agree," said Kira, touching the side of my head with her palm.

I clicked my mouth, shished the waiter, and made a circular motion with my hand. The waiter rushed over with three fresh beers, as Stevie stared on in wonder.

"Dude," he said, "you've changed so much. You're like a local now."

We flew to Managua in the morning, their adventures in Nicaragua had come to an end, while mine were just beginning. I hugged Stevie and Amy and said goodbye, then pulled in Kira and squeezed her tight. We'd traveled a thousand miles together, both literally and physically. But we both knew it would never work between us—we were just different people. Stevie was right, I had changed. Whether I was a local or not, was beside the point, I now viewed life from a completely different angle. Regardless, it still hurt to say goodbye, and I was going to miss her. We gave each other a final kiss.

"You're a special person Kira. Whoever you choose will be a lucky guy."

"You're right," she said with a playful grin. Then she kissed my cheek and walked away. I watched as she passed through immigration, waiting for her to look back. She never did.

CHAPTER SEVENTEEN

THE FLOOD

Life mellowed considerably after my return to Estelí—a stark contrast from my manic days of training, and although I was sad that my friends had left, I was excited about where life would take me next.

Ramón appeared to have enjoyed my two weeks away as much as I did. He stopped fussing about me working with the socios, so I split my time between the bank and three businesses. I finished setting up my house, making it as comfortable as possible, even buying a fridge on my limited stipend.

I still had the dull, tingling sensation in my hand, but I was now able to move all my fingers, removing the fear I'd be called Captain Hook for the rest of my life. I'd managed to wean myself off valium, and I was picking up the language. I guess you could say I was hitting my stride.

One warm evening, as I sat in my living room listening to the croons of Frank Sinatra, a steady rain began to fall. I watched the water pool on the other side of my iron bars as I took sips from my Victoria beer.

I never thought about rain much before coming to Nicaragua. San Diego averages a paltry ten inches a year, and when it does come—which is rare—it walks in quietly, does its business and moves on, a polite guest on its best behavior. Nicaragua's rain, in contrast, enters like a pack of wild boars, fighting for scraps of food. Or rather, a litter of unruly children, running about and screaming just feet above their grandmother's head.

The storm picked up, banging and clattering atop my tin roof, drowning out *The Lady is a Tramp*. I took a long, pensive sip from my beer, as thunder rumbled overhead like an angry bear. The wind began whistling and howling, mutating into screams of a demon. I clenched the rails of my chair, digging my fingernails into the wood, as the rain grew stronger and louder—a monster at birth.

I thought Estelí might blow away at any moment. It sounded like a freight train was barreling towards my house. A bullwhip snapped the top of my roof, followed by a flash of lighting. I stood up and screamed, but the wind screamed back, louder, mocking me. Ha, ha, ha!

Relax, I told myself. You arrived during the dry season, and you're getting your first taste of the wet season. This is all normal, just ride it out.

Thousands of moths and creepy bugs flew inside, seeking shelter around the light bulb in my living room. That's normal, right? A trickle of water rolled across my bare foot. I looked towards the door and saw a stream of water moving through the bars. This can't be fucking normal!

I froze, paralyzed by the sight of water creeping to every corner of my house. But, as the cold water rose above my calf, it pried me loose from my statuesque pose. It was time to act. I splashed through the water to the fridge, pulled the handle and reached for my last four beers. Water rushed inside, and the light began to blink. I peeked behind the fridge and became alarmed at the sight of water inching towards the outlet. I rubbed my fingers on my shirt to dry them, and then yanked the cord from the wall. Wading back to my chair, I felt content. I was safe from electrocution and of being beerless. Mission accomplished!

As I opened a fresh beer, indifferent to the water nipping at my knees, I was startled by a loud banging. A man in a neon-yellow vest was rapping on the bars of my door with a metal flashlight. "Salga su casa! Leave your house, it's flooding!" he screamed, as rain splashed off his helmet. The panic in his voice shook me from my apathy. Definitely not normal!

I stood and began searching for the keys to the padlock on the gate. The water was now up to my thighs. As I splashed around, I was pissed I still felt the need to lock myself in every night. My once safe, cement house now felt more like a Samoza prison cell—or worse, my watery grave.

"Hurry!" the man shouted, as I frantically patted tabletops and reached inside drawers. "Hurry!"

I stopped and gathered myself, attempting to find order within the chaos. Breathe. I scanned the room. A sparkle on top of the fridge caught my eye, the keyring shimmering in the moonlight. Thank god! I pushed through the water—now above my waist—grabbed the keys and worked my way back to the gate. The man's headlamp beamed into my eyes as I fumbled with the keys. He wrapped a rope around his waist and tugged on the bars. "Vamanos, Vamanos!" he yelled, making me even more nervous than I already was. I jabbed the key into the lock, but it slipped and splashed into the water. FUCK! The rescue worker stared in disbelief at his horrible victim.

I dropped to my knees and stuck my face in the muddy water, feeling all around, but unable to find the key. I came up for air and caught a glimpse of the river now flowing through my house. This was real—I was in a life or death situation! I plunged my face back into the frigid water and submerged my body, swimming in different directions while feeling all around for the keys. Nothing! I came up for another breath of air and heard the rescue worker screaming and banging on the door. I sunk back into the water, desperate now, and moved my hands with a fury back and forth. I felt something jagged and clutched onto it like a pair of vice grips. Bursting from the water, as if I was a breaching whale, I held the key in my hand and cautiously stuck it in the hole and opened the lock.

The rescue worker tied a rope around my chest and another to the bars on my gate. He guided me outside and along a cable attached to a Red Cross jeep parked up the hill. The river was halfway up its doors. If the vehicle washed away, it would drag me down the river behind it. Rain beat down on our heads as we worked our way, hand over hand, in front of my house. The tortilla lady's hut had disappeared, along with the vegetable stand. I was now standing in the middle of the River of Blood.

I clutched the rope tightly as I neared the edge of my house. Two Red Cross workers were waiting to guide me to higher ground. I made it out of the river and sat in the middle of the street, exhausted and emotionally drained—a front row seat to the raging river now tearing through my neighborhood. I began to laugh as the rain dumped all around me, but it came down harder, drowning out my voice. I looked to the sky and screamed, "Touché!" Life is a funny thing.

Forty minutes later, the rain finally stopped, she could laugh no more. Before I knew it, the river had receded, and I was staggering back to my house. Six inches of mud was caked to the tile floors, along with tables and chairs toppled over and strewn about. My lumpy mattress was now a giant river sponge. For once, it actually paid not having any worldly possessions. My neighbor came over and helped me sweep out all the mud. When she left, I lay on the cold tile floor and closed my eyes.

Stephanie's blue eyes peered down at me. She was in a raft, floating down the river. I reached for her, but she drifted away. I swam after her, but the current pushed her downstream. She stretched her hand back towards me, but I was too far. A wave splashed over my head, and I woke up breathless.

In the morning, I rode my bike to the telephone office and sent her a telegram: *Coming today—Kevin—Full stop.* I took the dream as a forewarning, to take control of my life. I'd let it slip through my hands once before.

I put on a clean t-shirt and pair of shorts, stuffed an extra set of clothes in my backpack, and climbed aboard the Express Bus heading south. The regular buses would stop for anybody, anywhere, anytime, making for long trips. The Express Bus was direct and would shave an hour off the three-hour trip. It cost a few extra córdobas, but it was well worth it.

The lady in the seat next to me held two live chickens upside down by their skinny legs. I stared into their eyes and wondered why Stephanie had never responded to my letter. Did she not have feelings for me? The chickens seemed cagey, reluctant to give me the answers, so I devised a new strategy. I'd determine whether she liked me or not, by how she reacted to my arrival. Content with my ingenious plan, I closed my eyes and dreamed of Kentucky Fried Chicken.

Ciudad Darío was a sleepy, cowboy town, named after the famous Nicaraguan poet, Rubén Darío. "Donde vive la gringa?" I asked two boys kicking a soccer ball in the dirt. Their eyes lit up, and they motioned for me to follow, kicking their ball down the dusty road with me hot on their trail. After several blocks, the boys came to a stop and pointed to a brick house, "La gringa!" A man on a black and gray horse trotted past as I searched my pockets for a córdoba to thank the boys. I pulled out some coins, but they were already halfway down the block, passing the ball back and forth.

I rubbed my clammy hands on my shirt and walked to the door. It was easily fifteen degrees hotter here than Estelí. I wiped my brow with the side of my forearm and knocked. Nobody answered, so I knocked again, wondering if she was even in town. But then, the door opened, and an older Nicaraguan woman with long, gray hair stared out at me. "Esta Stephanie?" I asked. She squinted and began talking rapidly. I couldn't follow her, so I blurted out, "La gringa?"

"Oh, sí, sí, sí, la gringa!" She grabbed my hand and led me inside. We went through the living room and down a hallway to a partially opened door. The room was dark inside, but I could make out a person lying in bed. The woman motioned for me to go in and walked away.

"Steph?" I called out, entering the room slowly. She was lying on her side facing the wall.

"Stephanie?" I repeated, moving closer to the bed. She turned over, and I realized it wasn't her.

"No, I'm Beth."

"Oh, I'm sorry, I…" I stopped moving forward, confused.

"It's ok, she just lives a couple blocks away."

"Oh, ok. I'm Kevin by the way."

"Hi, I'd walk you over there, but I'm sick." She was curled up in a ball, her long, blond hair matted to her forehead.

"It's alright. Are you a volunteer?"

"Yes," she said, sitting up on her pillow.

I moved closer, noticing her pretty eyes, "What's wrong with you?"

"I'm not sure, my stomach is messed up, and I'm running a fever. I hope it's just the flu. I was working in a town last week that had an outbreak of cholera."

"Oh shit!" I took a step backward when she looked away. "I take it you're a health volunteer?"

She reached for a glass of water. "Yes."

"How long have you been in Nicaragua?"

"About seven months," she said, taking a sip of water. "You?"

"Four."

I was surprised more than one volunteer lived in the same town. There were only about fifty volunteers total in the country, but new groups were arriving every three or four months. I suppose they had to go somewhere. The Peace Corps pulled out of Nicaragua in the 1970's due to the Sandinista uprising and had only recently returned in 1990, after the country's first democratic election in decades. Peace Corps Nicaragua was still in its infancy, attempting to gain a foothold.

"Well, get better!" I told Beth, and then followed the directions she gave me to Steph's house.

And this time, when I knocked, I was greeted by Stephanie's giant smile. "Welcome to Ciudad Dario!"

"Thanks, cool town."

"You think?"

"Why yes ma'am," I said, fake tipping my ten-gallon hat, "I reckon so."

"Come inside, you goofball." She was renting a large room inside a house. "Here's the grand tour," she said waving her hands around at a bed, a few chairs, and a table used to store her food and dishes. "You like?"

"Impressive. Hey, I met your neighbor."

"What neighbor?"

"Beth."

"Beth, really?"

I told her about our brief meeting as we sat down.

"What do you think about her?"

"She seems nice."

"All the guys love her. If you want, we can visit her later." Wait, now she wants to set me up with Beth? Had she even read my stupid letter?

"That's ok," I said, leaning back in my chair and taking a deep breath. My super-smart, ingenious plan wasn't going as planned. I still had no clue where we stood.

"Well hey, I have to go back to work for a couple hours, but I'll be back tonight, and we can go out for dinner."

"Ok cool. Yeah, sorry, I know this was kind of last minute."

"It's ok, I just can't bail on work, since I just started. But you can hang out here until I get back."

"Is there a bar around?"

She pointed me to the local bar, and returned to work, at yet another Savings and Loan. I grabbed my journal and spent the rest of the day drinking Nica Libres and writing gibberish in my journal, the spirit and words of Rubén Darío resonating within, "I seek a form that my style cannot discover; A bud of thought that wants to be a rose."

"You're still here?" Stephanie asked, appearing out of thin air. "I was waiting for you at home. Did you still want to go out for dinner?"

"Woah! Where'd you come from? You're a fucking magician!" I peered at her through bloodshot eyes. I was nice and lubed by then, having long since concluded she wasn't into me.

"Come on dork, let's get some food in you."

I gulped down the last half of my rum and coke and followed her out the bar, swaying as I hit the streets.

"Why'd you stay there all day?"

"I don't know, just thinking I guess." I looked down at my feet, making sure I wasn't staggering too much.

"About what?" Steph slowed down and looked at me seriously for a moment. Her eyes were so pretty. I wanted to tell her everything, share my entire, twisted tale. My knee buckled, but I caught myself.

"Ah, just stupid shit."

Steph looked at me funny that evening as I piled blankets on the floor next to her bed. "You're going to sleep down there? On the cement?"

"Yes."

"Oh, that should be good for your arm."

"I'll be fine."

"You can sleep up here," she said, tossing aside the sheet and scooting back on the bed.

My brain began to swirl, battling itself. A ping-pong match of yes, no, yes, no playing out in my head. "It's better if I just sleep down here," I finally said.

"Are you sure?"

"Yes," I said, lying down on the cold slab. It reminded me of being on a gurney in the Hospital Bautista.

"Well if you change your mind, you know where to find me."

I squirmed around on the floor, fighting off every urge in my body to crawl into bed and wrap my arms around her. Thankfully, mercifully, I passed out.

When I woke, just before dawn, my body ached from head to toe. I was dehydrated, hung over, and sad. Stephanie was sound asleep. An internal battle raged inside me: Show my emotions and risk being rejected or play it cool and continue to feel empty inside. I chose the path of least resistance—also known as the coward's approach—kissing her lightly on her forehead and setting off to find a bus back to Estelí.

CHAPTER EIGHTEEN

MARI

For many locals, I was the first white person they'd ever seen in real life. I tried breaking down the invisible barrier by bullshitting with the neighborhood kids as they shot marbles, like sharpshooters, in the dirt around my porch. I hooted when they made good shots, and they would laugh and shout back, "Oy chele, regalame un peso - Hey whitey, give me a dollar."

"Oy chavalo, regalame sus orejas - Hey kid, give me your ears," I'd joke back.

The children called me "gato" or cat, for my blue eyes. "Oy gato... va pues!" they'd yell out as they jogged past my house spinning bicycle tires with a stick. Sometimes I felt like a sideshow, but mostly I enjoyed the attention and wanted to become part of the community.

I would say "Adiós" to people as they walked by. The word was used interchangeably to mean hello or goodbye, much like "aloha" is used in Hawaii. And, if you said it in a singsong way, placing a heavier accent on the last syllable, it meant you were flirting.

One unusually mild day, as I sat on my porch reading Michener's *Mexico,* daydreaming about flapping a red cape and yelling, "Olé!" a mosquito buzzed by my ear and pulled me out of the bullring. I looked up, trying to spot my prey, and noticed a pretty girl with dark curly hair walking by.

"Adioooooos," I said, but she didn't reply—didn't even look up— just continued moving quickly on down the road, towards the river. The bullfight beckoned, so I put my nose back in my book and returned to old Mexico.

A week later, I noticed the same girl coming down the hill. I moved my chair at an angle which would face her and puffed out my chest.

"Adiooos," I said as she neared, putting less stress on the flirty "o." But, she kept her head down and motored past as if I was invisible. This cat-and-mouse routine kept up for the next couple of weeks. My flirty "Adióses" being rebuffed each and every time, until I finally gave up.

Ramón and I resumed butting heads. It irked him that I wasn't in the office from 8 to 5 every day, even though he'd never given me any specific jobs or tasks to do, which is why I had looked outside of the bank for ways to make myself useful.

Through other business volunteers, I learned about a program—funded by the U.S.—that provided computerized accounting training to banks in developing countries. Upon completion of the program, the bank would be eligible for free computers, equipment, ongoing training and possibly even a new building. The perfect solution!

I got to work filling out the thick packet, back in my element again. Jonny helped in his free time, and after a few days, I was down to the final form. With the papers spread out over my desk, and me busily scribbling away, Ramón strolled by and picked up a couple of pages, pretending he could read English.

"What's all this?" he grunted.

I'd only planned on telling him about it if the application was accepted, but now that he had it in his scrawny little hand, I figured what the hell.

"It's computer training for the Cooperative," I said, reaching for the papers.

I could see the disdain creeping over his face as I tried explaining the program to him. He tossed the papers on my desk and shouted, "You have to get my permission before you do something like that. It's a waste of time!"

Strangely, my anger didn't bubble up. I leaned back in my chair and looked Ramón directly in his eyes. "What exactly is your problem with me?"

"I'm the boss here!" he screamed, then stormed back to his office and slammed the door.

I shook my head and chuckled inwardly, calling him every swear word I could think of under my breath. I grabbed the papers and straightened them into a neat pile. Then, I turned them sideways, and was about to tear them in half, when I caught Jonny eyeing me from his desk, and shaking his head, "no." I scowled, but he continued shaking his head, his eyes wide with empathy. I gave a Ramón-like grunt and shoved the papers in my backpack. Jonny smiled, and gave an approving nod, as I raced out of the building and jumped on my bike.

I rode towards the waterfall, cranking hard on the pedals and snaking my way up the mountain. The air rushed against my face, soothing me. I followed my usual route, no longer needing to stop for directions. I moved through the barbed wire gate and past the blue house. When the trail narrowed and began its descent, a pig—covered in mud—cut across my path, squeezing his head, and eventually his butt, through a thicket of shrubs.

I pulled aside the branches and discovered a pig trail hidden within the vines and plants. I stashed my bike in a bush and squeezed through, following the overgrown path a short distance to a row of Yucca bushes. I scraped my arms and legs pushing through, but was rewarded on the other side; greeted by pools of crystal-clear water carved into slabs of granite, and waterfalls flowing off boulders. It was a hidden oasis.

I stripped down and waded in, the water acting as an amnesiac to my frustrations and anger. I climbed up boulders and jumped into the chilly water. When I grew tired, I laid on the warm slabs of rock, feeling the energy spread across my back, and the sun's rays beating down on my chest. This area was much sunnier than the main waterfall, where the high cliffs blocked out the sun. I closed my eyes and continued working on my poem in my head…

Lost, confused, yet gentle the hand,
cast all aside, like a statue I stand.
Pure of mind and fresh of soul,
baptized in the mar of old

The heat became too much, so I dove into the water and splashed around like a kid, happy with my new discovery. I climbed back up, and followed the flow of the water downstream, jumping from boulder to boulder, until I heard water exploding and thundering like a locomotive. I stopped, as a cloud of mist kicked up and surrounded the area. I was on the precipice, the ledge of the main waterfall, which had once pounded my head like a thousand wooden spoons.

My heart raced as I took a step closer and peeked over the ledge. Water was crashing into the lagoon far below. My stomach quivered, and I had to crouch down and collect myself. After a minute, I stood back up, took a deep breath and held it in, and looked back over the cliff. The water was unrelenting, gushing with all its might—frightening. I walked to the side and sat on a rock. *Don't do it Kev!*

The lagoon must be deep, I reasoned. The waterfall had been carving a hole down there for thousands and thousands of years. *Don't do it!* The jump would be insane. Imagine the thrill. *Don't do it!* I stood and peeked back over the ledge. *Too risky!* My brain screamed at me to back up and walk away. *Don't fucking do it!* But, I was tired of being logical, tired of trying to stack the world into neat little boxes. Fuck all that! I looked over the cliff one last time and jumped!

I kicked and screamed the whole way down, finally splashing into the lagoon and plunging into the dark depths of the water. When my body finally stopped sinking, I kicked and swam as hard as I could to the light above me. As my head popped through the water, I gasped for air, and screamed out at the top of my lungs. A sense of euphoria and freedom spread over me unlike anything I had ever experienced before. I looked back up, to the ledge high above, watching as the water rushed over it. Happy to be alive.

*　＊　＊　＊*

I pedaled hard back to the bank, jumped off my bike and marched into Ramón's smoke-filled office. He looked up with surprise.

"Ramón, walk with me!"

He followed me around the corner to the side of the warehouse. I turned and backed him against the cement wall. "Listen, I'm a volunteer here, I am NOT your employee." I raised my finger and pointed it at his chest, "You're my counterpart, not my boss!"

His face turned beet red, but before he could say anything, I continued. "I've already spoken to Mike, and he is more than willing to drive up and talk to you directly if you like. Perhaps we could all figure out why the default rate is so fucking high."

Fear flashed through Ramón's eyes, the lines on his face grew deeper, forming dark caverns. I could almost see his mind spinning, trying to decide which way to go—fight or flight?

"Ok, ok, ésta bien," he finally said.

"Bueno, pasa buen día," I said with a smile. As I grabbed my bike, I saw Jonny smiling at me through a louvered window. I gave him a quick nod and grin and then headed off to work with the Nintendo owner, stopping for a beer along the way.

At my final physical therapy session, my therapist told me I no longer needed to wear my brace. It was so dirty and stinky by then, it posed a health risk. She smiled when I thanked her for bringing my Frankenstein hand back to life. "Continue the massages and exercises on your own," she said. "And no mas Diazepam!" I gave her a big hug and thanked the entire staff. They had all been amazing.

When I got home, I took off the brace and was attempting to clean my arm while listening to reggae, when I spotted the pretty girl with curly hair coming down my road. I decided to give it one final shot and hastily maneuvered my chair into position. When she reached the corner, I called out, "Adiós" in my best Spanish, removing all traces of the flirty "o."

As she passed by me, she lifted her head, revealing large almond eyes, and said, "Adiós," then disappeared down the block. I ran inside and cranked up Peter Tosh as loud as it would go, dancing through the living room and back onto my porch. The neighborhood kids laughed and shouted, "Gato loco. Chele loco!" as I kicked up my legs and moved my arms.

Weekends were spent hiking into the surrounding mountains, always careful to stay on trails and avoid the landmines. I found hidden spots, between the trees, where I could look out on the city far below. I'd be sure to be home by dusk, so I could sit on my porch and watch the neighborhood end its day.

Money was always tight. Fortunately, my local pulpería allowed me to purchase items on credit. And every month, when my stipend came in, I'd grab a wad of cash and head up the block to pay my tab. The elderly woman would pull out the spiral ring notebook and flip through the pages until she found the one titled, "Kebin," spelled phonetically. Under my name, was a list of all the items I'd purchased, with chicken scratches next to them representing the quantity purchased. She would read off the items line by line: "one toothpaste, one package of mortadella, two pounds of cheese, one bottle of oil, three pounds of beans, two pounds of rice, eight bags of chips, and…"

There would be a long pause as she counted, "ten, eleven, twelve…" she would look up occasionally, with questioning eyes, then back down, "twenty-one, twenty-two…" Eventually, after hitting the forties, she reached for a calculator and proceeded to punch in so many numbers, I thought she was adding up the GDP for Nicaragua. Finally, she set the calculator down, and with a tone of confidence, said, "and eighty-seven cervezas."

"Qué!" I exclaimed, "That can't be right." I grabbed the notebook and began adding up all the dashes next to the word, *Victoria*. After the fiftieth dash, I realized she was correct. Wow, how had that happened?

I paid the bill and headed for the door, a mild sense of shame trailing me. But then I stopped, and turned back, "Oh, I almost forgot, I'll take six beers."

I eventually convinced the Victoria beer truck to add an additional stop to his route—my house. Thus, preventing any further shame. And, as an added bonus, cutting out the middleman would now allow me to get my beer wholesale, as opposed to retail. Hey, I am a business guy after all!

I hadn't seen the girl with the almond eyes in weeks, and I'd almost given up hope entirely. But then, I saw her approaching one evening and knew I had to make a move. "Adiós," I said jumping to my feet and walking alongside her. She sped up, practically jogging, but I kept up.

"What's your name?" I asked. She ignored me, so I asked again and again.

"Why do you want to know my name?"

"So I can say more than Adiós to you." I was breathing hard and struggling to keep up as we continued motoring down the street.

Finally, she slowed and said, "Maribell," and then sped up even more. I stopped to catch my breath, watching as she disappeared over the river.

Over the next couple of weeks, our conversations grew from quick hello's to five-minute chats as she sat out on my porch and drank Coca-Cola with me. She was patient with my Spanish and helped me with the words I didn't understand. She taught second grade at the local elementary school across the river.

She was curious about the United States and my job. I tried telling her what I did, and why I was in Nicaragua, but I could barely explain it in English, let alone Spanish. But then I got an idea.

"Hey, what if I come to your class and put on a presentation about the Peace Corps?"

Her eyes lit up. "Que bueno!" she said.

We set a date for the following week. I was excited, but as the day neared, I became nervous. My Spanish still sucked, and I hated speaking in public—even if it was to a class of second graders. I walked to the Telcor Office and called Craig at his bank.

"Oy, Gregorio, it's Kevin."

"Hola, Kebin... como estás?"

"Good, how's life in Condega?"

"As boring as a blind man watching a silent movie."

"Ha, Ha! Hey, how'd you like to help me put on a presentation to a bunch of second graders?"

"Wait, you're giving a presentation? Is it in remedial Spanish?"

"Wow, you're on fire today. That's why I need you, for your amazing Spanish abilities."

"That makes sense. Sure, when is it?"

Craig showed up the night before the presentation. We worked up a little speech about the Peace Corps and found some pictures that reflected American culture; baseball, fast food, movies, different cultures. Craig came up with the idea of buying a few big bags of candy to pass out to the kids.

In the morning, I put on my best clothes, a pair of beige Dockers and a white collared shirt, then we headed out the door for the short walk to the school. The sun was blazing, and within minutes, I had sweat stains under my armpits and running down my back. We entered the school and found Maribell's class. My pulse quickened when I saw her writing spelling words on the chalkboard. She looked so beautiful and professional. The students stared at us through the windows and began to murmur. Maribell motioned us inside.

The students fell silent as we entered. Maribell introduced us, and we walked to the front of the class. A sea of brown faces was now fixed on us, their eyes burning into us like lasers. My temple twitched as I began talking about the Peace Corps and its mission throughout the world.

Craig sensed my nervousness and jumped in, "Why should your teacher always wear sunglasses in the classroom?"

The kids looked at each other, puzzled. One little boy giggled, and asked, "Why?"

Craig replied in a flat, emotionless voice, "Because her students are so bright."

The boy looked at Craig curiously for a second and then chuckled. Moments later, another student laughed, and then another. Soon, the entire class erupted in laughter.

We spent the next twenty minutes discussing the Peace Corps and life in the United States while the students roared with laughter. They thought the two sweaty, white guys—one babbling incoherently in Spanish, and one telling dry, silly jokes—were hysterical.

Teachers from other classes came by to see what all the commotion was about. Maribell tried to hush the students, but it was no use, they were too wound up. She decided to take them out on the playground so they could calm down. Once outside, Craig and I opened the bags of candy and began passing them out. The children converged on us, pushing and shoving to get a piece of candy. The force of all their little bodies swayed us from side to side. They moved in even closer, squeezing us, a million hands thrust in our face. My body was being crushed, and I was in fear of falling and being trampled by eighty little, brown legs.

Maribell pulled a fistful of candy from one of the bags and threw it over the children's heads. They turned and sprinted after it, giving us space to breathe. Craig and I looked at each other as if we'd just escaped a gruesome death. We reached into the bags and chucked the candy as far as we could. As the kids scattered, Maribell grabbed our shirts and pulled us from the mayhem before our candy ran out. We raced into her classroom and locked the door behind us. Craig and I fell to the ground, laughing hysterically. Maribell and I started dating shortly after.

CHAPTER NINETEEN

LIFE & DEATH

One rainy night, during my freshman year of high school, Mom came into my room and shook my shoulder as I slept, "Come in the house." My three sisters were all sitting around the dining room table, eyes wide with worry. Shit was going down, and guaran-fuckin-teed, it wasn't gonna be good!

I sat next to Mom and gazed at her profile. Lines in the corner of her eye spread like wildfire as she looked from one of my sisters to the next. Time came to a crawl as I watched the words form on her lips, "Your father died tonight."

The words hung in the air, like a wisp of smoke in an airless room. You couldn't blow it away. Death had made his appearance. He pulled up a chair and leaned back, plopped his feet on the table and clasped his hands behind his head. Cocky motherfucker!

I looked from sister to sister, staring into their eyes, into their souls. They didn't move. A moment frozen in time.

"Don't be afraid to cry," I heard Mom say through the ice and fog. "He was your father."

Kerry let out a sob, shattering the silence, and soon all three of my sisters were crying. Clocks began to spin once again, and a fire now burned inside my nostrils. Mom looked my way, waiting for my reaction, but I stared straight ahead, avoiding her eyes, fearing they might unleash a flood of pain and heartache stowed deep inside my heart. A hurt that only a boy whose father doesn't care enough to be in his life can know. A hurt that grows like weeds inside a person.

Later that night, as I counted pleats in my parachute ceiling, desperate to find order in the world, I tried to make myself cry. I tried recreating the same pain that had burned inside my nose earlier, but the tears wouldn't come. My emotions had all been neatly packed away by then. Hidden so well, that even I could no longer find them. Still, something had been triggered inside me. I'd always envisioned my dad and me walking hand in hand down a beach one day, laughing and discussing life.

How could my dad have left me? Over the years, in some absent-dad twisted way, I'd turned him into a fictional character in my head; Brave, daring and strong as an ox. Nobody fucked with my dad. I learned how real men acted by watching TV: how to shoot guns from Little Joe on *Bonanza,* how to make blow darts from Charles Bronson, and how to kick ass from Clint Eastwood.

I learned how loving dads acted from *Eight is Enough, Brady Bunch* and *Leave It to Beaver.* My favorite show was *Courtship of Eddie's Father.* In the opening, the father holds Eddie's hand as they walk along the beach, smiling and having deep talks. My fictional dad took on all these traits, he was calm, cool and loving. Unfortunately, my reality was nowhere even close.

My parents had split when I was in diapers. I don't even recall seeing my dad until I was five or six years old. Even then, all I had was fuzzy memories of him taking my sisters and me to an arcade or bowling alley for an hour or so. We'd hug his giant thigh and big neck, smelling of Old Spice, and he'd reach into his big pockets and pull out mounds of change, which we'd use to play Space Invaders and pinball. After, he'd drop us back off with our mom, and then disappear for another six months or a year. Whenever Mom and I fought, I'd lash out about how great my dad was. One fight, in particular, pushed her over the edge.

"I hate you, I want to live with my dad!" I screamed.

"Your dad doesn't want you. He's a piece of shit. When's the last time he sent me child support?"

"He's better than you are!"

"Fine, you want to go live with your dad so bad? Pack your bags!"

That wasn't a threat to me. I ran into my room, shoved some clothes into my backpack, and slid my favorite baseball card, Pete Rose, in the side pocket.

"You're sure you want to do this?"

"Yes!" I shouted.

We got into Mom's green Lincoln Continental and drove to Santee.

"You're really want to do this?"

"Yes!" I repeated. She thought I was bluffing, but I wasn't.

Mom slowed and came to a stop in front of my dad's condo.

I reached over and opened the door, but before I could step out, she began driving off.

"What are you doing!" I shouted.

"We're going home."

"NO!" I screamed, "I want to live with my dad!" I mean, come on, who wouldn't? My dad was a combination of the Incredible Hulk, Clint Eastwood and Eddie's fucking Father!

Mom stopped the car, "Fine, I'll go to the door with you." As we walked up the stairs, I could tell she was nervous. She lit a cigarette, and then knocked on the door. We waited a minute, but there was no answer. She knocked again, but nobody came.

"Nobody's home. Get in the car, we're going home."

"No, I'm staying. I'll wait outside."

"Get in the damn car!"

"No!"

"Ok, fine, stay!" she said, walking down the stairs. "I'm going now."

"Ok, bye."

"I'm really going," she repeated.

"Bye!"

She got into the car and slammed the door. A moment later, she lowered the window on the passenger side and hollered out, "I'm leaving now, Kevin. Have a good life!"

"You too," I called back.

Then she started the engine and drove out of sight. I leaned back against the door and slid down, planting my butt on the floor. Five minutes later, the green Continental reappeared and stopped at the curb. "Get in the goddamn car," she yelled through the window, "we're going home!"

"I am home!"

Even from the porch, I could see her eyes wince in pain. I felt terrible, but I wanted to be with my dad. "Fine," she said, "stay there with that son of a bitch." Then she drove away, this time for good.

I sat on the porch for several hours. When the sun dipped, and the air turned chilly, I became scared and sad. Nobody wanted me.

"What are you doing here?" I woke to my dad staring down at me, his eyes wide with shock. My arms were wrapped around my body, and I was shivering.

"I'm..." I stood and grabbed my backpack. "I'm moving in!"

He brought me in and asked me what happened. As I warmed up, he made me a sandwich, and then we went outside and played catch football in the dark. Later that night, we went out to dinner and talked about school and girls, and all the important things in a boy's life. I knew it was meant to be when he told me that he and Susan were separated. It was how I'd always imagined it—my dad and me.

The next day we went to a florist and bought a bouquet of flowers. He had me write "I'm sorry" on the card and drove me back home. Back to Mom. I felt as though I was suffocating the entire ride, as though I'd been punched in the gut and was gasping for that first breath—struggling to survive.

My dad wasn't a fictional dad, he wasn't Mike Brady or Eddie's father. No, he was just a regular guy who didn't want me. And now he was dead. We'd never walk hand in hand on a beach. He'd never give me fatherly advice or hug me or tell me how much he loved me.

I reached under my bed for my pipe and baggie of pot, but they were gone, only the lighter remained. Oh right, I quit. Well, fuck me! I grabbed the lighter and threw it against the wall as hard as I could. It smashed, splintering into a thousand shards of cheap, red Bic plastic. A splotch of lighter fluid smeared the wall, as a bolt of pain shot through my arm from the force of the throw. The stain grew darker, as did my anger. I liked the feeling; It gave me comfort.

I made an important decision that night: I'd only allow myself to feel anger from that point forward, stay far away from pain. Why should I run from my anger anyway? Isn't it a manly feeling? Only pussies feel pain. I would soon learn to love my rage, embrace it, and feed it. As a result, it grew deeper and darker.

They say that when life throws you a curveball, lean in. I started listening to Punk and breaking shit, instead. And fighting—lots of fighting. I had a short fuse and would never back down from a fight. But over time, punching people became boring, so I began to take risks, instead; climbing up the sides of buildings, walking on ledges—drinking booze until I passed out in canyons and parks.

When shit grew dicey, I welcomed my old buddy Death back into my life. He didn't scare me. We hung, we were boys. One drunken night, on a bridge overlooking the 805 freeway, he walked me to the edge of a concrete pillar and made me stare down into the abyss. I didn't turn away, I looked closer. The end of my life was floating down there like a turd in a toilet. I could've jumped—could've said, "fuck all this shit!" But I wasn't no fucking pussy. Just ask Chip! No, I wanted to see this through, and, besides, I still had shit to prove.

Hoover High made a change that year which would affect my life forever. They switched from 10th-12th grade to 9th-12th grade, and I would be in their first 9th-grade class, providing the opportunity for a fresh start at a new school. Perhaps—just this one time—I could use "change and chaos" (which seemed to follow me everywhere) to catapult me forward, instead of allowing it to continually drag me down.

The arrival of winter in San Diego was usually only a blip on the radar—a passing of a date, followed by a drop in the temperature from the mid 80's to the mid 70's. This year, however, it meant wrestling season would soon begin at Hoover High. I hadn't wrestled in five years, but I was eager to get back on the mats and throw people around.

The first day of practice was a thrill. The smell of the gym and the sound of bodies being slammed to the ground brought me back to my youth. Here, instead of letting my anger run wild and unchecked—where it would become destructive and risk my life or my freedom—I could channel that anger, using my muscles and wits to overpower my opponent. I was a good wrestler, and the sport suited me. It had nothing to do with personality or seniority, or your lot in life. It was about two men facing off and using their strength, speed, agility, and smarts to overpower the other guy. On the mat, I alone decided my fate. I was in charge. But first I needed to make the team, and only the best wrestler made Varsity. Regardless if you were rich or poor, a senior, or a former pothead.

Each wrestler's name was written on a round tag and hung on metal hooks attached to a wooden board under thirteen different weight classes. Coach Stone wrote "Cromley" in blue ink and placed my tag on the very bottom hook under the 112-pound class. Seven people were above me, and I'd have to beat all of them to get to the top.

We had wrestle-offs at the end of practice every day, where I'd wrestle the person directly above my tag. I beat the first guy and Coach moved my tag up one hook. Six hooks above me—five now—was "Jones." I'd heard other guys on the team whispering about Brandon Jones. He was the top wrestler in my weight class, and also one of best wrestlers on the squad. He was a senior and had been varsity for the last two years. But I really didn't give a fuck.

I kept winning and working my way up the hooks until the day came when Coach Stone placed my tag just below Jones and yelled, "Kevin and Brandon, wrestle-off!"

The other wrestlers formed a circle around us, as Brandon and I crouched into our stance and waited. Coach blew the whistle and I quickly tied up, working my arm under his in an "underhook." Then I waited, letting him get comfortable. I pushed on him a few times and felt him push back. Finally, I pushed harder, and when he stepped into me, I dipped my hips and flung him over my back. He flew in the air and landed on his back with a loud boom. The entire gym vibrated. I could hear the other wrestlers screaming and shouting as I squeezed Brandon's head.

Coach Stone dropped to his big belly and watched Brandon's back getting closer and closer to the mat as I ratcheted down on his head. He was pinned, but Coach was reluctant to call it, so I squeezed harder, with all my strength, laying him out as flat as a pancake. Finally, Coach blew his whistle. I had just stuck Brandon Jones! A freshman nobody pinned the stud senior in front of the whole team. Brandon jumped to his feet and barged out of the gym, slamming the door against the wall.

But the next day, towards the end of practice, Coach pulled me to the side, "You're going to have another wrestle-off with Jones."

It didn't seem fair, none of the other wrestlers had to have more than one wrestle-off with the same opponent. My face became red hot, as if somebody had doused it in gasoline and lit a match. All the old rage and pain came flooding through me. I wanted to fight, wanted to break something.

The wrestlers formed a circle around us for the second time, and Coach blew the whistle. My anger was on the surface, ready to explode. My mom, my dad, all the shit I'd gone through, was all percolating, a volcano ready to erupt. But then I remembered my moves, my speed, my wits, and a sense of calm came over me. I was in my element here.

But I didn't want any uncertainty this time, so I toyed with him, drawing out the match, harnessing my anger and using it to my advantage for once. I threw him from one side of the mat to the other, letting him up and taking him down at will. Eventually, he got so pissed off he didn't even finish the match, just ran out of the gym. I puffed out my chest as Coach placed my name tag on the top hook. Brandon never returned to wrestling.

I figured it was about time to find some peace in my life, to cut me some slack and learn to live a little. So, I had a little chat with Death, and told him to go fuck off for a while.

CHAPTER TWENTY

CHASING BULLS

I put up fliers around my neighborhood offering free English classes, and the first night I had eight students come through my door. I think most came just to get a better look at the crazy gringo living in the neighborhood. I taught conversational English with a dose of American culture mixed in. I tried using the same teaching techniques I'd observed in my Spanish classes, but I pretty much just made it up on the fly.

We met every Tuesday and Thursday in my living room. I tried making the classes fun, by listening to American music and discussing the words or walking through the neighborhood and calling out the things we saw in English. During one class, I taught the students how to play hacky sack while shouting out adjectives with each kick.

I became friends with two polite and eager students, Fabrício and Ervin, who worked in a leather shop where I was also working with the owner on exporting beautiful leather, snake and iguana boots. I'd visit their shop and watch them make wallets, boots, and saddles while giving an impromptu lesson on the art of cursing and slang. Although, I probably learned more Spanish cuss words and slang from them, than they learned English cuss words from me.

I was still going into the bank, and even finished the application for computer accounting. When I gave it to Ramón, I figured he'd probably just throw it in the trash, but when I mentioned the free computers and possible new building, his eyes lit up like a kid at Disneyland for the first time. I'd had enough of Ramón and the bank. I'd given them about as much as I could under the circumstances, and the completed application, for all intents and purposes, was my letter of resignation.

The Peace Corps has three goals. The first, to provide technical assistance to countries in need. Second, to promote a better understanding of America while in those countries: The Peace Corps wasn't a Monday through Friday job, we represented the United States at all times and in all places. In fact, we would be volunteers the rest of our lives, as the third goal of the Peace Corps was to share our experiences about the countries we served in upon our return to the U.S.

Ultimately, each volunteer makes his or her mark in their own unique way, often in manners far different than originally intended. Counterparts fall through, work situations change, real life emerges. It's up to the volunteer to adapt and find a way to make a difference. Teaching English, working with small businesses, being a part of my community: all gave me the sense of purpose I needed.

I came to love living in my newly adopted Estelí; going to the restaurants and markets, the different stores and discos. But every so often, the draw of adventure would tug at me, like an itch that had to be scratched. And when the travel bug bit, the only cure was to shove a change of underwear in my backpack and get moving.

When I mentioned my hikes into the mountains to Fabrício and Ervin, they told me about an annual pilgrimage people made from Estelí to El Sauce each Christmas. I'd always thought El Sauce was hundreds of miles away since it took over four hours to get there by bus. They pointed out that the buses had to make a giant loop around the mountain range, and El Sauce, was basically, on the other side of the mountain. A twenty-seven-mile hike. Well that certainly fell under the adventure category, and, as further incentive, Susan (a volunteer in my group) lived there. Itch scratched.

I woke just before dawn, stuffed my backpack with water, tomatoes, avocado, a couple of tortillas, and a pair of boxers; tightened my pack around my midsection, and headed off at first light. As I crossed the bridge, I took a moment to look out at the River of Blood. She seemed so peaceful now; calm. No sign of the thundering monster who had crashed through my house and neighborhood.

The morning was sunny and peaceful as I began my ascent, sticking close to the trails to avoid land mines. The front side proved a much tougher climb than I'd anticipated, steeper, forcing me to stop several times. But after two hours, I approached the summit, my shirt soaked with sweat. Waves of dark, ominous clouds rolled over the peaks, turning the sky a dark, foreboding gray. And just as I reached the crest, it began to rain. The back side of the mountain leveled off. I found a road and followed it through the hills. Farm trucks and tractors were parked alongside it. The rain continued to come down.

Two men ran past me, their boots kicking up water as they stomped through puddles. I looked back to see if someone was chasing them, but there was nobody there. The skies turned from gray to black as I continued down the road. Then, another man sprinted by. When he was ten feet ahead, he turned back and gave me a worried looked, then sprinted away.

I picked up my pace, scanning the road from side to side like a soldier in battle. The wind picked up, whistling and lashing at my face. A man and woman ran by, motioning for me to run and pointing up towards the rain. I didn't understand their alarm, it was just rain after all.

In the distance, I saw a large truck parked on the side of the road, and huddled underneath, were all the people who had sprinted past me; All motioning for me to get under the truck. My brain was trying to process the scene when an explosion rang out overhead. It sounded like a bomb had gone off. The ground trembled under my feet. Lighting suddenly shot from the sky and hit the ground fifty feet away. I froze, wondering what to do, rain flooding down. Thunder cracked overhead as if God himself was screaming. I was in the middle of a lightning storm.

I heard the screams from the people and ran for my life. But the truck was over a hundred yards away, and an electrical plant was raging overhead, churning up power and spitting it out. Lightning bolts struck on either side of me as I ran the gauntlet. Sheer terror! Nearing the truck, I jumped in the air and slid head first in the mud, like Pete Rose, coming to a stop in a puddle of muck underneath the chassis.

I spat out a mouthful of muddy water, and peered out along with the others, watching as God unfurled his power. The show lasted another thirty minutes, while the people around me said Hail Mary's and waited for the truck to get blasted. When the storm finally passed, we crawled out from underneath the truck, muddy, wet and trembling, and gave each other hugs. I continued on with my journey, while they set off in different directions, some still making the sign of the cross on their chests.

I hiked for the next ten hours over rugged terrain, as the sun returned and beat down on my face. Arriving in El Sauce, I made my way down the main road, as children ran out of their houses and trailed behind me like I was Jesus of Nazareth arriving in Jerusalem.

"Donde vive la gringa?" I asked my flock. They grabbed my hand and dragged me to Susan's house. She was on her porch laughing hysterically.

"What's so fucking funny?" I asked, dropping my backpack to the floor.

"The town already has a nickname for you," she said while lighting a cigarette.

"Oh great! What?"

"La Langosta Sucio. Have you looked in a mirror lately?"

"Uh, no, I've been a little busy hiking for the last twelve fucking hours through a freaking electrical storm!"

"Ahhh, poor baby." She took my pack inside and came back with a hand mirror. "Take a look, Guapo."

I put the mirror to my face. My skin was bright red, fried from the sun and splotched with mud. I almost didn't recognize the skinny kid looking back at me. I began to crack up. They were right, I did look like a "dirty lobster."

Susan smacked me on my shoulder, "Come on lobster boy, it looks like you could use a drink."

She showed me around town, pointing out the church and park. People shouted "Susana" and waved frantically wherever we went. El Sauce was a small, but lively community and Susan had made her mark. The vibe was much different than in big, metropolitan Estelí, where I could blend in and remain anonymous.

She led me to a little bar, where I proceeded to drink beers at a brisk pace, content in the knowledge that God had spared me that day. Susan was from Pennsylvania, and like Craig and Stephanie, was fresh out of college. She was tall and skinny, with short black hair and a quick wit. She was like your tomboyish little sister that might kick your ass if you're not careful.

"So, you really hiked here from Estelí? Did that Dengue Fever fry your brain or something?"

"I think so," I said, signaling to the bartender for a new beer while giving a play-by-play of my near-death experience.

"Oh my god, you're crazy!"

"I think you're right." I held my fresh beer in the air, "Here's to The Sauce!"

Susan clanked my beer, and then grinned, "So, what's up with you and Stephanie?"

"Nothing," I said, squirming in my chair. I'd been trying to get Stephanie off my mind, telling myself that she was young, and we were different people. "I met a local girl."

"Uh oh!"

"What? She's nice." I told her all about Craig and I's presentation, and about how we almost got crushed to death by the children.

Susan smacked at a mosquito on her ankle. Little red welts covered her legs. She saw me looking with concern. "Don't be alarmed, the mosquitos fucking love me and my pale, white skin."

"Must be all that sarcasm dripping from your pores like honey."

"Yeah, must be that lobster boy, now back to the girl. Are you guys dating now or what?"

"Dating? Hmmm…"

A few days after the presentation, I snuck back into Maribell's classroom while she was busy scrawling fractions on the chalkboard. Her eyes lit up when she turned around and saw the bouquet of flowers in my hand. I asked her to dinner right there in front of all the children. They squealed and shouted, "Sí, Sí, Sí, Sí!" as we all waited anxiously for her answer. Maribell blushed and said, "Sí." I was in a daze the entire walk home.

When I arrived for our date, I was greeted by her twelve-year-old niece, Johana, who was to be our personal chaperone for the night. The three of us walked to a restaurant a few blocks away. Once inside, Maribell hid behind the menu, barely looking at me for the first ten minutes while I chatted with Johana about jump rope and her friends.

"Order anything you want on the menu," I said, raising my head and trying to peek over her menu. When the waiter came over, she ordered an appetizer and water. "You don't have to get the cheapest thing on the menu, you know."

"Sí señor."

"And stop calling me señor," I said. "It makes me sound like an old man. I'm only 26."

"Ok," she said, "but only if you stop calling me Maribell, everybody calls me Mari."

A few days after our date, Mari stopped by my house, and after a short conversation began cleaning. "Oh hey, you don't need to do that, I have a lady that cleans." She ignored me and started mopping the floors. And, once they were clean, she washed my clothes and made some rice. I tried explaining how I'd grown up with three sisters and a mother who had taught me how to cook and clean for myself. And, how they'd keel over and die before waiting on a man. But, nothing I said would stop her. In the end, Mari did what she wanted. Curiously, my cleaning lady stopped coming.

Susan burst out laughing, beer spewing from her mouth, "Well don't expect me to cook you any fucking dinner tonight."

"Ok Betty Crocker," I chuckled. "I'm on a liquid diet anyway."

The next morning, after breakfast, I boarded a bus to Estelí. The "langosta sucio" wasn't walking back!

* * *

I got a wire from Jason. His town was gearing up for their annual Fiestas Patronales festival. He was giddy at the prospect of booze, women and bulls. And, since I always try to support my friends, I hopped on a bus and journeyed to Chontales, a dusty ranching town in the middle of nowhere.

The bus zigzagged our way south through muddy detours and potholes until we were just outside Managua. Then we headed east, for another bumpy ride, through fields and dusty towns. When the paved road turned to dirt, we just kept right on going—barreling along past horses and cows—bouncing from side to side as I held on tight to the metal rack above my head. I gazed out the back window, it was as if we were driving through the Dustbowl.

The bus rattled to a stop in a small speck of a town called Santa Teresa. And when the dust finally settled, there stood Mitch, smoking a cigarette and looking my way, while Jason was busy hopping on one leg and slapping at mosquitoes on his ankles. I slung my backpack over my shoulders and headed off the bus.

"What's up?" I shouted, slapping high fives.

We strolled down the dirt road to a pulpería for a round of beers. I held my bottle up towards Jason, "Dude, you live in the middle of fucking nowhere, literally."

Jason gave my bottle a loud clank, "Yeah, I like it that way, the girls have nowhere to run."

"Cheers to that!" Mitch said, cracking both our bottles.

"Susan and Stephanie should be here soon," Jason said.

I coughed, and spit out a mouthful of beer, I hadn't realized Stephanie was coming.

"Dude!" Jason said while pushing my chest, "Drink much?"

"Sorry," I said, "I guess I'm just so happy to be in Chontales; Dirt capital of the world."

"Wait till you see all the cows," Mitch said.

"Hey, stop bagging on my lovely town, I think you're both just jealous."

"Yeah, that's it," I said. "Hey, you guys interested in taking a real trip, like around Central America?

"Hell yeah, I'm in," Mitch said.

"Me too," Jason chimed in. "Somebody's gotta babysit you clowns." I pulled out my Lonely Planet guidebook, and we sketched out a trip through Honduras, El Salvador and Guatemala. Then we all clanked beers to confirm it.

We bought some fresh tortillas and quesillo (a stringy white cheese) and walked back to the dirt lot. We grabbed some shade under a palm-thatched roof and waited for their bus, taking bites of fresh tortillas and warm melted cheese. We didn't have to wait long before we heard the roar of a diesel engine, and sputtering of gears, as a bright purple bus rolled up. Stephanie and Susan were smiling and waving from the side window. My eyes locked on Stephanie as she exited the bus, wearing wrinkled jeans and a big goofy grin. She shot me a smile as I reached for her backpack.

"Hey," I said.

"Hey back," she said with a laugh.

We took turns hugging, then skipped down the road, arm and arm, like actors in a musical. After a round of beers, and an intense argument over which was the best beer in Nicaragua, Victoria or Toña—I made a strong case for the former—we made our way to the bullring. A big hodgepodge of scrap wood and tree branches that had been recently, and by all accounts—hastily—nailed together. Stephanie was huddled close to Susan, no doubt conspiring to pull some practical joke on Jason. Whether I liked it or not, I still carried a torch for her.

The Fiesta Patronal of Santo Tomás was legendary, attracting revelers from around the country, and they were all pouring into the arena. The walkway encircling the bullring was sketchy at best, but a wild and frantic energy rose from the crowd as we moved up the rickety stands. I got an uneasy feeling, envisioning the entire structure toppling over. We found seats near the top and looked around.

"What'd they let the third graders build this monstrosity?" I asked.

"Osha certified, I'm sure," said Susan.

"As long as Jason doesn't shift his weight too much," Stephanie added, "we should be ok."

Jason stood up, and started jumping up and down, as we all screamed, "Stop, Stop, Stop!"

"You guys want more?" he asked.

"No!" we all screamed at once.

Mitch took a swig of rum from his flask and passed it around. "Look over there," he said, pointing down.

Three bulls were running wild, chasing drunk men from one side of the ring to the other. With their horns in striking distance, the men jumped in the air and clung to the flimsy wood fence, as the massive animals rammed their heads into planks just below their feet. When the bulls got bored and turned away, the men jumped back in the ring and sprinted off, bulls in hot pursuit.

Some men—by virtue of being braver, or perhaps just drunker—stood in the middle of the fray, scooting out of the bull's path at the last second, and slapping them on their haunches as the crowd roared with delight. The energy was electric. I'd never seen a rodeo like this!

"I've got to take a leak," I said to nobody in particular.

"Thanks for the update," said Susan, as I stood to leave.

"Hold on," Mitch said, "I'll go with you."

After making our way down and around the creaking wooden platform, I asked a guy where the bathroom was. He pointed to a row of plywood, lined up together vertically. We walked behind, expecting to find a restroom, but saw a line of guys pissing on the other side of the wood.

"Oh nasty!" Mitch said as we looked for spots along the plywood toilet. The stench of urine blasted my nostrils, conjuring up images of my pretty nurse and my bucket of piss during my stay at Managua's Juan Bautista Hospital. I deleted the images from my head and unbuttoned my jeans. But, as I began to piss, nearly every fly in the world arrived to greet me. I shook my head in disgust, and said to Mitch, "Dude, I'm the Lord of the Flies."

After leaving the open-air, communal urinal, we purchased a round of beers for the four of us and made our way back to the stands.

"Beer?" I said, holding out a bottle for Stephanie.

"Thanks."

I sat down next to her. "So, how's Ciudad Darío?"

"Good, what happened to you the other day? You just disappeared."

"Yeah," I took a long swig of my beer, "I just had to get back."

"Well, thanks for saying goodbye, dork."

"I always aim to please ma'am," I said, fake tipping my imaginary hat. She rolled her eyes and shook her head.

I knew deep down she wasn't that into me, and keeping up my illusive pretense, was just a slick way to avoid outright rejection. But, for now, I was content living in my little fantasy world, where anything was possible. I looked at the mad spectacle unfolding below and suddenly wanted to be down in the scrum, mixing it up with the bulls.

"I'm going in!" I said, jumping to my feet.

"No, you're going to be killed!"

"Well, at least I'll die in Chontales."

"Yo, where are you going?" Mitch said.

"Dude, I'm going in!"

He handed me his flask. "Here, take another swig before you die."

I climbed up and straddled the fence, scanning the ring for an opening. A big muscular bull, black as velvet, came near as I flipped my leg over and held on for dear life. He stepped closer, and I could see the sweat beading on his snout, as he huffed and grunted and dug his hoof in the dirt. A man wearing a straw hat came over and smacked him on his rump. The bull turned and gave chase, charging hard. The man's sombrero flew off as he zigzagged across the dirt. The beast caught him before he could reach the fence and flipped him in the air with his horns. He flew like a rag doll and crashed to the ground. The bull skidded in the dirt, spun around, and rushed back after him.

People waved their shirts in the bull's face, trying to distract him, as the man struggled to stand. But he kept moving forward, muscles bulging, and right as the man stood, he launched him into the air for a second time. He landed with a thud and rolled through the dirt, his shirt torn and streaked with blood. A group of men dragged his limp body away as the bull chased another man.

I stared out into the madness, heart pounding, trying to force myself to jump. The crowd screamed with delight as four more bulls entered the ring. It was a free for all now: Men waving red bandanas, bulls galloping every which way, and the stands trembling every time their muscular shoulders crashed into the walls.

I looked at my friends; Stephanie seemed concerned, Susan indifferent, and Mitch and Jason were egging me on. I let go of my grip and landed in the dirt, then ran as fast as my legs would carry me. I heard a bull charging and looked back. The velvet beast was hot on my trail, the ground vibrating from his massive body as he galloped behind. I could almost feel his horns piercing my ass. I leaped as high as I could, and grabbed onto the fence with a death grip, pulling up my legs as the bull plowed into the wall.

I scrambled higher and tried to catch my breath. I looked across the arena and saw my friends cheering me on. I raised my arm in triumph. Moments later, Mitch and Jason climbed over the fence and raced across the dirt, bulls giving chase. They climbed up the wall and stood next to me, screaming and slapping high fives, as we waited for our next opening.

The girls watched from the stands, laughing and drinking beers, as we ran like drunken fools around the ring. We moved toward the center, and waited for the bulls to get close, then smacked them on their rumps and ran, just like all the other idiots.

I looked up and saw Stephanie talking with Susan. She was so natural, so friendly... so beautiful. She looked down and caught me staring. I pretended to be a matador, waving a cape from one side of my body to the other, daring her to run through it. She gave me one of her big beautiful smiles, but I knew it was time for me to move on.

CHAPTER TWENTY-ONE

FINDING HIGHER GROUND

I was listening to Bob Dylan and fooling around with a harmonica when Mari knocked on the door. We went into my backyard and sat in the shade.

"How was class today?"

"Good, the children miss you and Craig. They want him to come back and tell more jokes."

"Oh, I'm sure he'd love that!"

A leaf fluttered down and landed on her head. "Oh, look at that," I said, "it means good luck is coming your way."

She grabbed the leaf, and held it up, "Really?"

"Sure, why not," I said, leaning back in my chair and smiling.

She flipped the leaf over, "Do you know what kind of leaf this is?"

"A tree leaf?"

She smiled and shook her head, "No, this is Sapote, see the fruit growing?" She pointed to dark oval-shaped pods growing on the branches."

"Oh yeah, I never noticed those before."

"Inside is a sugary, orange and red pulp." She twirled the leaf in her fingers, "My family and I ate the fruit every single day for a month. And when the fruit was all gone, we ate the leaves."

"Why?"

"We had nothing else to eat. After we'd eaten all the fruit and leaves from the Sapote tree, we moved onto the Guayaba, and ate all the fruit and leaves on that tree. Then we ate Mostaza leaves."

"But the land here is so fertile, and I see farms growing food everywhere."

"Yes, but this was during the war, after the soldiers came to our house."

I sat up, "Oh really, what happened?"

Mari's face grew serious, and she looked around, just as Yolanda had the day she told me about Samoza's troops invading Monimbo. Even the sky sensed trouble, as gray clouds rolled in and covered the sun, as she leaned in and told me about the day the Sandinistas came to her farm in Las Sabanas, one of the highest and coldest mountains in Nicaragua.

Her family was gathered inside, listening to a radio station from neighboring Honduras—desperate for news on the recent war. Nicaragua had been thrown into chaos, but due to their remote location, they could only receive the one radio signal. The Sandinistas, however, had forbidden Nicaraguans from listening to any Honduran stations. They didn't want them getting outside, biased news. Further, the Contras—the militant group they were fighting against—trained there.

Soldiers, patrolling the area, overheard the radio and kicked in their door. They rushed in with rifles drawn, shouting profanities and accusing them of supporting the Contras. Mari's father, Don Gabino, stepped in front of the family and was butted in his face with the end of an AK47. Blood spurted from his nose as he fell to the ground. A soldier pointed his rifle at Gabino's head. Mari, only eight-years-old at the time, raced over, screaming and crying, and latched onto his bloody head.

"Don't shoot him inside," the leader of the squadron said, "take him outside and do it away from the family."

The soldier kicked Mari away and dragged Gabino across the floor by his collar. She ran back and wrapped her arms and legs around her father's leg. The soldier kicked at her, but she wouldn't let go. Growing frustrated, he let go of Gabino's collar and forced the family to sit against the wall, while he and the other soldiers ransacked the house.

They stole all the food and valuables from inside the house, then went outside and took their chickens and pigs and uprooted all the vegetables. After the soldiers had taken nearly everything the family owned, they told Maribell's brother, Miguel, to: "Get up! You're fighting against the Contras now." They forced him out the door, and then they all left.

I could see the pain in Mari's eyes. The gray clouds were turning black, and a breeze was picking up. I reached out and squeezed her hand as she continued her story.

Mari's family had nothing left, and over the next few weeks, they grew hungry and pulled the few remaining vegetables left in the ground. When the greens were gone, they scavenged the land, eating fruit and leaves from the surrounding trees to survive. Nicaragua fell into a desperate state, with much of the country's food going to support the war.

The Sandinistas began handing out food vouchers to each family.

They'd wait in long lines, for several hours, to receive basic staples, such as beans, rice and soap. The monthly rations weren't enough to feed Mari's family, and they continued to scavenge.

Before the war, her family always had plenty of food stored in the home and planted in the ground. They ran a pulpería, and her mom sold tortillas to the neighbors for extra money. Now, with battles raging in the mountains surrounding their home, and the war growing, life was hard for the proud family.

It got even harder when news arrived that Miguel had been shot and killed in the mountains near Honduras, where the CIA was running secret bases training and arming the Contras. The U.S. had determined—in its infinite wisdom—that by fighting Sandinistas in Nicaragua, they were preventing the spread of communism, and stopping the Russians from getting a toehold in the Americas.

The thing is: most Nicaraguans just wanted to farm their land and live their lives. They didn't understand what was happening around them. The CIA recruited young, poor men from small towns, enticing them with money or a new pair of boots. They gave them rifles and pitted them against their "new" mortal enemy, who also happened to be from Nicaragua.

So Nicaraguans fought Nicaraguans. For reasons neither of them understood. And, brothers, often found themselves on opposite sides of the battlefield, shooting and killing each other at will, oblivious to the actual proxy war being waged: a battle of two Super Powers and their ideologies, with neither side spilling a drop of their own blood.

It began to sprinkle and we moved under the patio awning. It seemed like with each story that Mari told about Nicaragua, another layer was peeled back, revealing her true identity; A country beaten down and stained in blood, yet strong and majestic—tough and proud—resilient and complex.

Nicaragua; like the coffee growing through its mountains was a blend of both beauty and strength, and for those willing to search long enough and deep enough: they just might find the magic that lies hidden within.

The skies opened up, and the rain came pouring down—Nicaragua was crying as she unveiled her secrets. We moved inside and listened to the thunder rumbling overhead and the rain slashing against the roof. After an hour, the first dribbles of water crept under my metal gate and moved towards our feet. Mari's eyes widened with alarm, and then fear as the water crept above her ankles. "Just relax," I said unplugging the fridge and grabbing a bottle of rum, "I've been through this before."

I put on Judas Priest's, *Screaming for Vengeance*, as Mari crawled onto my table, looking as though she might faint at any moment. "Don't worry, it'll be ok," I reassured her. A blast of thunder rang out overhead. I screamed, "Woohoo!" and toasted the heavens, water now at my knees. But then, as if Nicaragua was exhausted—depleted of tears and sorrow—the rain stopped.

The water began to recede. Lower and lower it dropped, until only a thin layer of mud remained: a reminder of all that Nicaragua had suffered. I squeezed Mari's hand and drank my last swill of rum. Then I shook my head and began laughing uncontrollably. Life is a fucking comedy!

* * *

A month later I moved to higher ground in the middle of the city. Living in the path of a river had lost its charm. The new house, although safe from rising floods, was a real shithole! The toilet was outside, twenty yards up a dirt hill. The shower, also outside, was in a three-foot by three-foot wooden structure, with no roof and cement floors that drained into the yard. A water hose, attached to a post by bailing wire, served as the showerhead.

The back patio had a cement floor and a corrugated tin roof. I turned it into a kitchen by setting out a table and filling it with spices, my propane stove and a few pots and pans. Whenever it rained—which seemed like "always" now that it was the wet season—the yard flooded, forcing me to scatter two-by-fours around the newly formed lakes, and using them as bridges to get to the shower and the toilet.

One day, hot and sticky from a torrential downpour which caused the humidity levels to soar, I made my way to the shower, tiptoeing cautiously like a gymnast on the balance beam, over two-by-fours. Mari, stirring beans in my makeshift kitchen, looked over and laughed as I entered the "shower."

The bailing wire which kept the hose above my head had broken, forcing me to hold it while I showered. After struggling, but finally managing to wash my body, I placed the hose between my knees and lathered up my face. But it shifted, and icy-cold water shot up my balls, causing me to shuffle my feet. I felt something slimy touch my foot and jumped three feet in the air. But when I landed, the slimy thing was still there, resting against my foot. I tried looking down and seeing what it was, but the soap was blinding me. The hose began spraying in all directions, and the slimy thing hopped up and down on my foot.

In a panic now, I wiped frantically at the suds in my eyes and peered down through squinted eyes. There, sitting nonchalantly on my foot, was the biggest, wartiest toad in the world. I immediately ran from the shower, naked and coated in soapsuds, screaming like a little girl. I splashed through the lake, making it only a couple of steps before I tripped and fell head first into the muck. Lifting my head, I wiped away the mud from my eyes and saw Mari staring at me with alarm.

I jumped up, covered in mud, and ran towards her—screaming like a wild man, and trying to remember the Spanish word for toad. Her eyes filled with terror when I grabbed her hand and pulled her towards the shower. Flinging open the curtain, I pointed to the giant toad. Mari screamed and jumped in the air, then hopped through the miniature lake like a wounded bunny. After making it across, she ran into my room and hid under my mosquito net. It turned out, I was dating the one girl in Nicaragua who was more afraid of slimy animals than me!

* * *

My neighbor's dog barked incessantly. I'm talking nonstop, all day and all night. Apparently, nobody else in the neighborhood had a problem with it, but me. The poor dog was tied to a fence by a two-foot leash and forced to sit in his shit and piss all day. I'd probably bark all day too. I'd made the rookie mistake of moving from my old house in the flood zone, to my new hovel without doing my due diligence. In my rush to avoid another Noah's Ark type flood, I moved without checking out the neighborhood or the house very well.

To add to my misery, a parrot lived in the house behind me who squawked all freaking day. The combination of the two made life almost unbearable: barking and squawking, squawking and barking, on and on. I'd scream "¡Cállate!" all day and throw in "Shut up!" from time to time in case either of them spoke English. But they ignored my pleas and went right on driving me insane; Dog barking, bird screaming, gringo cussing— each trying to out-scream the other.

One day it all became too much for me, and I went to the neighbors and told them they had to do something about their animals. The dog's owner solved the problem by moving him fifteen feet to the other side of the yard. The bird's owner solved the problem by telling me to fuck off. I began devising plans to kill them both: a secret, night operation involving rat poisoning in ground beef and ground up valium in bird seed.

But, before I could put my plan in motion, I had a sudden

epiphany—a profound realization—that the Peace Corps might frown on my killing of the local people's pets. So, I gave up my devilish, scheming ways, and decided to move instead, enlisting the help of Mari and her friend to help me in the search.

A week later, I made a big pot of spaghetti for Mari and her friend, Mirna, as a way of saying thank you for all the time they'd spent scouring Estelí for a new house for me. We'd only managed to find three homes available in the central part of Estelí. Two were even bigger shitholes than my current dump, and the third was nice, but outside my price range—costing a whopping $120 a month. Way too much for my $200 stipend. I mean, come on, a man needs his beer and cigars after all.

We'd all just sat down to eat when there was a knock on the door. I was surprised to find a tall, blonde kid, hunched over with his hands on his knees. He was wearing Dockers and a Polo shirt, which seemed a little overdressed for me—of course I'm from San Diego where we wear shorts and t-shirts 365 days a year.

"Are you Kevin?" he asked breathlessly.

"Yes," I said taking a swig of beer, "Who are you?"

"I'm... Robb," he struggled to say, "I'm... a new business volunteer. Just got here today."

"Are you alright man?"

"I... don't know. I'm not... feeling so good."

"Dude, come in," I pushed the door open. "We were just having dinner. Come in and have a beer."

"No... I'm just going to go back to my hotel room. I just wanted to introduce myself."

"Bro, just come in. What's wrong with you?"

"No, I'll be ok. I just need to rest."

"Well, where are you staying, just in case?"

"I'm at Hospedaje Sacuanjoche."

"Yeah, I know the place, it's just a few blocks away. You sure you don't want to come in and relax for a little while?"

"No... I'll see you around town." Robb turned and left, breathing hard, almost panting as he walked down the street.

I figured he'd be ok. Volunteers were always getting sick. But I did have mixed feelings about sharing my city with another person. After all, this was my town—I was the King of Estelí. I'd done all the heavy lifting to break it in.

But, on the other hand, he was a fellow business volunteer, and it might be nice to have somebody to talk to. Worst-case scenario: we split the town in half, him on one side and me on the other.

"No, twirl it," I said laughing, as the girls shoved large strands of spaghetti into their mouths, tomato sauce smearing across their faces. I showed them how to roll the pasta with their fork and use the bread as a stopper, as we laughed and enjoyed the night.

Early the next morning, I woke to somebody banging on my front door. I struggled to open my bloodshot eyes and crawl out of bed, as the banging continued, louder and more intense. I swatted at a mosquito having breakfast on my ankle and stumbled towards the door.

"Qué!" I barked, flinging open the door.

The blonde kid from the night before (What was his name again?) peered at me sideways, in the same bent position from the night before, and whimpered, "You have to help me, man. I'm sick… I mean really sick."

I scratched my throbbing head, "What can I do?" I could barely see straight myself.

"I don't know, I think… I need a doctor."

"A doctor, really?" This might be more serious than I thought.

"Yes, maybe you could call the Peace Corps."

"Call the Peace Corps!" Oh shit, this must be serious.

"Yes…"

"Alright man, come inside." I helped Robb into a chair and grabbed my bike.

If he was willing to get the Peace Corps involved, he must feel like shit. I sympathized with him, knowing exactly how it felt to be alone and sick in a strange country. I cranked down hard on the pedals, racing to the Telcor office, where I had the dispatcher patch me through to the Peace Corps office. She pointed me to a booth and signaled for me to pick up the phone.

"Buenos días, Cuerpo de Paz Nicaragua," I asked the secretary to transfer me to Samantha, my favorite nurse in the world—Yes, she was still there.

"Samantha, it's Kevin in Estelí. A new volunteer named Robb just came to my house. He's really sick and says he needs a doctor."

"What's wrong with him?"

"I don't know, but he's bent over moaning in pain. What should I do?"

"Ok… um, I'll send an ambulance up there to bring him back."

"What!" I said shaking my head. Now, don't get me wrong, I was digging Samantha's whole new sense of urgency towards deathly-ill volunteers, but apparently math wasn't her strong suit. "Samantha, that doesn't make sense. It'll take over eight hours, four up and four back, to get him to the hospital. How about if I just send him down on the bus, and he could be there in four hours?"

"Ok, but wait, I don't want him going alone."

I hesitated for a minute, as my brain (like somebody seeing their life flash before them) envisioned the long, hungover day ahead of me. I let out a sigh and said, "I'll go with him."

After racing back to my house, I found Robb still doubled over, sweating and dazed. I helped him up by wrapping his arm around my shoulder. I was becoming quite adept at lugging around passed out volunteers. I leaned him against the wall of my house, locked my door and then hailed a cab to the bus station.

After struggling to get Robb into a seat on the bus, I tried catching some sleep by putting my head on the cushion in front of me, but Robb was breathing hard and talking incoherently. I took a deep breath, trying to collect myself, and caught a whiff of my body odor: a foul mixture of day-old sweat, rum and cigars. I smelled like a cow in the pasture, with the sun baking down, kicking off the morning dew.

The bus ground to a halt and a group of women got on board selling pancake-sized tortillas. "Güirila, Güirila," they called out, making their way down the aisle. I handed one of the ladies a wad of bills and took my sweet, corn tortilla topped with dry, crumbly guajada cheese. I pointed to her apron and the row of soda bottles shoved in the pockets. "Una Fanta Naranja y un Pepsi, por favor." I now had the perfect hangover cure.

I gulped down half the Pepsi with one swig, and then put the chilled bottle to my forehead. Condensation and sweat dripped from my scalp, as the bus lurched forward and pulled back onto the highway. I tapped Robb on his shoulder with the Orange Fanta, but he didn't move. I shook him gently and put the bottle in front of his eyes. He mumbled and reached for the bottle. After taking a couple of sips, he leaned towards me and began to speak, "I'm g... I'm gonna..."

"What?"

"I'm gonna ra..."

"You're gonna what?"

"Ralph!"

"Dude, we're only halfway to Managua, can't you hold it?"

"No," he said, gagging and moving his shoulders back and forth. I jumped from my seat, pushed through all the people standing in the aisles until I reached the front of the bus, then kneeled down next to the driver. "Perdón señor, mi amigo es muy enfermo. He's about to throw up all over the bus."

The driver looked straight ahead, ignoring me.

"Can you please pull over for a minute?"

He looked at me with a scowl and returned his gaze to the road.

"Señor!" I screamed, loud enough for the whole bus to hear.

He slammed on the brakes, (nearly sending me flying through the windshield), pulled into a patch of dirt and cranked opened the door. I went back and peeled Robb off his seat, walked him down the aisle and out onto a field—a mere ten feet from the busy Pan American Highway.

He hunched over and heaved his guts out for the next five minutes, with a hundred passengers looking on, and the driver blowing his horn every thirty seconds.

I knelt beside him, "Robb, we have to go, the driver's going to leave us."

He nodded "ok" in between gasps of air and retching. I stood him up and walked him back to the bus. He took a deep breath and made his way up the stairs. The driver grumbled, "Estúpido maldito gringos!" as we passed by, and slammed the bus in gear, nearly knocking us off our feet. I got Robb into his seat, where he quickly passed out, his head flopping from side to side as if he might keel over and die at any moment.

The stench of Robb's vomit, combined with my sweaty-rum-cigar body odor, hung over us like a dark (stinky) cloud, causing the people in the aisle to back away; All except for a short, fat guy with curly black hair and a nose like a pig. He didn't seem bothered at all by our foul smell, as he stood over Robb shoving cabbage, carrots and fried pork into his mouth with his chubby little fingers. And with each bite, bits of cabbage and carrots fell onto Robb's head.

Robb, his head still bouncing from side to side like a giant bobblehead, was oblivious to the vegetable garden raining down on him. Mr. Pig could have been dumping piles of shit on his head for all he cared. But I cared, what with me being his newly appointed brave protector. And, I wasn't having any of that shit under my watch.

"Oy, hombre, Muévate - Move it!" I yelled in my toughest voice, sitting up tall in my seat. But he just grabbed another handful of food, and shoved it in his mouth, while another clump of cabbage landed in Robb's blonde hair.

I switched to English, "Hey fucker, move over!" That caught fatty's attention. He looked down at me for a moment, grunted like a sow and then shoveled more food into his mouth. The chunks of cabbage and carrots were piling up on Robb's head, and each time we hit a pothole, tiny bits fell off and landed on the floor. I didn't know whether to burst out in anger or laughter.

I stood up and screamed every cuss word I knew at fatty—in English and Spanish—while flailing my arms and acting like a crazed man ready to take on the world. Satisfied with my superhero-protector work, I sat back down.

I looked up, expecting to see Mr. Pig sprinting down the aisle. Instead, chubby lifted his shirt, revealing a rather large, black pistol sandwiched between a roll of belly fat. My face turned hot as an iron, and my heart skipped a beat.

I instantly lowered my head and shut my mouth, like an obedient dog; And didn't say another word the entire ride to Managua. I kept myself busy, picking out pieces of food from Robb's head like a mama ape pulling fleas from her baby's hair—having officially retired as "Peace Corps Protector."

In Managua, a driver helped me load Robb into a cab, and we made our way to the Juan Bautista Hospital, my favorite place in Nicaragua.

Robb was rushed inside and hooked up to an IV. A doctor came over and told me he had Dengue Fever. Before they wheeled him away, I bent down and said, "Have fun with the sponge baths."

I hailed a cab back to the bus station. My hangover was starting to go away, and for some odd reason, I had a craving for fried pork, cabbage and carrots.

CHAPTER TWENTY-TWO

LOVE

What pissed me off the most about that night Mom pulled me out of bed and told me my dad had died, was the thought of never feeling a father's love... never having that bond I so craved.

Before that night, I'd always envisioned life—at least my life—straightening, becoming linear, as opposed to the downward arc I'd always known. There just had to be more, had to be a bounce. All the stupid movies I'd ever seen were a testament to that upward trajectory and the notion that the struggle is always rewarded.

My father's death was a dagger to the heart of those childish ideologies; An unveiling of the cruelties and harshness of life. A cement truck filled with cynicism backed up and poured its contents over my body, creating a rock. A rock void of love. A rock so solid and impenetrable, I thought I'd never find love again. But then came the summer of 1985, and it was magical.

Michelle, my middle sister, was dating Javier. He was a nice guy, who always gave me rides to school and dances. On the last day of school of my sophomore year in high school, I came home to find him sitting on the couch with Michelle.

"Hey, what's up Kevin?" he said with a big grin on his face.

"Hey," I replied, looking at them curiously. Something was up.

"Hey man, how'd you like to work at the beach this summer?"

"Work at the beach?" I'd just turned sixteen and was eager to work and make my own money. Plus, I'd been spending nearly every free minute surfing and hanging out at the beach, anyways. "Are you serious?"

"Yes, I'm serious," he said. "I wouldn't bullshit you. I'm the manager at Hamel's and we need an extra person."

My eyes lit up, Hamel's was a surf shop in Mission Beach—well, actually, *on* Mission Beach. I'd learned to surf in the waves right out front.

"Hell yeah!" I jumped over the couch to shake his hand.

"You start Monday, I'll pick you up at 7:30 a.m. Be ready!"

"You got it. Thanks, man!" I ran off to call my friends.

Javier picked me up bright and early Monday morning, and we drove to the beach. He set me up in the rental section: a little shack facing the boardwalk and Pacific Ocean where I rented bikes, skateboards, skates, surfboards and other items to the public.

Tourists, mostly from Arizona who we referred to as "Zonies" or "Zoners," and military guys on leave were our primary customers. They rented out the bulk of our inventory in the morning, and then, for the rest of the day, I pretty much just kicked back in a beach chair—watching girls in bikinis walk by—and waited for the renters to return the bikes and surfboards at the end of the day. At which point, I'd hand back drivers licenses to wobbly, sunburnt tourists and sailors, and call it a day.

One warm day, hours after the morning rush, as I stared out at the waves listening to Howard Jones, *she* came by. The most beautiful girl I'd ever seen. She had short blond hair, cut diagonally in the back, a summer tan and beautiful light brown eyes.

"Hi," she said, in a sweet, happy voice, "I have a coupon for one free hour of bike rental." I would have given her every bike in the shack if she asked.

"Ok... um... what's your name?" my voice cracked.

"Marlo," she said with a smile. "Can we get a tandem?" I hadn't even realized she was with another girl. I fumbled through the paperwork, trying to steady my hand, my heart fluttering. I finally gave up and wheeled out a tandem bike.

"Here, take it for as long as you like," I said.

The sun glimmered off her brown shoulders as she and her friend struggled to get the bike moving. I ran over and held the bike as they mounted and gave them a shove. They rode off down the boardwalk, her blonde hair growing fainter in the distance.

I waited nervously, calculating how long it would take them to ride to Crystal Pier in Pacific Beach and back. My heart began racing the moment her turquoise bikini top came into view. As she passed by, she made eye contact and waved, her sarong fluttering in the ocean breeze. I nearly collapsed.

They rode up and down the boardwalk, sending me into a tizzy each time she passed by, until finally, they stopped to turn in the bike. Her friend said goodbye and took off as I came around to get the bike.

"Hey," I said, my face flush and mouth barely able to form words.

She leaned the handlebars to me, "Do I owe you anything for the extra time?"

"No," I said wheeling the bike away.

"Ok, well thanks. Say hi to Ray for me."

"Wait, you know the owner?"

"Yes," she said, "I just live a few blocks away."

She turned to leave and I blurted out, "Can I have your phone number?"

She smiled, "You have a pen?"

My heart swelled, and I couldn't wait to get back to work each day, hoping she might stop by. After a few days of not seeing her, I decided to call. Later that evening, I steadied my hand and punched the numbers into our phone. Every muscle in my body wanted to slam the phone back onto the receiver, but I fought them all back.

"Marlo? Hi... it's Kevin from Hamels."

We talked on the phone for hours. It seemed so natural, like we'd known each other forever. We discussed our families and our problems, our dreams and hopes for the future. It took twenty minutes just to hang up, "You hang up." "No, you hang up."

We spent the rest of the summer together, kissing and holding hands. I fell hard, and deep in love. Vowing I'd be with her forever. It felt like for once in my life, I was getting that bounce—that lift I'd always waited for. Everything in perfect order.

Our relationship was a secret. Her parents were strict, and she was younger than me. But we blended in on the beach with thousands of others during the day and talked on the phone at night.

"Spend the night," said Marlo, one day out of the blue.

"What?"

"Spend the night with me."

"How?" I said, looking at the freckles on the bridge of her nose and running across her cheeks.

"I'll sneak you in."

"You're crazy!" Her parents lived in the Penthouse of a five-story building overlooking the bay.

"Come on," she said, staring at me with her big, brown eyes, "there's a side door with a key code, and my room is right next to the door. They'll never even know you're there."

It sounded like a bad idea, but I would've been insane to say no. "Are you sure?" I asked.

"Yes!"

Around ten o'clock that night, I had my buddy, J.D., drive me to her building and drop me off in the alley. "Dude, are you sure about this?" he asked.

"Shit man, I don't know," I said nervously. "Just do me a favor: Wait five minutes. If I don't come out, go ahead and take off."

I crept up the stairwell and punched in the code. A green light flashed. I opened the door, ever so softly, and stepped inside—a burglar on the prowl. After waiting for my eyes to adjust to the dark, I tiptoed down the narrow hallway and opened the first door on the left. Marlo looked up, and my heart sprang to life. She jumped up from her bed and came to me, kissing me long and passionately while pulling me blindly backward.

We fell into bed and began ripping each other's clothes off. I fumbled for a condom and then we made love, staring into each other's eyes and telling each other how much we loved each other. It was perfect; That explosion of love I'd heard about, dreamed about. We fell asleep, wrapped in each other's arms, only to wake in the middle of the night and make love again. She whispered in my ear, "You're everything I've ever dreamed of and more."

Early the next morning, I ran my fingers through Marlo's hair, "I should leave before your mom gets up."

"No, don't worry," she reassured me. "She sleeps late."

I pulled her in close to my chest and sank my head back into the pillow—content with life.

Less than five minutes later, there was a loud knock on the door. I jumped out of bed, wearing only my boxers, and stood next to the door. The second knock was even harder, and then the doorknob rattled.

"Why is this door locked? Open the door right this minute young lady!"

Marlo sprang out of bed, rushing to put on her t-shirt and panties. I looked around the room for a better place to hide, but there were none. The doorknob rattled again.

I watched in horror as Marlo walked to the door and turned the lock. The door flung open, stopping just inches from my face. I could see her mom through the crack, and watched as she scanned the room, praying she wouldn't look towards the hinges of the door.

"What's going on in here?"

"Nothing, I'm just getting dressed."

"I thought I heard you talking to somebody."

"No…"

"Well get dressed and come down for breakfast."

My heart beat a million times per second as her mom scanned the room one last time and shut the door. I dipped my head in relief, careful not to let out a sigh, or make even the slightest noise. Everything was going to be ok.

But, then, the door flung open once again. Her mom stepped into the room and looked behind the door. Our eyes met, and shock tore through her pupils. She glanced down at my boxers and flung her head up.

"What in the hell is going on here!"

She ran out of the room screaming for her husband. Marlo and I began dressing as fast as humanly possible, as all hell broke loose downstairs. I was pulling up my pants when her step-dad burst into the room, shouting and waving his hands in the air.

"Downstairs, both of you!" he ordered.

We went downstairs and sat on a plush white couch. I looked over at Marlo, but she had her head down.

"Explain to us just what in the hell is going on," he said.

I lied and told them that I had just come to the house.

Her mom stood with her hands on her hips, "If you just came to the house, then why weren't either of you wearing any clothes?"

I told her Marlo had taken off her clothes when she knocked so that she could pretend to be asleep.

"What?" She took a step forward and leaned towards me. "So, why didn't *you* have your clothes on?"

That one stumped me, the adrenaline coursing through my body was slowing, along with my excuses. I was caught—straight up.

"Well, we didn't have sex!" I bellowed, attempting to go a different route. I was in deep shit, and there was no way out.

"What's your mother's phone number?"

Beads of perspiration oozed from my scalding hot forehead as I sat there waiting. Thirty minutes later, there was a knock at the door and Mom walked in. I stared into her eyes, looking for a sign.

When she passed by Marlo, she reached down and squeezed her hand, and gave her a big smile. All of my fears disappeared at that very instant. Mom, with that one act of compassion (and having never met Marlo) had suffocated the fireball raging around us.

Mom and I had learned to co-exist by then. Our raging battles having all but disappeared since she'd given me the space and freedom I needed. We never discussed the shitty years of my youth, and at times, it felt like it had transpired in another lifetime. She had remained sober over the years, and I respected her for that. And as the years passed, I learned to love and trust her anew.

Now, here she was, squelching a fire that could have easily consumed me. It was determined that Marlo and I would never see each other again, but I knew deep down that would never last. As we drove away, I told Mom the truth about everything, including how much I loved her. When we got home, she hugged me tight and said, "Kevin, you know I love you, and I want you to be happy. But Marlo's mother will never—ever—let you two be together. I'm sorry."

But I wasn't worried, not in the least. I knew love would overcome all. And soon, just as predicted, Marlo and I were back on the phone, talking for hours and writing love letters. We snuck underneath the lifeguard tower and kissed, our toes wiggling in the sand. Our love could never be stopped.

When I got my driver's license, I raced down to the beach and picked her up. We drove down a dirt road and into a restricted area of Fiesta Island on Mission Bay—the perfect hidden spot.

We crawled into the backseat, grinding on each other and kissing as deep as our tongues would go. When we finished making love, we lay back, looking up at the ceiling and giggling. We loved each other so much, nothing could ever separate us.

Then, there was a loud tap, tap, tap on the window. I cleared away the fog with the palm of my hand. Two cops with batons in hand were peering in.

"Get out of the car," one said forcefully.

"Wait," I said, "let us get dressed first."

"Hurry up!" he said, rapping on the window again.

I sat up, "Well can you at least turn around?"

We dressed quickly and got out of the car, heads bowed. He asked our ages and then put us in the back of a Police Bronco.

"Please let us go," I pleaded. "We're good kids."

The officer driving turned and faced Marlo, "Where do you live? And is anybody home right now?"

Through sobs, she gave him her address and said her step-dad was home. When we arrived at her building, he said to go up and bring him back to the Bronco, then he got out and waited by the front of the vehicle.

Marlo returned with her step-dad—his face tense and questioning. The cop told her to tell him everything we had done. Her shoulders slumped as she began telling him all the sordid details. I thought she might disappear at any moment. Her stepfather's face became redder with each word, to the point I thought he might explode right there in the alley. He turned and stared into the Bronco—a murderous, bloodthirsty stare. Then they turned and walked into the building. Marlo didn't look back once.

They drove me to a police substation and made me call my mom. When she arrived, they read a list of charges they'd press if I ever tried seeing Marlo again: littering (the used condom), off-roading and public nudity.

"He's lucky he's only sixteen," the officer said, "or we would've charged him with statutory rape." I didn't feel lucky!

Mom and I drove back to Fiesta Island. It was dark by then, and we spent the next thirty minutes driving through scrub brush trying to find the car.

Marlo's real father, an Admiral in the Navy, showed up at my house one day while I was in school and threatened my step-dad, "If that son of a bitch ever tries to see my daughter again, I'll beat the shit out of him."

I got a call from Marlo later that night. When I heard her voice, all the pain I'd been feeling faded away. I knew true love could never be stopped.

"Kevin," she said, "this is the last time you'll ever hear from me again." Wait, what? I felt her hand reaching into my chest and ripping out my heart. Tears flowed down my face, and I felt myself floating away.

"No Marlo," I cried. "I love you so much, please don't leave me!"

"I'm sorry, but it's over. Please don't ever contact me again." The sound of the phone hanging up reverberated through my ears and rattled around in my head. I wrapped my arms around my body and wept as molten lava dripped over my head, enveloping my world, morphing me into solid rock yet again. I never saw Marlo again.

CHAPTER TWENTY-THREE

JUST BREATHE

Robb got better and came back to Estelí. I let him visit my side of town, and we began hanging out, drinking beers and bullshitting, eventually becoming friends. One day, Robb brought up the idea of us being roommates; He was still living in the Sacuanjoche Hospedaje, and I was still living in the City Zoo. The problem was the Peace Corps had a rule against volunteers living together—some bullshit about not getting the real "Peace Corps experience." But the way Robb and I figured it: if we got any more of the "Peace Corps experience," we might be dead.

After searching Estelí for several days, and not finding a place to live, Mari reminded me of the house near the center of the city that went for $120 a month. Robb and I went up to have a look. It had a toilet, running water, two rooms and a pulpería that sold beer and rum next door. Perfect!

So a week later, I shoved all my shit into my duffel bag and said goodbye to my two dear friends: the parrot and the dog. I took one final look at the shithole and cranked down on my pedals, eager to escape the zoo. The dog began barking as I rode away, and I swear I heard that godawful parrot scream in perfect English, "Shut the fuck up! Shut the fuck up! Shut the fuck up."

Robb and I cracked a beer and made a toast, "To roommates!" Fuck the Peace Corps rules, by pooling our money, we'd be able to afford luxuries such as a TV and even a phone. It would take months for the Telcor office to process the work order, and run a telephone line to the house, but for the moment, we were ecstatic.

Life settled into a nice little rhythm. Mari and I were officially dating, and Robb found himself a pretty girlfriend named, Norvis. My English classes were going well, and even some of the neighborhood children came by for help with their English homework. On the surface, all appeared well. Deep inside, something was skewed.

Robb was dedicated to his job, working Monday through Friday 8-5, coming home only for lunch. He was young and ambitious—with something to prove. He also had something I didn't: a counterpart that cared.

Ramón and I had never patched up our relationship. How could we? He didn't want my help, and I felt like a fraud showing up for work only to sit at my desk and do nothing. I was still working with small businesses, but even that began to slow. Surprisingly, very few owners wanted advice from a twenty-seven-year-old gringo who'd never owned a business.

Caribbean Mike made trips into town every couple of months to see how things were going. And since I'd almost entirely stopped going into the bank, his visits were always filled with dread, wondering if he'd find out. Fortunately, he almost always came towards the end of the day, when I had a reason for not being at work. But, now that Robb and I were roommates, I had one more thing to worry about.

Anxiety, that little fucker, crept back into my life. And no matter how hard I tried to cram him back into his hole, he kept emerging. I spent several days at the waterfall, contemplating my life and my next step; Concluding, I'd no longer participate in the charade with Ramón and the Cooperative. I decided to tell Mike I was quitting my job on his next visit to town, which meant I'd probably be booted out of the Peace Corps.

* * *

My favorite ride at Disneyland isn't Space Mountain or any of the roller coasters—it's Pirates of the Caribbean. There's just something about the pirate lore, the call of adventure, traveling from one exotic island to the next, chucking law and order into the sea.

I suppose it might have had something to do with me reading Robert Louis Stevenson's, *Treasure Island* at the time, but I was eager for some swashbuckling adventure by the time Mitch and Jason arrived in Estelí for our trip around Central America. I figured I'd get one last adventure in before I had to pack my bags and go home.

I convinced Robb to give up his Dockers and Polo shirts for a few weeks, and travel with us to meet some real pirates, on our very own adventures in the Caribbean. We even planned on getting certified in scuba diving at some point on the trip. Although, just the thought of being down in the water with only a tank and hose keeping me alive, kept my friend, anxiety, frothing at the mouth.

On the first leg of the trip, we traveled to the ancient Mayan ruins of Copán in northern Honduras, close to the Guatemalan border. That evening the fog rolled in, bringing visibility near zero. I thought about how this site was once the heart of the Americas, pumping its lifeblood through the jungles and beyond. An eerie feeling hung in the air—as if the ancient spirits were whispering in the wind.

"This place creeps me out," Jason said.

Mitch lit a clove cigarette and passed him his flask of rum, "Pussy!"

"Oh yeah, well let's see how brave you are when Quetzalcoatl comes for your heart tonight."

"Wrong civilization, genius."

Jason took a slug of rum and twisted the cap back on, "Aztecs, Mayans, Incas: they'll all rip your heart out."

The next morning, we woke early and entered the ruins. The mist hung heavy in the air, and only the outlines of pyramids were visible. I imagined the Mayans moving about the city, trading goods and socializing.

We entered a narrow court with seating on either side. Tall poles, with small hoops attached, stood on each side of the court. Here's where they threw around eight-pound rubber balls and tried to throw them through the circles—an ancient version of basketball. Only in this game, the captain of the losing team had his head cut off with an obsidian axe, and his heart ripped out and placed on an altar.

We were walking in the footsteps of a culture over three thousand years old, studying hieroglyphs etched on stone columns in the Acropolis and gods carved into statues in the Great Plaza. Spiritualism flowed inside me as I ran my fingers along the carvings—this was my worship, this was my church.

The sun burned away the clouds, unveiling the pyramids. We climbed to the top of the tallest one, where people once worshiped a Sun God, represented by a Jaguar who spit up the sun each morning. I looked out at the jungles surrounding Copán. One day it would creep inside and turn the city to rubble—burying her secrets within. Will it all have mattered, this ancient civilization?

"Imagine," Robb said, "they sacrificed bodies right here at this very spot."

"Yep," Mitch said, "I read they also pierced their tongues and genitals with the barbs of stingrays, mixed the blood with hallucinogenic plants and then burned them in a big bonfire."

"Sounds like fun," Jason said.

"They inhaled the smoke to see sacred images and receive messages from the Gods."

"Yeah," Jason said, "the message should have been to keep stingrays away from their balls!"

From Copán we traveled to La Ceiba, a rundown port near the Caribbean Sea, where we caught a puddle hopper flight to the small Caribbean island of Útila. When we walked across the tarmac, we were met by a group of tall, white men with long, blond dreadlocks and blue eyes speaking pidgin English, "Eh man. Come down here. We got food and bed. Dive shop. We go now."

"What?" I asked.

"I say. You come. Dive blue water."

Real pirates! Or at least, the descendants of pirates—who'd left Europe and sailed across the Atlantic over 500 years ago, attempting to make their fortunes by raiding Spanish cargo vessels, and sacking them of their gold. They built settlements on this small island and called it their home for the last five centuries. They spoke Creole-English, Spanish and Dutch. Having only heard black people talk that way, it came as somewhat of a shock when I listened to these white, pirate-reggae-dudes speaking in broken English.

We hopped in their jeep and headed to the edge of town, where several small motels and bed-and-breakfasts were offering rooms for $3 a night if you signed up for a scuba certification class. We found an old bungalow style motel and ordered a round of beers.

"I'm going to find Captain Morgan's lost treasure," said Jason as he plopped down on a chair on the front porch.

"Good luck with that," I said. "I'm just gonna try not to fucking drown."

"Don't worry man, there's nothing to it," he said.

Jason's words provided little to no comfort. Being forty feet underwater, with weights around my waist and a tank on my back, seemed like a bad idea.

Robb and I signed up for the basic certification class, while Jason, already certified, enrolled in the advanced diving class. Mitch, apparently the only smart one in the group, decided to skip the diving altogether. He'd keep busy drinking beers and reading books while swinging in a hammock.

I was restless all night, thinking about breathing through a regulator while deep underwater. It didn't seem logical. I reminded myself how I'd left everything behind for adventure and new experiences; And what could be more adventurous than diving, and discovering a whole new world?

At breakfast, I tried to calm my stomach by eating waffles covered in mango and passion fruit syrup while listening to excited backpackers discuss their day's dive schedules. I drank the last few sips of my macadamia nut coffee and headed nervously to dive class. Robb and I were paired up as dive buddies and spent the first half of the day inside a classroom, learning about air pressure and oxygen, and working on time charts.

"Dude," I said, turning anxiously towards Robb, "I'm a little confused on the timetables."

"Don't worry about it," he said. "We won't really use them."

"What? What do you mean we won't use them? That's the whole point of the class. We have to know how to use them. What if we get the bends?"

"Just relax mon', we're in the Caribbean bra."

"Oh great, I'm going to fucking drown with Bob Marley!"

After lunch, we loaded the dive gear into a boat and headed out into the blue waters. An hour later we pulled into a cove, with water so clear it looked like a swimming pool. But, suddenly, thousands of tiny flies began buzzing all around me, biting my arms, neck and legs. And within seconds, everybody on the boat was cussing and slapping at their arms and legs.

"Sand fleas!" screamed the dive master. "Get your gear on and get in the water."

Robb and I began putting on our gear and checking the equipment like we'd been taught, while the fleas continued to terrorize us. Several people jumped in the water, trying to escape the pain of their skin being ripped from their flesh.

"You ready?" Robb asked.

"No!" I screamed, slapping at fleas and fidgeting with my weight belt.

"Come on man, it's going to be ok."

The fleas kept tearing at my flesh. It was either die by drowning and asphyxiation or be scourged to death by these devilish pests.

"Ah, fuck it!" I finally said, putting my regulator in my mouth and falling over the side. I splashed under the water and instinctively held my breath, trying not to panic as I somersaulted through the water. As I searched for sunlight to guide me back to the top, I remembered the respirator in my mouth and breathed in cautiously. Crisp, clean air entered my lungs, calming me. I kicked my fins and surfaced. I looked around and found our dive instructor and gave him the "ok" signal with my fingers.

Our group formed a circle, and then the instructor gave the thumbs down sign. I pushed the deflate button on the buoyancy control device, releasing air from the vest, and let the weights around my hips drag me to the bottom of the sea.

We made our way down fifteen feet and formed a circle on the sandy bottom. A school of purple and yellow fish swam through our group and hid in a patch of seagrass swaying in the current. Robb was next to me, his hair floating above his head. The instructor gave hand signals to each person, "Are you ok?" I signaled back, "Yes I'm ok."

I could hear my breathing through the regulator and looked up. The sun's rays were piercing through the water. Somebody shot up to the surface, and then another person followed. The instructor put out his hands for everybody to remain calm and then swam after them. The rest of us sat on the sea floor staring at each other. My breathing became louder, and I fidgeted with my mask. Inhale, exhale, inhale, exhale. I adjusted the regulator in my mouth. Breathe, breathe…

The instructor swam back, bubbles trickling from his mouth. I could hear my breathing growing louder and faster. Should I shoot up? No, just hang on, calm down, relax and breathe. He looked my way, pointed and gave me the signal, "Are you ok?"

Breathe, breathe… just breathe, Kev. A sudden wave of calmness washed over me. I smiled and gave him the "ok" sign. I was ok, in fact, I was more than ok—I was amazing! I'd come to the realization that by veering off from the life set out for me, and learning to live in a world of both order and chaos, I was no longer weighed down, no longer suffocating. No longer drowning in pain. And, as a result, I'd emerged into this magical world of color and life. On the adventure of a lifetime!

* * *

Caribbean Mike showed up in Estelí shortly after returning from my trip. We went to a restaurant that served Nacatamales, a traditional food made from corn masa filled with potatoes, pork, rice, achiote and other spices. I ordered a beer and flipped the bottle cap around in my hand, waiting to get my nerve up.

"Look, Mike," I finally blurted out, "I can't work with Ramón anymore. I'm done with that place. He's a thief. If you guys want to kick me out of the Peace Corps, then go ahead. But I'm not going to pretend to work at some stupid job anymore. I didn't join the Peace Corps for that shit."

Mike took a swig of beer and set the bottle down gently. "First of all, calm down, nobody's kicking you out of the Peace Corps."

I relaxed my shoulders and let out a long, deep sigh. Air I'd been holding inside me for months, perhaps years.

"What exactly is going on?" Mike asked.

I gave him a summary of everything I'd discovered: Ramón's unpaid loans, board members in default, the bank's side businesses. I told him about how Ramón had never given me a work assignment, but still didn't want me looking at the accounting ledgers or working with the socios (small businesses).

"Look," Mike said, "you don't have to work there. Just do whatever you want."

"Really?"

"Of course, it's no big deal."

"Don't worry, I'll finish out the week," I said, "and I'm still teaching English and working with a couple of businesses."

He took a big bite of pork and masa, "I'm not worried, Kev."

Yeah, mon' I was finally on my own; You just had to love Caribbean Mike! Before I left the bank for good, I followed up on the application I'd submitted for assistance. It had been approved. And during my last few days working with the Cooperativa, a technical team arrived and began computerizing their entire accounting system.

"Jonny, I'm going to miss you, man."

"Everything's cool, dude." He pointed to Ramón's office with a big smile. Two men were inside with him pouring over all the loans, file by file.

I decided to celebrate my new-found freedom by visiting Craig in his town. But instead of busing it, I would ride my bike the 49 kilometers down a steep, winding mountain road to Condega. I filled a small backpack with water and a little food and set out early in the morning.

After leaving Estelí, I pedaled up a few hills before hitting a straight-away, where I was able to check the bike for any problems. I pumped the brakes several times and shook the frame from side to side. Everything felt solid.

Nearing the top of the mountain, a sun-soaked valley of tobacco came into view many miles below. I tucked my body in and began my descent, picking up speed immediately. I checked the brakes one last time, put my head down, and let the bike go. Faster and faster I rode, wind blasting, lips flapping, the bicycle hugging the road. I swiveled from side to side around each turn, trees whooshing, asphalt whipping by. I looked to the side: no guardrail and a mile drop.

"YES! YES!" I screamed, my heart hammering away.

A car came roaring up from behind, forcing me to the edge of the cliff. Breathing rapidly now, and squeezing my knees against the bicycle frame, the tobacco plants came into view, thousands of feet below. The car whizzed alongside me. My brakes were useless at these speeds, so I put a death grip on the handlebars and waited for him to pass. Fear set in as I flew like the wind. Any wrong turn would send me over the cliff, careening to an early death.

As the car blew past, the bike felt wobbly. But I maintained control, racing to the bottom of the mountain and pumping the brakes. The thrill ride was over.

I climbed hills for several kilometers, before spotting an old bullet-ridden plane located on a knoll—a remnant from the Revolución, and a signal that I'd reached Condega. I rode into town and searched for Craig's house, aka the Bank. The sleepy Savings and Loan was located in the town square.

"Estás Craig?" I asked an old man half asleep at his desk.

He went in the back, and a minute later, out walked Craig. He began to laugh the moment he saw my bike and sunburnt face. "Wait, don't tell me," he said. "Estelí ran out of rum!"

I had a harrowing tale to share with him over our favorite snack: cream cheese, mayo and mashed up garlic. Choices were slim in Nicaragua. Craig and I ended up taking a 12-hour bus ride to Tegucigalpa in Honduras for the sole purpose of going to Taco Bell and McDonald's.

While our friendship started off somewhat rocky in Miami, it grew over time, forming a strong bond. Similar, I suppose, to Felix and Oscar in the Odd Couple. Opposites, yet each holding a high level of respect for the other.

CHAPTER TWENTY-FOUR

ONE LAST ADVENTURE

I ran through our living room one day and stopped dead in my tracks. A calendar filled with black slashes hung on the wall, but it was the bright red ink that drew my attention. It was circled around my last day as a volunteer, and it was approaching rapidly.

I'd been in Nicaragua for well over two years. Although, at times, it felt like I'd been there my entire life. Nicaragua was my home. I spoke fluent Spanish, had a Nicaraguan girlfriend and had adapted to the culture. The United States now seemed like a strange, foreign land. I feared leaving Nicaragua and returning to the 9-to-5 grind. How could I go back to that? How could I live any other lifestyle?

Mari had been acting weird lately, picking fights about trivial things and then disappearing for days. I'd track her down at her house and apologize for things I never did, "I'm sorry for, um, you being mad at me."

"You have another girlfriend," she said. "That's why you're always traveling."

"No, I don't have another girlfriend," I'd explain over and over.

"You're lying."

"I'm just visiting my friends." I'd come to love Mari deeply but found myself growing tired of the pointless drama—finally telling her I needed to take a break.

Robb and I finally got a phone installed, and one evening, Stephanie called, "Hey you!"

"Hey back," I said.

"I'm throwing myself a birthday party, and I'm inviting everybody. You better be there!"

Almost all of Nica 6 showed up to celebrate, elated that our service was coming to an end. We sang and danced to the local music, and our conversations wove in and out of Spanish. Many volunteers had brought their Nicaraguan boyfriends and girlfriends. We were seasoned veterans now, and we all shared a special bond. Nicaragua flowed through our blood.

"I'm going to miss you Steph!" I yelled over the merengue music. She grabbed my hand and pulled me into the center of the living room where everybody was dancing. We twirled around and threw our arms into the air. Craig was laughing and doing the chicken dance, while Susan and Mitch danced in circles around an inebriated Jason.

We formed a conga line, shaking our butts and kicking our feet, as we moved through the house and out onto the street. Jason serenaded the neighborhood with his best Pavarotti, then proceeded to lie down and take a nap—using the curb as a pillow. But, before his impromptu concert, Jason, Mitch and I planned one final adventure: a bike ride along the Nicaraguan coast.

* * *

We met in the town of Diriamba a week later. Our first task was to divvy up our packing list: a pot, skillet, mini-stove, gas, water, tent, sleeping bag, food, rum, etc... With the weight equally distributed, we wheeled our bikes to the back of the bus.

I climbed up the rusty ladder to the roof of an old school bus. A wire cage, soldered around the perimeter, held empty cases of beer and wicker baskets filled with peppers and onions.

Mitch lifted my mountain bike above his head. I grabbed it by the rim and laid it on the roof. Then I pulled up Jason and Mitchs' bikes. Mitch had some half ten-speed, half mountain bike conversion. The tires were skinny, and I couldn't see it making the trip.

"What's this Frankenstein piece of shit?"

"Don't worry about it," he said climbing up. "It rides good."

We sat down and rested against the frames of our bikes. Mitch pulled out a flask of whiskey and we made a toast to the journey ahead. The diesel engine rumbled, and the bus began to move. We grabbed the metal cage and held on tight, as we were jostled from side to side.

Arriving in La Trinidad, we could almost smell the sea. Itching to begin our adventure, we practically threw our bikes off the bus. Seconds later, we were zooming down a hill at thirty miles per hour, wind racing through our hair. Free birds soaring through life.

I thought back to that day, years ago, when I hid from my step-mom in the mountains. I remember laying on my back, with the sun beating down on my face, watching the clouds move through the sky. I felt so free in that moment. Safely tucked away, immune from the belts and wooden brushes of a step-mom who resented me. Free from the screams and anguish of a broken mom. Free to be a boy exploring his world, and innocent in its pursuit. I suppose I'd been searching for that freedom my entire life.

We climbed a hill, and there she was: the magnificent Pacific Ocean. Pure beauty. For three boys from California, life couldn't get much better. We were hard-core explorers living in the present, and our journey had just begun. We stopped for water in the little beach town of La Boquita.

"That was awesome," Jason said.

"Dude, we were flying," I said, opening the map and pointing to a squiggly line near the coast. "We keep moving south, and we should find a dirt road here."

We were making great time and still had plenty of sunlight left. We took a last drink of water and pedaled south along a coastal road lined with colorful houses, passing the town of Casares and onto Huehuete, where the pavement ended at a pulpería. We stopped and drank a beer, letting the sun bathe us in her warmth.

After refilling our water bottles, we rode south down a dirt path running parallel to the ocean. After an hour, the trail veered into a stretch of thick, overgrown foliage. Soon, the road bogged down, turning from dry hard dirt to soft mud, and forcing us to walk our bikes for the next hour. Pissing and moaning, we trudged through the mud, cursing our luck. And just when we thought it couldn't get any worse, the road petered out altogether. It seemed our adventure was over before it'd started.

I opened the map and stared hopelessly at the squiggles and lines, "This is bullshit!"

"Who picked this road anyway?" Jason asked, turning and looking my way.

Then Mitch looked at me too. I threw my bike to the ground and began searching through the brush for a path. "Well how the fuck was I supposed to know there was no road here? Look at the map, it shows a line running along the coast."

"That's like some ancient cow trail or something," Mitch said, "you know you can't trust the maps down here."

"Give me the flask," Jason said, reaching out to Mitch. But then he moved his hand and pointed, "Wait, look over there... between those two trees. It's a trail!"

"See, I told you!" I bellowed. "Now give me that fucking flask."

We carried our bikes on our shoulders through a meadow of tall grass to the other trail, which wasn't much better than the first. Deep mud bogs caked our shoes and socks in the muck, making it hard to walk. The straps on my backpack ground into my shoulders, causing me to cuss at every single item I'd brought. I wiped at the sweat rolling down my forehead and wondered if I could be any more miserable. But we pushed on, seeing only the occasional hut along the trail. As we made our way deeper into the bush, the shelters disappeared altogether, along with any further sightings of the ocean. We were completely alone and lost.

"Dude, are we going the right way?" Mitch called out.

"I don't know man," I said kicking at the mud, head down. Our adventure had turned into a sweaty, mud-bogging, crapfest. Pushing our bikes through mud and cow shit was not what we'd envisioned when planning the trip. I wanted to just sit down in the mud and drink rum.

"This isn't looking good," Mitch said.

"Yeah man, this is rough," Jason added. "Maybe we should turn back."

"Let's just give it another ten minutes," I said.

The mud dried up, just long enough for us to climb back on our bikes and pedal for a distance. We hadn't seen the ocean in over an hour and weren't even sure we were still heading south. The mud returned, forcing us to walk our bikes again, this time through razor-sharp reeds and thorny bushes, while swatting at mosquitos and wiping away sweat. Then the trail ended.

"Fuck!" I shouted, throwing my bike in the muck. I was defeated. Our adventure had come to an end. All the old emotions of fear and pain, and not having control over my life, began to bubble up. Mom dragging me away from my life and friends to drive cross country. My dad not wanting me in his life. Marlo ripped from my arms at the height of my love. It was all too much. "Fine, let's just turn back!" I screamed.

But then I heard Jason say, "Come on man, let's push through."

And then Mitch added, "Yeah, maybe we can pick up the trail again."

I stared at the ground, fighting back the tears, feeling the pain burn in my nose—the same pain from my youth. I shook my head "ok" and picked up my bike, avoiding their eyes. They moved ahead of me, leading the way now, shoving bamboo and banana trees to the side. We slogged forward, brush slicing our arms and legs, dragging our bikes through the dense brush.

Jason let out a scream, his voice ringing through the jungle. I thought for a moment that he cut his foot open or had been bitten by a snake. I saw him disappear into some bushes and rushed down the path after him, pushing aside the branches and poking my head through. Waves were crashing on the beach, and the beautiful Pacific Ocean stretched out as far as the eye could see.

"Woo Hoo!" we screamed, running around the beach and giving each other high fives. We were alive. Mitch pulled out his flask and we drank a toast, "To the Pacific Ocean!" The rum tasted even sweeter than usual as we stood there on our little slice of paradise. Letting go of control and accepting help, had proved not to be a sign of weakness, but of strength.

"I didn't think we were going to make it," Mitch said.

I took another drink from the flask, "Well, technically, we haven't made it. We still have fifty miles to go."

Jason reached for the flask, "Well there's no more trail, so I guess we just ride along the beach from here on."

"Stick close to the water where the sand is compacted," Mitch said.

We pushed our bikes over the white sand to the hardpack at the water's edge, then pedaled along the beach following the curves of the tide—the wind spraying mist and grains of sand against our arms and legs.

Looking inland, a wall of palms rose up like an impenetrable wall, not a human in sight. Swallows and pelicans flew overhead, splashing into the ocean as they searched for a meal. We maneuvered around driftwood, broken branches, and washed up tree trunks scattered up and down the beach. After pedaling for several hours in quiet solitude, we passed a rock outcropping. "Hey look," Mitch said, pointing towards a group of huts camouflaged amongst the palm trees. "It's a village."

Tired and hungry, we pushed our bikes across the soft sand to the village. As we approached, we realized it wasn't a village, but just a couple of huts. A group of men, sitting in the shade of a blue panga boat, were stitching up fishing nets.

"Buenas, hay comida o cerveza?" Jason asked the men. They seemed surprised to see us.

An older man approached me, "Que querés?"

"Is there a pulpería nearby where we could buy food and beer?"

He stroked his scruffy white beard for a few seconds. "No, this is my house, there are no stores nearby. But we have beer we could sell you, and my wife could make you fish."

"Que bueno," I said. "Muchas gracias!"

"Come and sit over here," he said.

We followed him to a patch of sand between two huts. Tree branches and palm thatch served as an awning, blocking out the hot sun. We sat in the sand, with our backs against the hut. A little boy ran over and handed us each a beer. We clanked bottles and nodded in delight. A small dog came over, gave us a sniff and curled up in the sand.

Thirty minutes later, the boy came back with plates of fried fish, rice and beans. We tore into the delicious food with our fingers, consuming every last morsel. When we finished, we let out big burps and sank into the sand. Life was good.

After a quick nap, we decided it was time to move on. We thanked the family for their hospitality. Then Mitch reached into his fanny pack, pulled out a wrinkled fifty Córdoba bill, and handed it to the bearded man. His eyes lit up, and he said, "Good journeys to you, but watch out for thieves on the beach."

We pushed our bikes to the waterline and continued south. The sun began to dip, so we found a stretch of beach to make camp. After setting up the tent, we split up in different directions to search for firewood. Within an hour, we had a stack of wood six feet high. Jason got the bonfire roaring, and Mitch broke open a liter of Gran Reserva.

"Here's to great adventures," I said, holding the bottle in the air. The sun disappeared beyond the horizon, and the sky turned purple.

"And friendship," Jason added.

"Salud!" Mitch said.

"So, what's everybody's plans after the Peace Corps?" I asked.

Jason had been accepted to grad school, and Mitch wanted to travel. I was lost and uncertain about my path forward. I was sad and somewhat confused about my relationship with Mari. I loved her and knew she was acting strangely because I was leaving soon, but I didn't know where to go from there. We had talked about her coming to visit me in the United States. But would that really happen?

It depressed me just thinking about going back and falling into the same rut. Part of me wanted to stay in Nicaragua, but the other part wanted to go home and make my mark on the world.

"Hey," Jason said, "let's take a big trip after we C.O.S." He was using the acronym for Close of Service, the last day of Peace Corps service.

"Where to?" I asked.

"Let's go to Machu Picchu in Peru!"

"Oh man, that would be awesome," I said.

"Cheers to that," said Mitch.

And there it was, I had a plan. I wasn't sure what I'd do after the trip, knowing how life has a funny way of throwing obstacles and curves in your path when you least expect it. So, for now, I'd be content conquering one thing at a time. We got rip-roaring drunk and crammed into the small tent. I woke up in the middle of the night and crawled out to take a piss.

"What the fuck are you doing!" Mitch screamed at the top of his lungs. I looked down and realized I hadn't made it out of the tent. I was pissing all over his head. Oops! He ran off to the ocean. We packed up early the next morning and continued south. Mitch made me carry all the heavy shit!

This became our routine: riding along the beach during the day and making camp near a fishing village at night. After eating our dinners of fish and rice with the families, we'd head back to our campsite to drink and bullshit around a raging fire late into the night.

One night, around midnight, we put on headlamps and set off in search of sea turtles. After stumbling around in the dark for over an hour, and not finding anything, we called off the search. We had just turned around and begun to head back when Jason tripped and rolled into the water.

I turned and began to laugh. "Are you alright?" My headlamp caught something moving across the sand. Moving closer, my light illuminated upon a giant black-and-gray turtle emerging from the ocean. The ridges on her shell glistened in the moonlight as she scooted along. She must have weighed three hundred pounds.

After hobbling up the beach a few feet, she stopped and began digging her flippers in the sand, carving out a deep hole. When she finished, she moved over the hole and squatted. We huddled around and waited. Minutes later, she sat up on her haunches and began dropping her eggs into the sand: plop, plop, plop, plop. Then she moved forward and used her flippers and legs to kick wet sand over the eggs. When they were completely covered, she turned and crawled back to the ocean.

It was an amazing scene, watching the ebb and flow of life play out before us. A mother protecting her young, and then leaving them to fend for themselves. Survival of the fittest. We pushed away some sand and looked at the mound of eggs. They were shaped like ping-pongs and stacked one on top of the other. Hundreds of eggs it seemed. Which among them would survive? Perhaps one of these turtles would come back to this very beach one day and leave their own pile of eggs. We covered them back up and returned to the tent, only to discover that somebody had stolen the skillet we'd left out.

"Who'd steal a dirty skillet?" Mitch asked. "Hide the other pan and silverware under the tent."

The next morning, we realized that all of our kitchen supplies were gone, stolen literally right out from underneath us as we slept. But nothing could deter our adventure, and we continued riding south down the coastline. Until, that is, we ran into a giant, impassable cliff jutting into the ocean. There was no way around it, or over it.

It seemed as though life had been placing barriers in front of me since the day I was born, some more challenging than others. I was beginning to learn, however, that not every cliff needed to be scaled, and not every obstacle was a battle needing to be won. Sometimes, you could just change course and go with the current, let life push you along.

Our beach adventure had come to an end, but nobody complained. We had traveled long enough, and far enough. We moved past the palms and back into the brush, eventually finding a cow trail heading inland. After several hours, we came out on the road and caught a bus to the tranquil little beach town of San Juan Del Sur. Over rum and cigars, we made a pact to never forget the sense of freedom we had felt while riding along the ocean, with the mist blowing in our face and the sun beating on our skin.

CHAPTER TWENTY-FIVE

FULL CIRCLE

I was accepted to UC Santa Barbara, my dream college on the beach, but life followed its customary downward trajectory when Mom told me she couldn't afford to send me. After high school, I floundered around San Diego; working, partying and half-assed going to junior college.

One day my buddy Stevie called, "Come up and visit me." He was attending college in the small rural town of Chico, located in Northern California, a ten-hour drive from San Diego. I drove up that weekend, taking Hwy 99 through the farms of Central California, known as the "heartland," and past Lake Oroville and Feather River. After passing through hundreds of almond orchards, all planted in perfectly straight rows, I arrived in Chico.

Maple and walnut trees lined every street, and the fragrances hung heavy in the air. The campus and surrounding streets were alive with activity: students walking to classes, skateboarders hopping off curbs, bikes—their riders loaded down with backpacks—zipping into the houses and apartments nearby. The college vibe permeated every nook and cranny of the town, and it blew me away. I knew right away I had to go to school there. I wanted that experience, needed that experience.

I returned to San Diego and started busting my ass—working longer hours, saving money and pulling up my grades. I was on a mission and couldn't be stopped. I used the $4,000 I received from my father's death to put a down payment on a convertible X19 Fiat. I suppose convertible Fiat's ran in my blood; like mother like son.

The big day finally arrived. I put the top down and pointed the Fiat north, ready to make my mark on the world. I cranked up Depeche Mode and The Cure as the wind blew through my hair. Life was wide open.

I wasn't even enrolled at Chico State, so I attended Butte

Community College for one semester while begging and fighting with the admissions office to let me in. They finally relented, and I transferred to Chico in the Spring.

Money became tight, I was just barely surviving between financial aid and odd jobs. The repo man began circling the Fiat, I hadn't made a payment in months. Before they could snatch it, I gave it to my sister, Stephanie, attending law school in nearby San Francisco. I grew jealous watching my roommates open their monthly checks from their parents. They would buy Chico State sweatshirts and go out to eat and drink, while I was struggling to pay for my Marketing and Accounting books. At parties, while kids were busy doing beer bongs, I was stealing cans of corn and fucking tuna from their cupboards. Shhhhh...

College was tough. I had to work my ass off and force myself to scrap it out. It stripped me down and left me butt-ass naked. Humble, yet solid and confident. Sink or swim motherfucker—I swam.

I scraped $300 together my senior year and bought a beat-up Karmann Ghia. Everything was broken on it except the engine. The engine, like me, was strong and solid. I stripped the car down to metal and worked on its brakes and transmission throughout my senior year—getting it to run just days before graduation.

In May of 1992, I graduated from college, skipping out on my ceremony. After a few quick goodbyes, I drove off in the unpainted Ghia. She puttered down the I-5 and rattled over the grapevine—a metaphor of my life: a tale of two cars. I'd raced up to Chico as a brash, cocky kid in a sports car, only to return as a broke—yet wiser—young man, in a clunker.

I received my degree in Business; Specifically, a Bachelor of Science Degree in Business Administration, with an option in Management. It sounds fancy, but it's really just a mouthful of words: a scrap of paper with my name in fancy script. Something to pin on a wall.

I expected a lot from the world when I arrived in San Diego. I had just spent a tough, but amazing four years attending college and it was time to reap the rewards. I held my diploma high in the sky like it was a torch. "Here I am world, you may now commence to throw money at my feet!" Man was I in for a rude awakening.

I arrived home during a recession and learned rather quickly that people didn't give a shit about my little scrap of paper. In fact, it represented money which employers couldn't afford to pay. I was under-qualified and overeducated, a toxic mix in a recession.

I mailed out hundreds of resumes, and the rejection letters poured in. I became convinced that the whole world was conspiring against me.

When it all seemed hopeless, the government took a chance on me.

They hired me as a caseworker for people receiving government assistance. The work was rewarding and gave me a sense of pride. I tried to be kind and treat the people with respect, many of them were just down on their luck—something I could relate to. Some took advantage of the system, I wasn't naive, but they were the exceptions, not the rule.

For the next two years, I sat in a windowless cubicle working for the Department of Social Services, staring into a computer monitor as fluorescent lights flickered overhead—trapped like a caged animal.

My boss, a smart and direct woman, sensed my angst and switched me to a ten-hour, four-day-a-week schedule. I took advantage of my three days of freedom by wandering around San Diego and finding hidden beaches, parks and trails that I never knew existed. And when I ran out of places to discover in San Diego, I traded in my Ghia for a VW van and began traveling south into Mexico.

I'd pack the van with fishing poles, a cooler of food and my surfboard, then cross the border at sunrise and drive south for hours and hours. I'd make camp at different locations along the beach, always seeking remote spots, devoid of people.

The deeper I drove into Baja, the more solitude I was able to find. My van didn't move fast, but what it lacked in speed it made up for with practicality. It was a home on wheels. I could park anywhere, hop in the back, and lay down for a nap.

I surfed deserted waves by day and stared into fires at night, free from obligations, free from mankind. Always thinking, always searching.

And that, friends, is how I came to be on that deserted stretch of beach that night in El Socorro, Mexico. I'd been born into a whirlwind and tossed about from one chaotic even to the next. Weathering the storms, I'd been seeking a safe harbor ever since—following the parting clouds and setting suns to reach this very spot.

I didn't join the Peace Corps on some fucking whim. My whole life had been leading me there. I just needed to shut up and listen to the call for once in my life.

CHAPTER TWENTY-SIX

FREEDOM

Mari knocked on my door one morning. Her head was down and her eyes puffy and red.

"Yes?" I asked, trying to hold back my emotions. We hadn't seen each other in two weeks, and I had missed her fiercely.

"Kevin, I'm very sorry," she said. I almost fell over, she'd never said she was sorry for anything before. It was the first time I'd seen a crack in her tough exterior.

I tried speaking, but nothing came out. I flung my arms around her. There was no use fighting my feelings. I loved her and couldn't stand to see her in pain.

My time in Nicaragua was almost up. I had a big adventure to South America planned—the perfect beginning to life after the Peace Corps. But what then? Where would I go? I couldn't just walk away from this new reality that existed inside me, this sense of adventure and thirst for knowledge about the world around me. No, I was a changed man, and this 'thing,' this 'new reality,' this 'spiritualism' was enmeshed in my DNA now—a symbiotic relationship, with each side feeding the other, depending on the other, for our continued existence.

I told Mari I needed to think and rode up to the waterfall. I lay back on the warm rocks, staring up at the sky, pondering how I could use this crazy adventure to shape my future. Would it even be possible to go back to the States and get a regular job? Pretend that this whole experience never happened? Maybe I should go back to college for my MBA, but why? I could stay in Nicaragua with Mari, but what would I do here? Mari and I had been through so much together. I loved her, and it seemed almost cruel to leave her behind. A cloud passed overhead. I waited for the answers to fall from the cotton candy fluff.

They didn't.

When I returned from the waterfall, I rode up to the Telcor office. My mom had done a bang-up job of fucking me up when I was young, but she had battled back strong and made me into the man I was today. Who in the hell else would I turn to?

"Mom?"

"Hey sugar, I was just thinking about you. Your time's almost up down there, huh?"

"Yep, you make it sound like I'm getting out of prison."

"Well, from some of the stories you've told me..."

"Mom, the good stories outweighed the bad a hundred-to-one."

"I know, I'm kidding. So, what's up?"

"I'm still trying to figure out what to do with my life."

"Aren't we all."

"Ha, ha. I'm supposed to go on that trip down to Peru, and then I was going to go back to San Diego."

"So, what's the problem?"

"Well, Maribell for one. I mean, I'm having a hard time thinking about just leaving her behind. And what am I going to do when I get back to San Diego? And what about—"

"Hold on, hold on, slow down. It seems to me that you need to prioritize your questions and find the answer to the most important one first, and then all the other answers will follow."

I looked out to the street, an ice cream man was pushing a little cart down the road and ringing a bell as he went. I thought about how my life had changed so drastically from the first day I stepped off that plane over two years ago. I was no longer that confused boy running around the fire, spitting Tequila into the flames and seeking clarity. "Mom, I know the question to ask!"

"You always did," she said.

I jumped on my bike and raced to Mari's house. When she opened the door, I dropped to one knee. "Maribell de Jesus Rodriguez de Videa... Will you marry me?" Mom was right, I only needed the answer to one question. I suppose I would always need my mother's affirmation, and perhaps that not a bad thing.

In the end, I loved Mari and couldn't see my life without her. Somewhere, up in those cotton candy clouds, I'd envisioned my life without her, and discovered it was incomplete.

There was a long pause, and then she finally said, "Yes."

We set a date and told all of our friends. I broke the news to Jason and Mitch that I wouldn't be going to Peru, and then Mari and I began planning for a wedding which would occur in just three weeks' time.

***

It was time to say my goodbyes. I rode up to the business owners and thanked them for allowing me to work with them. From there, I rode to the Cooperativa and said goodbye to Jonny and the other employees. The bank had received the assistance from the application and had moved from the outskirts of town to a modern building on the main drag of Estelí, near all the major banks. There were men inside setting up computer systems. Ramón came out and gave me a big smile and handshake. I'd long since given up any animosity I harbored towards him.

Jonny came out and gave me a hug. He pointed to the men and said, "Audit, dude!" with a big smile. I wished him and the bank well, and rode on to the leather shop, where I invited my two English students, Fabrício and Ervin, to the wedding.

Nica 6 met in Managua for the official Close of Service (COS) ceremony. It was a momentous occasion, like crossing the finish line after just completing 10 back-to-back Ironman Triathlons. Of the thirteen volunteers in our group, only ten made it through. Elena had left only a couple months after arriving at her new site, and out of the ten of us that completed our service, four of us married Nicaraguans, just as had been predicted years before during our orientation in Miami.

Our group celebrated in Montelimar, a beautiful resort on the Pacific Coast, complete with winding pool and a swim-up bar. We swam and laughed and congratulated each other over a two-day period. We were on top of the world.

"I'm going to miss you guys," I said, splashing water on Stephanie and Susan. They were headed off to Costa Rica. It would be the last time I'd see them for a long time.

"Oh no," Susan joked, "he's getting sentimental. Get him more beer, quick!" Stephanie laughed, sprayed me with water and swam off.

My smile masked a deep sadness. It was the end of a chapter in my life—our lives—and in some small way, I wanted to keep everything the same, freeze time. I looked out at the ocean, and the waves crashing onto the shore. Change was inevitable. The motion of life as constant as the surge of the tides, the gravitational pull of the moon and the rotation of the Earth. Our journeys had intersected in this magical place, at this moment in time, and within this sector of space. And now, it was time to move forward. Ever forward.

Later that night, I opened my journal and wrote the final words to my poem…

Thus comes the end of an adventurous voyage
The ship does sail in the dull moonlight,
Shhh… quiet, a dove takes flight.

Mari and I were married in my backyard beneath a mango tree, under a wedding arch made from palm fronds, surrounded by friends and loved ones. My heart nearly stopped when I saw her walking down the path towards me dressed in white. Robb and Jason shared best man duties. Mari's father donated a pig, and after we said our "I do's," we had a blow-out barbeque fiesta, which raged into the late hours of the night.

In the morning, it was time to say goodbye to my friends as they set off for their adventures. We kept it light, having already planned to meet back up in the States once we settled in.

"Don't fall off the cliffs in Machu Picchu," I told Mitch and Jason.

"Have fun with the ball-and-chain," Jason replied.

Mitch passed me his flask for one final toast. "See you in the States!"

I gave Craig a big hug, "I'm going to miss you, man."

"Yo tambien Kebin."

***

After some deep contemplation and a little soul-searching, Mari and I decided to start our new life back in San Diego. It took some time to get her Visa, and as she packed her belongings and prepared to leave Nicaragua, I could almost feel her pain and fear. Like me before her, she was heading to a new country where she didn't speak the language or know the culture. And she didn't know when, or if, she'd ever return to her friends and family.

The day finally arrived. It was time to go. I gave Robb a hug, he still had a few months left in the Peace Corps. "Don't get married," I told him, "you're too young!" He laughed and pointed to my ring.

Mari, with tears streaming down her face, said goodbye to her mother and father, her siblings, and all her friends.

As we adjusted our backpacks and prepared to set off, I wondered if I'd ever see Nicaragua again. Wondered if I'd ever lie on the warm rocks above the waterfall or watch the River of Blood flow through Estelí. I wondered what this amazing adventure had meant in the grand scheme of my life.

Mostly, I wondered where Mari and I's adventure would lead us next. What twists and turns lay ahead? For I'd discovered that it was within those twists and turns; atop the highest volcanos and within the densest of jungles, where life explodes inside you—and on rare occasions, when you feel as though you can't move another inch forward—it reaches out and gives you a nudge.

EPILOGUE

The Peace Corps motto is, "the toughest job you'll ever love." We used to joke that it should have been, "the easiest job you'll ever hate." The Peace Corps was both easy and tough, and you simultaneously loved it and hated it. It flipped my world on its head; teaching me to seize life instead of watching as it passed me by.

Jason went on to obtain his MBA from Georgetown, proving you can go from sleeping in the gutters of Nicaragua to graduating from one of the most prestigious universities in the U.S. Mitch joined the Border Patrol and worked his way up the ranks. He showed up at my house one day with his shiny badge and a gun. I wasn't sure whether to run and hide or get him drunk. I chose the latter.

Craig went on to work for Sun Microsystems and is working on his MBA. He learned to drink small amounts of beer and rum, but he prefers to be dry—like his humor. Robb moved to Panama and became Vice President of an insurance company, switching out his Dockers and Polo shirt for a suit and tie. Stephanie received her MBA in International Business and married a man from Puerto Rico. Susan works for the Feds on the East Coast, and Samantha—everybody's favorite Peace Corps nurse— was eventually fired for incompetence.

I received a message one day from my English student Ervin thanking me for teaching him English. He said that, because of my help, he'd been able to get a great job working on an oil rig in Texas. Life is a funny thing.

As for me, well, let's just say Mari and I's adventures had just begun. We would go on to experience twists and turns that often made my two-years in Nicaragua pale in comparison; from packing everything we owned in a camper and crisscrossing Mexico and Central America, to driving our F-250 through the heart of Hurricane Mitch. But, then again, those are tales for another day.

THE END OF AN ADVENTUROUS VOYAGE

I've crossed the waters of azure blue and dipped my head in its vibrant hue
Sullen and shaken I thus emerged, absent all tears, my emptiness purged
Lost, confused, yet gentle the hand, cast all aside, like a statue I stand
Pure of mind and fresh of soul, baptized in the mar of old
Cuerpo de Paz, Cuerpo de Paz
A flash blinds the night, darkness now, a bird takes flight
Carry on, carry on, winged doves of peace,
Your journey awaits, your light shall never cease

Thunder crashes upon our ears, embrace all fears.
Once said of time, thus be true, carry on, embrace all that is you
The Ocean Pacific I have traversed, from the tip of Costa Rica,
to the point of Potosi,
Across the plains of Boaco, and through the mountains of Estelí
Up Mombacho, down la Boca de Infierno,
Through the coffee fields of Matagalpa, to the bottom of Laguna Apoyo
From Selva Negra to El Sauce's trepid town,
I've seen the breadth of Nicaragua, and to it, I am bound

Nicaragua, to you I send
My blessings of peace, please never bend
With power comes light, now we share a common plight.
With a part of your country, thus buried in my soul,
A piece of my own, I leave as my toll.
An equal exchange of love untold, a love unsoiled, a love so bold.
Now I depart whiter my wings, and a tip of my hat for the song that I sing.

Thus, comes the end of an adventurous voyage
The ship does sail in the dull moonlight,
Shhh… quiet, a dove takes flight.

-Kevin Cromley

Chasing Bulls

Nicaraguan Market

The Savings and Loan

Streets of Estelí

Travelin' Nica style

Surround by Peace Corps volunteers at our wedding

(L-R) Aunt Janet, Mom, Grandma Nicaraguan Paradise

Epic bike ride World Traveler

At peace in Lago Atitlán, Guatemala

Acknowledgments

First and foremost, I must thank my beautiful friend and companion Laurel for all the hours spent reading and re-reading my book in my endless quest to get the words 'just' right. Thank you for allowing me the time and space to find those words. You are amazing!

To my sister Michelle, for all the hours spent formatting text, searching out fonts and optimizing old pictures buried away in the garage for twenty years: a thousand thank you's!

To Stephanie, Craig, Beth and the folks at the Mission Valley Writer's Club, thank you for being "beta-readers" and giving me the moral support needed to continue this endeavor. I raise a glass of Gran Reserva to you all.

To Mari, Kevin, Kristi, Stephanie, Kerry, Michelle and all the rest of my family and friends: thank you for letting me be a part of your journey. I love you all.

To Peace Corps volunteers around the world, working in some of the toughest conditions on this planet, I salute you.

Lastly, to the reader, thank you for traveling down this path with me and sticking by my side. Hope to see you in the mountains, or on some desolate beach sometime in the future.